The Letter to the Hebrews

David J. MacLeod

EMMAUS
WORLDWIDE

Developed as a study course by Emmaus Correspondence School, founded in 1942.

The Letter to the Hebrews
David J. MacLeod

Published by:

Emmaus Worldwide
PO Box 1028
Dubuque, IA 52004-1028
phone: (563) 585-2070
email: info@emmausworldwide.rg
website: EmmausWorldwide.org

First Printed 1998 (AK '98), 2 UNITS
Revised 2003 / 2005 (AK '03 / '05), UNITS
Reprinted 2007 (AK '03 / '05), 3 UNITS
Revised 2011 (AK '11), 3 UNITS
Revised 2015 (AK '15), 3 UNITS
Revised 2018 (AK '18), 3 UNITS
Revised 2020 (AK '20), 3 UNITS

ISBN 978-1-59387-503-9

Code: HEB

Printed in the United States of America

For My Beloved Parents,
Elwin and Elizabeth MacLeod

Abbreviations

AV	The Authorized Version of the Bible (King James Version)
i.e.	that is
LXX	The Septuagint, the Greek translation of the Old Testament
ms.	manuscript
mss.	manuscripts
NASB	Holy Bible: The New American Standard Bible
NEB	Holy Bible: The New English Bible
NIV	Holy Bible: The New International Version
NKJV	Holy Bible: The New King James Version
NT	New Testament
OT	Old Testament
J. B. Phillips	The New Testament in Modern English
RSV	Holy Bible: The Revised Standard Version
viz.	namely
cf.	compare

Course Overview

The letter to the Hebrews explains that the sacrificial system of the Old Testament is a picture of the ultimate sacrifice that Jesus came to fulfill. Hebrews weaves together these two realities in a profound way that shows the intricacy of God's plan throughout history. It also shows the Lord Jesus Christ, our High Priest, to be superior in His person, superior in His functions, and superior in His resources. We hope this course will help you understand the letter to the Hebrews and the themes in it to grow in your faith and encourage your life in Christ.

Lessons You Will Study

Student Instructions

This Emmaus course is designed to help you *know God* through a *better understanding of the Bible* and *how it applies to your life*. However, this course can never take the place of the Bible itself. The Bible is inexhaustible, and no course could give the full meaning of its truth. If studying this course is the end goal, it will become an obstacle to your growth; if it is used to inspire and equip you for your own personal study of the Bible, then it will achieve its goal. As you study the Bible using this course, prayerfully ask God to reveal His truth to you in a powerful way.

Course Sections

This course has three parts: the *lessons*, the *exams*, and an *exam sheet*.

The Lessons

Each lesson is written to help explain truths from the Bible. Read each lesson through at least twice—once to get a general idea of its content, and then again, slowly, looking up any Bible references given. You should always have your Bible opened to the verses or passage being studied. It is important that you read the Bible passages referenced, as some questions in the exams may be based on the Bible text.

To look up a Bible verse, keep in mind passages in the Bible are listed by book, chapter, and verse. For instance, 2 Peter 1:21 refers to the second book of Peter, chapter 1, and verse 21. At the beginning of every Bible, there is a table of contents which lists the names of the books of the Bible, and tells the page number on which each book begins. For practice, look up 2 Peter in the table of contents and turn to the page number listed; then find the chapter and verse.

The Exams

At the end of each lesson, there is an exam to assess your knowledge of the course material and the Bible passages. The exams contain multiple choice and/or True/False (T/F) questions. After you have studied a lesson, complete the exam for that lesson by recording your answers on the exam sheet at the end of the course. If you have difficulty answering the questions, re-read the lesson or use the Bible as a reference.

Please note, it is best not to answer the questions based on what you *think* or have *always believed*. The questions are designed to find out if you understand the material in the course and the Bible.

What Do You Say?

In addition to the multiple choice section, each exam also contains a *What Do You Say?* question. These questions are designed for your personal reflection and to help you express your ideas and feelings as you process the lesson's content. Your responses should not be written on the attached exam sheet, but rather, directly written in the space provided at the end of each exam.

The Exam Sheet

Use the exam sheet included at the end of the course to complete the exams. When you have determined the right answer to a question on an exam, fill in the corresponding letter on the exam sheet. If you have a group leader or instructor and he/she provides a different exam sheet, please use that one instead.

Write It Out!

The exam sheet also contains *Write It Out!* questions. These questions are designed to help you apply the course's content to your daily life.

Continued on next page

Write It Out! (continued)

The *Write It Out!* questions will address your *head* (thinking), *heart* (feeling), and *hands* (doing).

1. **Head.** The first *Write It Out!* question will be geared toward your head and asks you to respond to a critical question concerning the course in its entirety.

2. **Heart.** The next question asks how the course affects your perspective of or feelings toward God, yourself, or others.

3. **Hands.** The final question asks you what action you need to take in response to what you have learned.

Write It Out! questions will be reviewed and responded to by your group leader or instructor.

Prayer Requests or Questions?

You may include your personal questions on the exam sheet to help your group leader or instructor to get to know you and your needs better. Please let them know specific questions you may have about the Bible, God, or other spiritual matters. You may also include a personal prayer request and your group leader or instructor will pray for you.

Submitting the Exam Sheet

When you have answered all the exam questions on the exam sheet, check them carefully. Slowly tear out the exam sheet along the perforated edge near the course spine. Please note, do not tear out the exams from the lessons; submit the *exam sheet only*.

Fill in your contact information and submit your completed exam sheet to your group leader or instructor or the organization from which you received it (several options for submission are shown at right).

OPTION 1: Send to your group leader or instructor

If you know your group leader or instructor, give them your completed exam sheet or mail it to the address listed here (if blank, go to option 2).

OPTION 2: Send to Emmaus Worldwide's head office

If no address is listed above, or you do not know if you have a group leader or instructor and are unsure of where to send your exam sheet, you can:

MAIL the exam sheet to

Emmaus Worldwide
PO Box 1028
Dubuque, IA 52004-1028

OR

EMAIL a scan or photo

of both sides of the exam sheet
to this email address:

Exams@EmmauWorldwide.org

Receiving Your Results

You will receive your graded exam sheet back (through the same method it was submitted, either mail or email), including your final grade and personal response from your group leader, instructor or Emmaus Worldwide.

Introduction

You have chosen to study the Epistle to the Hebrews. It is a good choice. With the book of Romans, Hebrews stands out as one of the two greatest epistles (letters) in the New Testament. One well-known Bible teacher (W. G. Moorehead) called Hebrews "the profoundest epistle of the New Testament." Another (P. E. Hughes) described it as the most fully developed doctrinal writing in the whole of the New Testament. However we respond to remarks like these, we must agree with the Jewish Christian, Adolph Saphir, who called it a "grand and massive book."

Whenever we begin a study of a book of the Bible we should ask and answer certain questions: Who wrote the book? When did he write it? To whom did he write it? Why did he write it? When we ask these questions we learn why one writer (E. F. Scott) has called Hebrews "the riddle of the New Testament," for these questions are difficult to answer. Godly Bible teachers have differed in their answers. This should not disturb us, however, because it is possible to understand the epistle as a whole without reaching conclusions on these introductory matters.

WHY SHOULD WE STUDY HEBREWS?

We can begin with a question that is easy to answer: Why should we study Hebrews? Let me suggest a number of doctrinal reasons. First, this epistle exalts the person of our Lord Jesus Christ in a special way. Hebrews, says one well-known writer (David Gooding), is ablaze with His glory. The epistle insists on His full deity, His true humanity, and the complete sufficiency of His work on the cross. Unlike any other New Testament book, Hebrews refers to the priestly work of our Lord (no other New Testament writer calls Jesus a priest or high priest). Second, Hebrews is important for an understanding of the relationship between the Old and New Testaments.

Third, the epistle lays great stress on the need for endurance in the Christian life. And, finally, it focuses on the doctrine of faith and the life of faith.

The writer of Hebrews never separates doctrine from practical Christian living, so there are practical reasons for studying his epistle, especially in our day and age. First, this is an age of materialism and secularism. It is a day when the people of God need to be reminded that they are pilgrims on their way to the heavenly city (11:10; 13:14). Second, ours is also a day of "diverse and strange teachings" (13:9) which are answered by the epistle's portrait of the eternal Christ (13:8). Many false teachers in modern times are presenting heresies that are derogatory to the person of Christ, heresies that are refuted by the clear teaching of Hebrews. Third, it is a time when many Christian believers are drifting from the biblical teaching on the Christian life as set forth in Hebrews. They are drifting toward an unbiblical emphasis on religious rituals and ceremonies. Fourth, it is a day of uncertainty and soul sickness (as proven by the large number of Christian counselors and psychologists). Thus, believers need to be reminded of the free access and family welcome that is theirs at God's throne of grace (4:14-16). Finally, it is a day when many believers have replaced church attendance with religious programs and church services on TV, radio, and the internet. In such a time the message of Hebrews is a vital one. The epistle teaches that the Christian life is a life of mutual encouragement and fellowship with other believers in submission to local leaders (10:24-25; 13:1, 7, 17).

WHO WROTE HEBREWS?

Some Say Paul

Some of our Bible translations give as a title for Hebrews "The Epistle of Paul the Apostle to the Hebrews." The view that Paul wrote Hebrews is a very old one. As early as AD 200 there were Christians who believed that Paul had written the epistle. This is not surprising in that there is a clear Pauline spirit about the book. Yet most scholars today have concluded that Paul did not write Hebrews.

There are a number of reasons for rejecting Pauline authorship: First, although some translations have Paul's name in the title, this is not true of the Greek manuscripts. Second, from earliest times there have been Christians who have denied that Paul wrote the book. Third, the epistle s anonymous—that is, the author does not give his name, while Paul identifies himself in all of his thirteen epistles (2 Thess. 3:17). Fourth, unlike Paul's epistles, Hebrews lacks a salutation (a greeting) and does not name the group that received the epistle. Fifth, the plan of Hebrews differs from Paul's epistles. Paul, as a rule, structures his epistles with a doctrinal section followed by a section on practical Christian living. Hebrews, however, is arranged in such a way that the doctrinal discussions and practical applications are interwoven. Sixth, the style of Hebrews is different from Paul's writings. Hebrews is a polished, literary work, but Paul's letters have a rugged quality. Seventh, the author of Hebrews says something in Hebrews 2:3 that Paul would never have said. He says that he did not receive the Gospel from the Lord Himsel but from His disciples. Paul, on the other hand, strongly asserts that he received the truth from no man but from the Lord Himself (Gal. 1:12).

Believers need to be reminded of the free access and family welcome that is theirs at God's throne of grace.

There are also differences in doctrinal emphasis between this author and Paul: (1) Paul tends to emphasize the resurrection; Hebrews does not (13:20). (2) Paul never once refers to Christ as priest, while the priesthood of Christ is the theme of Hebrews. (3) Paul speaks of Christ's work in terms of justification and reconciliation, while the emphasis of Hebrews is on cleansing, sanctification, and perfection. (4) To Paul "faith" refers to the sinner's trust in Christ; in Hebrews "faith" has more to do with persevering faithfulness. (5) Paul lays great stress on the Holy Spirit's work in the life of the Christian; Hebrews has very little to say about the Holy Spirit. (6) Paul's doctrine of Christ as head of the church composed of Jews and Gentiles joined in one body is absent from Hebrews. (7) The author of Hebrews never uses Paul's distinctive expression "in Christ."

Some have argued that a denial of Pauline authorship is a rationalistic attack upon the inspiration of Hebrews. This is an unfair criticism for two reasons: First, the epistle nowhere claims to be Paul's. Second, the denial of Pauline authorship goes back to the early church. Men who are universally acknowledged to be godly teachers of the Word of God have denied in their writings that Paul wrote Hebrews. Others have argued that Hebrews is by Paul in that it quotes Habakkuk 2:4; the only other New Testament quotations of that passage are in Paul's letters (Rom. 1:17; Gal. 3:11). The fact that two New Testament books both cite the same Old Testament passage, however, is no proof that both were written by the same person (compare Matt. 27:46 and Mark 15:34).

Still others defend Pauline authorship by an argument based on 2 Peter 3:15-16. They compare 2 Peter 3:1 ("This is now the second letter that I am writing to you") with 1 Peter 1:1 ("To those who are elect exiles of the Dispersion"). Assuming that both 1 Peter and 2 Peter were written to the same group, they conclude that in 2 Peter the apostle Peter was writing to Jewish Christians. In 2 Peter 3:15 Peter says that Paul had earlier written to the same group—that is, he had written an epistle to Jewish Christians, or "Hebrews." There are two problems with this view: (1) It assumes that the "first" letter spoken of in 2 Peter 3:1 is 1 Peter. However, Peter's description of his earlier letter in 2 Peter 3:1-3 does not fit 1 Peter. It seems more likely that the "first" letter of 2 Peter 3:1 is one of the many letters of the apostles lost to posterity (see 1 Cor. 5:9 and Col. 4:16). It is very possible that the letter of Paul spoken of in 2 Peter 3:15-16 is the Epistle to the Romans. Compare the reference to God's patience concerning Christ's second coming in 2 Peter 3:9, 15 and Romans 2:4. (2) Even if 2 Peter was written to a group of Jewish Christians to whom Paul had also written, this does not prove that the letter Paul wrote was Hebrews. It is possible that the letter of Paul to which Peter refers was also lost.

Other students of Hebrews in the early church believed that Paul wrote the epistle in Hebrew and that Luke translated it into Greek. Most have rejected this view for three reasons:

1. Luke was a Gentile Christian (compare Col. 4:11 and Heb. 4:14), while the author of Hebrews most likely had a Jewish heritage.
2. There is no evidence that any other letter of the New Testament originated in this way.
3. As noted above, there are pronounced differences between Paul's thought and that of Hebrews.

Other Names Have Been Suggested

Other Christians in the early church felt that the author of Hebrews was Barnabas, the Cyprian fellow-worker of Paul (Acts 4:36; 13:1). As a Hellenist (that is, a Greek speaking Jewish man of the Dispersion), Barnabas may have had the literary qualifications for writing this epistle. His fellow Christians knew Barnabas as "son of encouragement" (Acts 4:36), which uggests that he could have written Hebrews, called by its author "my word of exhortation" (13:22). Acts 4:36 translates the same Greek word "encouragement" that is translated "exhortation" in Hebrews 13:22.

The only other writer with early traditional support is Clement of Rome, a church leader at the end of the first century AD who wrote an epistle to the Corinthian Christians. We may explain the similarities that some have noted between the letter of this church leader and Hebrews by the fact that he quoted Hebrews when writing to the Corinthians.

At the time of the Protestant Reformation, Martin Luther (1483–1546) suggested that Apollos (see Acts 18:24-25) was the author of Hebrews. This proposal has been accepted by a great number of people up to the present time. Apollos, it is argued, had many of the same characteristics as the author of Hebrews. He was an eloquent Jewish man, "competent in the Scriptures" and an accurate teacher. There is no early tradition in favor of this view, nor is there any known writing of Apollos with which to compare Hebrews.

Other names that have been suggested include Silas, the apostle Peter, Philip the evangelist, and Epaphras. Two twentieth-century suggestions are Priscilla and Mary, the mother of our Lord. Interesting arguments for and against these theories favoring a woman author have been presented. The most telling objection against the view is the fact that the author uses a masculine participle when referring to himself in Hebrews 11:32 ("time would fail me").

> "But who wrote the epistle, in truth, God knows."

Most modern scholars have come to agree with the ancient Christian writer who said, "But who wrote the epistle, in truth, God knows." That we do not know the human author of Hebrews is probably as it should be. The author of Hebrews had little interest in the human writers of Scripture he quotes throughout his letter. What was of utmost importance to him was that God had spoken, and this is what is of utmost importance in the Epistle to the Hebrews itself. What we can say with assurance is that the author was a Christian who had heard the Gospel from the apostles (2:3-4). He was a man (that is, a male) who was well versed in the Greek translation of the Old Testament (the Septuagint) which he regularly quotes. His writing style, vocabulary, and means of expression combined to produce a letter that is written in some of the best Greek in the New Testament. He was a Hellenist (Greek-speaking Jewish man of the Dispersion) who was part of the circle of Paul (see Heb. 13:23).

TO WHOM WAS HEBREWS WRITTEN?

The first thing we can say about the original readers of Hebrews is that they were Christians. This is clear from the terms the author of Hebrews uses to describe them. He calls his addressees "beloved" (6:9), "holy brothers" (3:1), "who share in a heavenly calling" (3:1) and "[who] share in Christ" (3:14). Furthermore, he says in 6:18 that they have "fled for refuge" to the Christian hope. Also, in 10:19-25 he exhorts them not as if he feels they need to be converted but as if they need to enjoy privileges that are already theirs. In addition, in 12:1 he encourages them not to enter the Christian race, but to run a race they have already entered. Finally, in 13:18 he asks for their prayers. This is a request he would not make of unbelievers. In short, the readers were, for the most part, at least, Christians.

We can be even more specific about the make up of the original readers of Hebrews. Although a number of scholars have argued that the original audience of the epistle was Gentile, the majority have always held that Hebrews was written to a group of Jewish Christians. There are several reasons for this conclusion: First, the title "to the Hebrews" appears in the oldest New Testament manuscript containing Hebrews, namely P46 (AD 200). There is no evidence that the epistle ever bore any other title. Second, there is evidence that the epistle was called "Hebrews" by early Christian writers. Third, the content of the epistle suggests that the original readers were Jewish. The following elements stand out:

1. The author seems to assume that the Old Testament is authoritative to his readers, which would make sense if they were Jewish.
2. The overall argument of the epistle stresses that the Levitical priesthood and offerings have been replaced by the work of Christ. This would be more meaningful to Jewish readers than to readers with a background in pagan religions.
3. The author of Hebrews argues that Jesus' priesthood has taken the place of Aaron's; this argument would be meaningless to Gentiles.
4. He also concludes that Jesus is superior to Moses, the Jewish lawgiver.
5. He insists that the old covenant given to the Jewish people is now replaced by a new covenant, a fact that would also be irrelevant to a Gentile audience.

6. He refers to believers as "the offspring of Abraham" (2:16). He refers to "fathers" of the Jewish race (1:1; 3:9). And he uses Jewish examples (for the most part) when illustrating the life of faith (chapter 11). The evidence seems to support the conclusion that the readers were Jewish Christians.

WHERE DID THE ORIGINAL READERS LIVE?

Some Say Rome

Opinions about the epistle's original destination have included Corinth, Antioch in Syria, Cyprus, Galatia, Cyrene in North Africa, and Spain. The majority of scholars, however, argue for either Rome or Palestine. Those who argue that the epistle was written to Christians in Rome present their case as follows:

1. The earliest quotations of Hebrews are found in a letter by Clement, the Roman church leader (AD 95).
2. In his conclusion the author writes, "Those who come from Italy send you greetings" (13:24). Those favoring Rome understand this to mean that believers from Italy are with the author in another part of the empire and are sending greetings home. The phrase could just as easily refer to believers in Italy sending greetings elsewhere.
3. Timothy, well-known to the readers (13:23), was well-known to the Roman Christians (Col. 1:1).
4. The allusion to the generosity of the readers in 6:10-12 and 10:32-34 agrees with the known history of the Roman church.
5. The reference to "foods" in 13:9 suggests a problem similar to that in Romans 14.
6. The plundering of property in 10:34 could be explained by the persecution of the Roman believers under Claudius (AD 49) or Nero (AD 64).

The arguments against a Roman destination are strong. First, the author's comments in 2:3-4 do not fit Rome. It is unlikely that the Romans were evangelized by eyewitnesses of Christ performing signs and wonders.

Second, the Roman church became known for its able exposition and defense of the faith, but the readers of Hebrews were spiritually weak and dull. Third, the persecution of the Roman Christians by Nero does not fit the Hebrews, for the author said to them, "You have not yet resisted to the point of shedding your blood" (12:4). Fourth, there is an early tradition (found in a notice added to some early manuscripts that says that Hebrews was written from Rome or Italy) that the epistle originated in Italy.

Others Say Palestine

A long line of commentators has held to the traditional view that Hebrews was written to Jewish Christians in Jerusalem or, more likely, a sister church in Palestine. The arguments in favor of this view are still compelling:

1. The epistle gives the impression that its readers lived near the temple. The fact that the author speaks of the tabernacle and not the temple does not weaken this argument. He does so in that he is dealing not just with the Judaism of his day but with the laws and rituals in back of the Levitical system as a whole.
2. Early Christian writers state that the Jerusalem church was made up entirely of "Hebrews" and was called "the church of the Hebrews."
3. The epistle implies that a crisis is about to take place (1:2; 3:13; 10:25; 12:27), and we might understand this as the approaching siege of Jerusalem.
4. The sufferings the readers have formerly endured (10:32; 12:4) may be explained by the Jewish persecution of Christians in Jerusalem.
5. No other church (Rome, Alexandria, Ephesus) has ever claimed the epistle. The Romans destroyed Jerusalem and dispersed (or scattered) nearby Christians in AD 70, just two or three years after Hebrews was written. This would explain why that city made no claim to it.

Some have lodged a number of objections against the Palestine theory. First, it is unlikely that Jerusalem Christians would have heard the Gospel secondhand as Hebrews 2:3 suggests was true of the readers of the epistle. This objection is invalid, however, if the epistle was written not to the Jerusalem assembly but to a nearby sister church in Palestine. Second, the criticism of the readers in Hebrews 5:12 would not apply to the mother church. This objection is also invalid, however, if the epistle was written to one of the sister assemblies in Palestine. Third, the group to which Hebrews was written had not suffered any martyrdom (12:4), yet the church in Jerusalem was where Christian martyrdom began (Acts 7:54–8:3). Again, however, this objection is not valid if the epistle was written to a Palestinian church outside Jerusalem. Fourth, a number of passages in Hebrews (6:10; 10:34; 13:2, 5, 16) suggest that the readers were a generous group, yet the Jerusalem church was poor. In response, we would only observe that poverty has never prevented Christians from being generous. Fifth, the author wrote in Greek, while Aramaic was the language of Palestine; and he quoted from the Septuagint and not the Hebrew Bible. This objection is not a strong one in that the author was most likely a Hellenist (Greek speaking Jewish man). Furthermore, quoting from the Septuagint was an accepted practice by Palestinians, as the writings of Paul (Jerusalem trained) and Josephus (Palestine born historian) show. I find no compelling reason to abandon the traditional view that Hebrews was written to a group of Jewish Christians living in Palestine.

WHEN WAS HEBREWS WRITTEN?

Although a few writers have dated Hebrews in the AD 50s, and a few more have dated it in the 80s, most have dated it in the 60s. Their reasoning is as follows: First, the date of the epistle has to be late enough to allow for the readers to be converted and become mature in the faith (5:11-14). Second, it had to have been written late enough to allow the first generation of leaders to pass away (13:7). Third, the date must allow for a time of persecution a considerable number of years before the author wrote his epistle (10:32). Fourth, Paul's name is omitted in chapter 13. This suggests that the apostle had died before the epistle was written. Paul's death occurred sometime between AD 62 and 68.

While the author must have written his epistle no earlier than the mid to late 60s, he could not have written it later than AD 70. The reasons are as follows: First, the author speaks of the sacrificial rituals using the present tense (7:8; 8:3-5; 9:6-7, 9, 13; 10:2-3; 13:10). We know that the Levitical sacrifices ceased in AD 70 when the Romans conquered Jerusalem and destroyed the temple. The use of the present tense, therefore, suggests a pre-AD 70 date. Second, there is no mention of the fall of Jerusalem in Hebrews. This would be very surprising if the epistle was written after AD 70. The whole point of the author in Hebrews 5–10 is that the Levitical priesthood and ritual have been replaced by the priesthood and offering of Christ. Had Jerusalem been destroyed before the epistle was written the author would surely have pointed to that fact as his clinching argument. Third, the author's statement in 8:13 that the old regime is "growing old [and] ready to vanish away" may imply that he anticipates the fall of the temple shortly. Fourth, the author refers (see Hebrews 3:7-9) to the forty years of Israel's wanderings in the wilderness. He may be implying that the day of Israel's grace was nearly over. Almost forty years had passed since Christ was crucified. Fifth, the exhortation to "go to him" (13:13) would have particular force if the doom of Jerusalem was soon. A date in the late 60s (AD 67–68), then, is likely.

WHAT WAS THE OCCASION OF HEBREWS?

The Spiritual Condition of the Readers

Spiritual Degeneration

As we read the book of Hebrews, we begin to learn what it was that prompted the author to write the epistle. He says in 5:11 that he would like to teach his readers about Melchizedek, but it is hard to explain. The problem, he says, lies with the readers and not with the subject. They "have become dull of hearing." The verb "have become" suggests that they were not always this way. The expression "dull of hearing" suggests that they are not now receptive to some of the more important teachings of the Christian faith. He gives the symptoms in 5:12-14; they cannot explain their faith to others; they are spiritual babies who only want "milk" and not "solid food"; they have no interest in the more profound teachings of Christianity such as Christ's sacrifice, ascension and high priestly work; and they have no skill in applying the Bible to the practical issues of life ("unskilled in the word of righteousness," (5:13).

Elementary Knowledge

The readers do know the basics of the faith, such as the fulfillment of the Old Testament prophecies in Christ ("elementary doctrine of Christ," 6:1-2). Beyond that, says the author, they have made little progress in the Christian life. He says that he wants to lead them on to maturity (6:1)—that is, a doctrinal and practical understanding of the high priesthood of Christ.

Intellectual Questions

As we study and seek to understand Hebrews, we must make every effort to put ourselves in the shoes of these early readers. They lived in a time of transition or change. On the one hand, they had become Christians. On the other hand, the outward forms of the old religion (altar, sacrifices, priesthood) remained, and the Jewish Christians were in a state of confusion over how the old and new related. As we read the book of Acts and the rest of the New Testament, we find Jewish Christians who still worship in the temple (Acts 3:1). They still offer animal sacrifices (21:17-26), and they still belong to the Sanhedrin (22:3). Some in the church (the party of the circumcision) attempt to force all Gentile Christians to become Jewish as well (15:1).

For many years Jewish Christians could argue that their participation in the temple rituals and offerings was only a traditional and cultural thing; it in no way interfered with their trust in Christ as Savior. The author of Hebrews has noticed, however, that they do not want to progress beyond the elementary

> As we study and seek to understand Hebrews we must make every effort to put ourselves in the shoes of these early readers.

doctrines that were Jewish as well as Christian (6:1-2). With the passing of time, God gave clear revelation concerning these things to the apostle Paul and others (such as the author of Hebrews). It became clear that devotion to the temple rituals was no longer an innocent thing. They must now break with Judaism and go to Christ "outside the camp" (13:13). God has now taken away the first covenant to establish the second (10:9). The readers must not be deceived by Jewish arguments (13:9) that there is saving power in the sacrifices and meat laws of the Jewish religion. Christians have another altar—namely, the cross of Christ (or Christ Himself) which is the source of saving grace.

We might summarize the intellectual stumbling blocks of the Hebrews as follows:

1. The relation of Judaism to Christianity.
2. The humiliation and sufferings of Jesus. Why, if He was Messiah, did He have to suffer?
3. The absence of a visible priesthood and sacrifices. Christianity, or so they thought, had no priesthood.
4. The delay of Jesus' return. If Jesus was now exalted to glory and honor, what was the purpose of His long absence?

Willful Apostasy

During his letter, the author warns his readers five times (2:1-4; 3:7–4:13; 6:4-8; 10:26-31; 12:18-29) of the danger of making a complete break with Christianity and falling back into Judaism. His concern is that they might "drift away" (2:1) from the truth and "fall away" (3:12) from the living God. Such a desertion of the Son of God would merit terrifying judgment (10:27, 31).

Every student of Hebrews must face the difficult question as to the precise spiritual condition of the readers. Some have argued that the readers are truly saved people who are in danger of losing their salvation. Others have concluded that the readers are not truly saved—that is, although they have professed to believe in Christ, they have never been truly born of God. This course shall adopt a third view. We shall proceed on the assumption that the author is confident that his readers are for the most part true believers (see Heb. 6:9; 10:39). This does not exclude the possibility that some of the group are rebellious in heart and on the road to apostasy. In other words, he is sure that his readers are true (although backslidden) believers, yet there is an element of doubt in his conviction. It is possible that a few of his readers have never come to saving faith in Christ. They have professed to believe in Christ, but that faith is not genuine.

The Historical Situation of the Readers

A Threat of National Disaster

Because of its date (around AD 67–68) and destination (Palestine) we must read Hebrews in view of the Jewish war (AD 66–70). The Romans began the war in September, AD 66, and the epistle was probably written as the war was going on. Throughout the epistle there is a sense of crisis: there is a "Day drawing near" (10:25); the "today" of opportunity is coming to an end (3:13); the temple rituals and sacrifices of the old covenant are "ready to vanish" (8:13). No doubt there would be solemn cursing of the Christians in the synagogues, and pressure upon the Jewish readers of the epistle to rally around the national cause and to forsake Christ.

An Expectation of Increased Suffering

The readers have suffered in the past (10:32-34), and there is the expectation of more to come (12:4). The author implies that the readers' powers of resistance are weakening (12:12).

A Loss of Church Loyalty

Some of the readers are beginning to neglect the weekly meetings ("to meet together," 10:25) of the church. The word "neglecting" (10:25) suggests that they were leaving it exposed to danger. The author implies that there is a growing selfishness among them. They are neglecting hospitality (13:2), failing to care for imprisoned believers (13:3) and showing a love of material possessions (13:5).

A Suggestion of Moral Danger

Some in the group, the author suggests, have become bitter and rebellious (12:15). There is a danger that such a person or persons will defile others. The author also mentions sexual immorality (12:16; 13:4) as a danger to which some might be exposed.

WHAT WAS THE PURPOSE OF HEBREWS?

It was not the custom of early Christian teachers to avoid dealing with practical problems and doctrinal error. The author of Hebrews does not open a "dialogue" with his readers hoping to arrive at a compromise solution. No, he deals decisively with their erroneous views by presenting the correct one. A careful reading of the epistle suggests a fourfold purpose:

1. To Establish the Supremacy of Christianity

The author explains the relationship of Christianity to Judaism and demonstrates from the Old Testament the superiority of Christianity. The revelation through the Son of God is superior to the revelation found in the Old Testament. In His person and authority Christ is superior to the custodians of the old covenant (Moses and Aaron). His priesthood is superior to Aaron's in the covenant He has established and the sacrifice He has offered.

2. To Exhort a Break with Judaism

The work of Jesus Christ has put an end to the Law with its covenant, priesthood, and offerings (see Heb. 7:11-12; 8:6-7). The author wants his readers to make a complete break with the Levitical altar and go "outside the camp" of Judaism (13:9-13).

3. To Encourage the Renewal of Effort

The author intends to "press on to maturity" (6:1, NASB) taking his readers with him. He wants them to again hear the living God through the Scriptures and move forward in their Christian walk. He reminds them that God's people have always been "strangers and exiles on the earth" (11:13). Their pilgrimage or journey will not be a disappointing one in that they will one day inherit "the land of promise" (11:9) and enjoy citizenship in "the heavenly Jerusalem" (12:22).

They must not allow reproaches and persecutions to discourage them (see Hebrews 10:32-33; 13:13). They need endurance (10:36), for the Christian life is a hard race (12:1). The sufferings and tribulations they face are not accidents outside the plan of God. They are the "discipline" (12:5-11) of a father and proof of their true sonship. The author reminds them of the example of the Old Testament heroes of the faith (Chapter 11). And he sets before them the example of the Son of God Himself (12:2, 7-10).

4. To Emphasize the Danger of Apostasy

The readers must not deceive themselves into thinking that by returning to Judaism they are lining up with the faithful of Old Testament times. If they desert Christ and Christianity, they will not desert *to* the faithful but *from* the faithful (10:39–12:1). Such apostasy (apostasy means "falling away") will not be *back to* but *away from* the living God (3:12). Such apostasy is the rejection of the Son of God (see Hebrews 6:6; 10:29), whose sacrifice is the only source of spiritual cleansing and access to God (10:1-22).

WHAT IS THE THEME OF HEBREWS?

Although there has been some difference of opinion, most scholars and Bible teachers have agreed that the central theme of Hebrews is the doctrine of the high priesthood of Christ. This is the "master idea" or "keystone" in the thinking of the author. One writer (C. F. D. Moule) has said that the whole burden of the epistle is wrapped up in two uses of the verb "we have": "we have such a high priest" (8:1) and "we have an altar" (13:10). Sanctuary and sacrifice are ours.

The following observations suggest that the high priesthood of Christ is the author's theme or central category. (1) The author says so in 8:1. "Now the point in what we are saying is this: we have such a high priest, one who is seated at the right hand of the throne of the Majesty in heaven." The epistle centers, then, in the thought of a seated priest. If you understand all that this means, you will grasp its message.

(2) This theme draws together and influences all the other teachings of the epistle. For example, God the Father dwells in the sanctuary (8:1-2). The author describes God's Son with priestly terminology. He describes

> **The central theme of Hebrews is the doctrine of the high priesthood of Christ.**

the angels as "ministering spirits" (1:14, lit. "Liturgic spirits"). He writes of Christ's work in the language of priestly sacrifice (for example 9:12; 10:12). He speaks of the application of Christ's work as forgiveness through blood (9:22). He describes God's people as those who, in priestly fashion, enter the Holy of Holies (10:19) and offer sacrifices of praise (13:15). The author's prophetic views are colored by the fact that he understands the king of "the world to come" (2:5) to be a priest-king (7:1-2).

Outline of Hebrews

I. Christ as High Priest: Superior in His Person (1:1-7:28)

1. Superior to the Prophets (1:1-3)
2. Superior to the Angels (1:4–2:18)
3. Superior to Moses (3:1–4:16)
4. Superior to Aaron (5:1–7:28)

II. Christ as High Priest: Superior in His Functions (8:1-10:18)

1. He Serves a Better Sanctuary (8:1-6)
2. He Mediated a Better Covenant (8:7-13)
3. He Performed a Better Ministry (9:1-28)
4. He Offered a Better Sacrifice (10:1-18)

III. Christ as High Priest: Superior in His Resources (10:19-13:25)

1. A Call to Steadfastness: Based on a New Access (10:19-39)
2. A Call to Faith: Based on Historical Illustrations (11:1-40)
3. A Call to Hope: Based on Christ's Endurance (12:1-29)
4. A Call to Love: Based on God's Grace (13:1-25)

Hebrews 1

The author's argument is that Christ in His person and work is better than (or superior to) the Levitical religion of the Old Testament (OT). At the heart of this argument is the author's contention that Jesus Christ is a high priest. His one sacrifice for sins (10:12) has obtained eternal redemption (9:12) and has opened the way of free, unhindered access to God (7:19; 10:21-22). The OT religion, on the other hand, failed to cleanse the conscience of sinners and establish intimate relations between God and man. Instead it kept people at a distance; the veil of the sanctuary symbolized this defect (9:7-8). The priestly sacrifice of Christ, however, has removed the veil, and there is now an accessible holy of holies (10:19-20).

Jesus Christ is a high priest.

Although the priestly work of Christ is the author's central theme (8:1), he does not immediately launch into it. Instead he lays the necessary foundation of establishing the superiority of the new revelation over the old. The comparison of old and new, therefore, has at its starting point the agents of revelation, and from there the author goes on to the agents of redemption. The author first deals with the personal superiority of Christ over these agents (1:1–7:28) and then develops His functional superiority over them (8:1–10:18).

I. Christ as High Priest: Superior in His Person (1:1 – 7:28)

SUPERIOR TO THE PROPHETS (1:1-3)

Hebrews does not begin like other New Testament (NT) epistles. It does not have a greeting for the readers, and the author does not give his name.

In fact, Hebrews does not begin to read like a letter until chapter 13. This has led most modern students of the epistle to conclude that Hebrews was originally a sermon. The author could not be with the readers in person, so he prepared this sermon for them. He then asked someone else to read it to them for him. He attached his personal greetings at the end (chapter 13).

In chapter 1 the author argues that the Lord Jesus Christ is the greatest possible agent of revelation because He is the Son of God. He is greater than the prophets of the OT, and He is greater than the angels.

The Superiority of His Revelation (1:1-2a)

Different in Method

Jesus Christ is God's final word to mankind. God did speak to His people in OT times, but the revelation given in His Son is superior. We can see the superiority of the new revelation over the old in their differences. First, the new revelation is different in method. The old revelation was partial and fragmentary; it came "at many times and in many ways." The expression "at many times" suggests that God's revelation through the prophets came over a long time (hundreds of years). The "many times" include the periods of OT history including the period of the patriarchs, the period of Moses, the period of the judges, the period of the kingdom, etc.

The old revelation came "in many ways." God used different methods to communicate revelation. For example, He used symbols, such as the tabernacle (Ex. 25–30). He used visions (Isa. 6:1-3). He used dreams (Dan. 2:1-3). He used angels (Dan. 8:15-17). He used direct, spoken communication (Num. 12:6-8), etc. In these "many ways" God's revelation was given bit by bit. Each inspired man had only a fragment of the truth.

During all that time (the OT era) "Jesus Christ had stood in the wings of history" (Roy Hession). When He appeared, all the threads of OT prophecy met in Him.

Different in Time

The revelation of the OT came "long ago." But now, God has spoken "in these last days." In the LXX (see abbreviations on page 4), the phrase "last days" refers to the times of the Messiah (Num. 24:14; Jer. 23:20). The OT prophets looked ahead to Christ's coming. We, says the author, live in the time of its fulfillment.

Different in Agents

In OT times God spoke "by the prophets." The author does not belittle that revelation—it was God who spoke through those men. But the revelation of the NT era is superior because God has "spoken to us by his Son." The original text says that God has "spoken to us *in Son*." The author words his phrase to fix our attention on the nature of the revelation. We have been given a son-type of revelation as opposed to a prophet-type of revelation. The readers of the epistle would highly regard a prophet; they must regard the Son of God even more highly.

The Superiority of His Person and Work (1:2b-3)

We might ask why a son-type revelation is better. The author of Hebrews now presents seven facts to show that superiority. The Son's revelation is better because of the following:

His Appointment as Heir

The prophets were servants, but the Son is the heir. As elsewhere in the NT (see Matt. 21:33-44; Mark 12:1-12; Gal. 4:7; Rom. 8:17), there is a link between sonship and heirship. Only members of a family may inherit. The Son's appointment took place before time in the eternal counsel of God. He has not yet entered into His inheritance (2:8); that awaits His second coming (9:28) when He will rule over "the world to come" (2:5).

His Lordship over History

The author goes on to say that God "created the world" through the Son. A more literal rendering would say "ages" instead of "world." The term refers to the periods or ages of history through which the purpose of God is unfolding.

> Jesus existed before the present created universe.

The prophets of old each appeared for a while in his own era. The Son of God, however, operates and manages the universe throughout all of its time periods. This implies that the Son is before all the ages of history. It implies the preexistence of Christ; He existed before the present created universe.

His Manifestation of the Divine Attributes

Not only does the author imply the Son's preexistence. He also goes on to assert His deity in verse 3, which many believe is an early Christian hymn. He speaks of the Son as "the radiance of the glory of God." The Greek word here translated "radiance" has a passive ("reflection") and an active ("radiance") sense. Here the active sense is more likely. The correct comparison would be sunlight, not moonlight. The Son flashes forth the glory of God. Light includes both source and radiance. Deity includes both Father and Son. The Son was of one nature with the Father. He is, therefore, more fully qualified than any prophet to reveal God.

His Embodiment of the Divine Essence

The author goes on to say that the Son is "the exact imprint of his [God's] nature." The term translated "imprint" here has the notion of absolute similarity. The term rendered "nature" here means "substance" or "real essence." The whole phrase stresses that the Son is a perfect copy of His Father in His divine nature. He personally and distinctly (that is, distinct from the Father) embodies the divine essence.

His Government of the Universe

There is another indication of the Son's deity in the next phrase. He "upholds the universe by the word of his power." The word translated "upholds" does not mean the passive and stationary support of a burden; it is an active term that means to bear along to a certain conclusion. The LXX uses the same word (Num. 11:14) of Moses praying for the people. He says, "I am not able to carry all this people alone [into the land]." The Son of God, however, is able to guide the universe of space and time to its appointed goal. In verse 2 the author has said that the Son is the Creator, the One who created the universe and fixed the boundaries of the ages through which the purposes of God would unfold. That looked primarily at His preexistent work. Now, however, in verse 3 he turns our attention to the present time and to the end time. At present He sustains the universe, i.e., He assures its continued existence (see Col. 1:17). And He is guiding the universe along in the way He has appointed. He is bearing history along to its consummation. "History and life are not purposeless ... He has programmed the universe and human history. All the pieces will come together when and as He has planned" (P. O. Wright).

His Provision of Purification of Sins

At this point the author briefly introduces the doctrinal center or main theme of the epistle. The Son of God, he says, "[made] purification for sins." The term "purification" is a priestly term and looks on to the discussion of Christ's high priestly work later in the epistle. All people are sinners. They are stained with guilt that separates them from a holy God. Only a sacrifice for sins can cleanse away guilt. At the cross Jesus Christ (as a priest) offered Himself (as a sacrifice) to remove the impurity of sins.

> **At the cross Jesus Christ offered Himself to remove the impurity of sins.**

His Exaltation in Glory

Following His priestly work on the cross, the Son of God "sat down at the right hand of the Majesty on high." This statement suggests two things:

1. The verb "sat down" implies that His work of purification was completed. This contrasts with the OT priests who never sat down because their work was never done.
2. The fact that He sat down at God's right hand means that He has been installed in a place of glory and honor. The place of highest honor in the ancient world was the right hand of a king (see 1 Kings 2:19).

SUPERIOR TO THE ANGELS (1:4–2:18)

Hebrews 1:4 marks a transition in the author's argument. It belongs to and concludes the first paragraph. In subject matter, however, it provides an introduction to the next paragraph. In this paragraph (1:5-14) the author affirms that the Son is superior to angels.

The original readers of the epistle were Jewish Christians. They shared the conviction of their fellow Israelites that angels were the highest beings in God's creation. The sacredness of the OT Law, they believed, was partly because it had been spoken by angels (see Acts 7:53; Gal. 3:19).

The readers were thinking of abandoning Christ and going back to Judaism and the old covenant. They argued that angels had a part in giving the old covenant, that is, the Law of Moses. They questioned if Christianity and the new covenant had anything to equal these messengers from God's own presence. The author of Hebrews now proves that Christ is superior to angels. He does this by quoting seven passages from the OT, the Jewish Bible. From these seven quotations he makes four points about Christ and angels:

Christ Bears the Messianic Title "Son" and Receives Angelic Worship (1:5-6)

Christ Is the Messianic Son

In verses 2-3 the author of Hebrews implies that Christ has always been the Son of God by nature. He goes on to say in verse 4 that He has inherited "the name … more excellent than" the angels. He immediately says (1:5) that the name Christ has inherited is, oddly enough, "Son" again. Clearly the author of Hebrews uses the title *Son* in two different senses: In verse 2 it indicates what Christ is and has always been by divine nature (eternal sonship); in verse 5 it is the messianic title He receives in connection with His human nature (acquired or messianic sonship).

There are three reasons for making this distinction between eternal sonship and messianic sonship:

1. The word "is" in verse 3 is timeless and suggests the eternal nature of the Son. The expression "having become" in verse 4, however, suggests that sonship is something He attained.
2. The order of events in verses 3 and 4 suggests that Christ acquired sonship after completing His work on earth.
3. In verse 5 the author quotes Psalm 2:7. Elsewhere (Acts 13:33) this psalm is associated with Jesus' resurrection and human nature. This would indicate that the title *Son* was inherited after His earthly work.

God has made Jesus—not an angel—His Messianic Son. In verse 5 the author quotes from Psalm 2, a coronation psalm of the Davidic kings. An OT king became God's "son" the day he was crowned. The angel Gabriel promised Mary that her son Jesus would "be called the Son of the Most High. And the Lord God will give to Him the throne of His father David"

(Luke 1:32). The OT kings were "begotten" (Ps. 2:7) as God's sons at their inauguration. Jesus was "begotten" (1:5) as God's Son at the time of His resurrection-ascension.

In verse 5 the author also quotes 2 Samuel 7:14 ("I will be to him a father, and he shall be to me a son"). In 2 Samuel 7 the Lord promised David that He would establish his son Solomon's kingdom. He then looked beyond Solomon to a greater king whose throne would be established forever. That greater king is Jesus Christ. At the time of His ascension into heaven, He was "appointed" as God's Son and installed as the messianic king. This messianic dignity will continue forever. God has never exalted any angel to such a high office.

Christ Will Receive Angelic Worship

The superiority of the Son to angels will be openly seen at His second coming into the world. Then ("when He brings the firstborn into the world") God will enthrone His Son as the Davidic king on earth. The title *firstborn* suggests dignity and sovereignty. At His second advent He will be openly revealed as the messianic heir and ruler. The author here quotes from the OT (the LXX and Dead Sea Scrolls of Deut. 32:43 or Ps. 97:7) which says of Christ's future coming: "Let all God's angels worship him." In the NT the term *worship,* with one exception (Matt. 18:26), speaks of worship addressed to God or Jesus Christ. The term implies that the messianic Son is in fact God the Son. The two senses of sonship merge in verse 6.

Christ Is the Divine King and Receives Angelic Obedience (1:7-9)

Angels Do the Divine Will

The fourth OT quotation (Ps. 104:4) is found in verse 7. There we learn that angels carry out the Lord's will with the swiftness of wind and the strength of "fire." As great as they are, angels are servants ("ministers") of God.

Christ Is the Divine King

Quoting Psalm 45:6-8 the author describes the Son in different terms. Verses 8-9 contain one of the strongest affirmations of the deity of Christ in the NT. The psalm directly addresses Him as God: "Your throne, O God, is forever and ever." The scene is prophetic and will be fulfilled at the second coming of Christ to the earth. Righteousness will characterize the Son's reign ("The scepter of uprightness is the scepter of your kingdom"). The scene in verse 9 is millennial (see Rev. 20:4-6). The psalmist's words describe a holy and lawful reign. It will also be a joyous time ("oil of gladness") for Christ, shared with His "companions." The word translated "companions" in verse 9 is translated "partakers" in Hebrews 3:14. It speaks of believers.

Christ Is the Eternal Creator, but Angels Are Mutable Creatures (1:10-12)

Christ Is the Eternal Creator

In verses 10-12 the author quotes Psalm 102:25-27. In that psalm the psalmist speaks of his own frailty and the possibility of death. He then meditates on the eternality and immutability (unchangeableness) of God. The author of Hebrews applies these words to the eternality and unchangeableness of Christ. He is the Creator of the universe (1:10). Just as most people outlive many suits of clothing in a lifetime, so Christ will live on when this universe grows old and perishes. The planets and stars "will all wear out like a garment," but He will stay the same. They will perish, but His "years will have no end."

Angels Are Mutable Creatures

The author does not specifically mention angels in verses 10-12. But because he has been contrasting Christ to angels, we may conclude that he has them in mind in his quotation of Psalm 102. In contrast to Christ, who is the Creator, angels are part of the creation.

Christ Is the Exalted Sovereign, but Angels Are Commissioned Servants (1:13-14)

Christ Is the Exalted Sovereign

A question introduces the seventh quotation from the OT (Ps. 110:1). The answer to the question is "No." God has never said to an angel, "Sit at my right hand until I make your enemies a footstool for your feet." He has, however, said this to His Son. At His ascension into heaven, the Lord

Jesus Christ was given the place of dignity and honor—namely, the place at God's right hand. Later in the epistle (7:25) the author tells his readers that Jesus presently carries on a work of intercession. Meanwhile, He waits for the defeat of His enemies. The devil and all that are hostile to God will be Christ's "footstool." This is a reference to the ancient custom of putting the feet on the necks of conquered enemies. Psalm 110, quoted here, looks on to the future kingdom of Christ when He will reign over His kingdom.

The Angels Are Commissioned Servants

In contrast to the exalted position of Christ, angels are servants. They are called "ministering spirits." The Greek word translated "ministering" is always used in the LXX of sacred service in the sanctuary of the tabernacle or temple. Angels are the servants of the One who sits in the heavenly tabernacle at God's right hand (see Heb. 8:1-2). The term "spirits" suggests three things:

1. They do not have material bodies.
2. They are beings whose essence is spiritual.
3. They belong to the heavenly realm, the realm of spirit. The term rendered "sent" carries the idea of a commission. They are under authority to discharge a service.

Their duty is to serve believers, called here "those who are to inherit salvation." The term "salvation" means "deliverance." In the NT, "salvation" is sometimes a thing of the past (see Eph. 2:8)—that is, a deliverance from the penalty of sin. It has a similar negative sense in Hebrews 2:14-15. It can also refer to a present "deliverance." In Hebrews 7:25, for example, the Lord is presently saving His people from all the evils that oppress them. In Hebrews 1:14, however, salvation is something future. It will take place at the second coming of Christ (9:28). Then Christ shall deliver His people into the kingdom, the promised inheritance of the "world to come" (2:5).

SUMMARY

The epistle to the Hebrews contrasts the old Mosaic covenant with the new covenant instituted by God's Son, the Lord Jesus Christ. In chapter 1 the author has argued that Christ is superior to the prophets of the old covenant (1:1-3). He is also superior to the angels who were involved in bringing the old revelation (1:4-14).

The epistle does not deny that God spoke in OT times. The old revelation was only partial and fragmentary. In the NT era, however, God has spoken through One who is greater than any prophet (1:1-4). His revelation is superior because He is God's Son. He shares the nature of His Father; He does the works of His Father; He shares the privileges of His Father; and He is on intimate terms with His Father. In these opening verses the author provides a survey of the nature and work of the Son. The author touches on:

> **Christ's revelation is superior because He is God's Son.**

1. His preexistence, eternal being and divine essence,
2. His incarnation (His coming in human nature) and His saving work and
3. His ascension and exaltation.

Using a series of seven OT quotations, the author then argues that the Son is superior to the angels (1:4-14). He makes four points:

1. Christ is the messianic and divine Son who receives angelic worship.
2. He is the divine King whom angels obey.
3. He is the eternal Creator, and they are mere creatures.
4. He is the exalted Sovereign awaiting His kingdom, but they are servants doing His bidding.

LESSON 1 EXAM

Use the exam sheet at the back of the course to complete your exam.

1. **In form, Hebrews reads like**
   A. a sermon.
   B. other New Testament letters.
   C. a tract or magazine article.
   D. a greeting card.

2. **In Hebrews 1:1-3 Jesus Christ is portrayed as superior to**
   A. Moses.
   B. Angels.
   C. Old Testament prophets.
   D. Old Testament priests.

3. **Hebrews chapter 1 views the Old Testament as**
   A. a false revelation.
   B. a Son-type revelation.
   C. a true revelation, but partial and fragmentary.
   D. a true and complete revelation of God's plan.

4. **Hebrews chapter 1 views Jesus Christ as**
   A. Lord of history.
   B. having the same divine essence as His Father.
   C. One who is preexistent.
   D. All of the above.

5. **Hebrews chapter 1 introduces the doctrinal center of the letter by the phrase**
   A. He is "the radiance of the glory of God."
   B. He is "the exact imprint of his nature."
   C. He has "obtained a more excellent name."
   D. He has "[made] purification for sins."

6. **The expression He "sat down" (1:3) suggests that**
   A. Christ's work of purification for sins was completed.
   B. Christ has been installed in a place of glory and honor.
   C. Christ's work differed from that of the Old Testament high priest.
   D. All of the above.

EXAM 1

7. **The New Testament uses the title *Son of God* to speak of**
   - (A) Christ's essential deity.
   - B. Christ's Messianic title.
   - C. Christ's human nature.
   - D. All of the above.

8. **Christ acquired His position as Messianic Son**
   - A. in eternity past.
   - (B.) at His birth.
   - C. at His baptism.
   - D. at His resurrection-ascension.

9. **Hebrews chapter 1 describes Christians as**
   - A. prophets.
   - (C.) companions of Christ.
   - B. angels.
   - (D.) sons of God.

10. **In Hebrews 1:14 the term "salvation" refers to**
    - A. deliverance from sin's penalty.
    - B. redemption from sin's slavery.
    - C. justification from sin's guilt.
    - (D.) deliverance into Christ's kingdom.

What Do You Say?

Why should we worship Christ and not angels, according to Hebrews 1?

Christ is Son of God, creator, King, Lord of history, preexisting. Angels are created, servants, spiritual, mutable. Christ is divine and human, Angels don't bring purification for sins. Christ does.

Hebrews 2

We learned in the introduction that the major purpose of the epistle to the Hebrews was to demonstrate the superiority of Christianity to Judaism. We learned in chapter 1 that the author of Hebrews accomplishes his purpose by pointing to a number of contrasts. Hebrews 1 presented the first and second of these contrasts. First, Christ has given a better revelation than the OT prophets (1:1-3). Second, Christ is superior to the angels who were also involved in bringing the old revelation (1:4–2:18). The argument that Christ is superior to angels covers chapters 1 and 2 of Hebrews. In chapter 1 the author has argued that Christ is superior to angels because of His deity. Now, in chapter 2 he will argue that Christ is superior to angels because of His humanity.

A Warning Against Drifting (2:1-4)

After reading Hebrews 1 we might conclude that the epistle is merely theoretical. In chapter 2, however, we learn that the author is very practical and serious. The teaching of chapter 1, that Christ is absolutely supreme, is of vital importance. To reject Him and His message is to reject all hope of salvation. In the opening verses of chapter 2, therefore, the author pauses in his remarks about Christ's superiority to angels. He now presents the practical implications of what he has been saying. His lesson is this: The old revelation was given through angels. To reject it brought punishment. How much more severe will the punishment be if we reject the revelation given through the Son of God Himself?

The Basis of the Appeal (2:1a)

Our chapter begins with the word "therefore" (or "for this reason," NASB). The author bases his appeal in verses 1-4 on what chapter 1 says about Christ. Because of His superiority the readers (including you and me) must pay close attention to the Christian message. The word "must" emphasizes the author's urgency.

The Substance of the Appeal (2:1b)

The author says that we must "pay much closer attention to what we have heard." It is likely that the author grew up by the sea. The Greek verb translated "pay attention" is a term that was often used by sailors. They used it to mean "to bring a ship to port" or "to dock a vessel securely." The author views our salvation as a safe harbor. The readers are to pay much closer attention to the words of the Son than to the words uttered by angels (the Law). By the expression "what we have heard" the author means the Gospel message (see Heb. 4:2).[1]

> **The author of Hebrews views our salvation as a safe harbor.**

The Seriousness of the Appeal (2:1c)

We must pay careful attention to the message of Christ "lest we drift away from it." Ancient writers used the Greek term translated "drift away" in a variety of ways. It was used, for example, of something slipping from the memory or of a ring slipping off a finger. The author of Hebrews uses it in the sense of a ship that drifts by a safe harbor. He fears for his readers. They have made a profession of faith in Christ, but there are no signs of life. He is afraid that some may never have truly received Christ as their Savior, so, he asks them if they are drifting past the safe harbor of Christ's salvation.

The Reason for the Appeal (2:2-4)

The author now gives the reason for his warning. Those who are drifting away are in great danger; to neglect the salvation offered by Christ will lead people to punishment.

The danger of punishment. Verse 2 says that punishment is a principle taught in the OT. God spoke to His people at Mt. Sinai, and He used angels to do so. That revelation was "reliable." This means that it was effective and forceful. It asserted its own claims. The Law was no dead letter. It enforced pains and penalties upon all who transgressed and disobeyed. Those who revolted against God's will ("transgression") and those who would not do what they were told ("disobedience") were punished. And the punishment fit the crime ("a just retribution").

Punishment is also a principle taught in the NT. In verses 2 and 3 the author argues from the lesser to the greater. If ("since") failure to respond in OT days brought punishment, how much greater the punishment will be of those who reject Christ. "How shall we escape," the author asks, "if we neglect such a great salvation?" By "salvation" the author of Hebrews means something future (see Heb. 1:14). He means the future deliverance of God's people from judgment and into the kingdom. How shall we escape that future judgment if today we neglect the message of salvation? This is a question for which there is no answer. We shall not escape if we neglect the Gospel message.

At this point we must pause to consider a question of interpretation. Of what is the author warning his readers? There are two interpretations of the warning in Hebrews 2:1-4. Some say that he is referring to divine chastening and loss of rewards in the future kingdom of heaven: those who live mediocre Christian lives in this age will suffer the loss of position and privilege in the next. Others say that he is speaking of eternal punishment; those who identify themselves as Christians but have never trusted Christ as Savior are in danger of destruction. The second of these views is the correct one in my judgment. There are five warning passages in Hebrews (2:1-4; 3:7–4:13; 5:11–6:20; 10:26-31; 12:18-29), and they must be studied consistently as a unit. In 10:39 the author clearly says that the danger is "[being] destroyed." Elsewhere in the NT this term describes an everlasting state of torment (see Matt. 7:13; John 17:12; 2 Thess. 2:3; 2 Peter 2:1, 3; 3:7, 16; Rev. 17:8, 11).

> **We shall not escape future judgment if we neglect the Gospel message.**

The greatness of salvation. Verse 3 calls the message of Christ "such a great salvation." The greatness of salvation is threefold. First, it originated with the Lord Jesus Christ ("It was declared at first by the Lord"). Second, it was proclaimed by the apostles ("those who heard"). The author's point is that the message of salvation is trustworthy because it came from those who had heard the Savior in person. Third, it was divinely authenticated by apostolic miracles ("God also bore witness by signs and wonders and various miracles and by gifts of the Holy Spirit"). Elsewhere in the NT (2 Cor. 12:12) the apostle Paul speaks of the "signs of a true apostle." These were special miracles and gifts in the apostolic age that were designed to authenticate the apostles and their message. Such miracles "attested to" the apostles' testimony. The term "attested to," or as other versions say, *confirmed*, was used in NT times of documents that were legally guaranteed.

SUPERIOR TO THE ANGELS (CONTINUED) (2:5-18)

Verses 1-4 are almost a parenthesis in the author's argument about angels. Using the word *for*, he returns to where he stopped in 1:14. At this point in the discussion someone might ask, "Does not the fact that Jesus was human prove that He is inferior to angels?" By implication, therefore, He would be inferior to the old revelation and to Judaism. The author's answer is something like this: "You do not understand God's plan. It is God's plan that human beings have a position in the 'world to come' (2:5) that is higher than angels."

Superior Because of His Destiny (2:5-9)

The Divine Intention for Man (that is, the human race) (2: 5-8a)

The author wants to get his readers' mind off angels. "Listen," he seems to say. "Think of the destiny of mankind. That destiny is glorious." Man, not angels, will rule over "the world to come" (lit. "the inhabited earth to come"). The phrase "world to come" does not refer to the blessing of knowing Christ today. Nor does it refer to the future life in heaven. Rather, it speaks of the future messianic age. Then all the nations will be subdued, and Christ will rule as King over the earth. The "world to come" is the millennial age (cf. Rev. 20:4-6) which will begin at the second coming of Christ. Then a man, not angels, will rule the earth.

> Mankind has been given an exalted place in the plan of God.

Like all good Bible teachers the author turns his readers to Scripture. In verses 6-8 he quotes Psalm 8:4-6. David probably composed this psalm at night as he gazed on the starry heavens above him. As David lay on his back, he meditated on the book of Genesis and the story of the creation of Adam. He considered the immensity of the universe and the frailty of man. Man is finite, but he has been given an exalted place in the plan of God. His status is just "a little while lower than the angels." The Lord has made him "the king of the earth" (E. Sauer). "You have crowned him with glory and honor." And Adam was no landless king. God gave him a territory (the earth) and subjects (all living creatures). God did this and so put "everything in subjection under his [Adam's] feet."

The Divine Frustration over Man (2:8b)

At the end of verse 8 the author summarizes the tragedy of man. The words "at present" introduce a contrast. The stuff of kings is in man, but there is sin in him as well. The author writes, "At present, we do not yet see everything in subjection to him." "There," says Ray Stedman, "is the whole story of human history in a nutshell." Man has not realized his destiny to be sovereign of the earth. The reason is that he is a sinner.

The Divine Realization in Man (namely, in Christ) (2:9)

The word "but" at the beginning of verse 9 introduces another strong contrast. It is obvious that man has failed, but the promise of Psalm 8 has not. The psalm has not yet been fulfilled by man. But it is on the way to being fulfilled by the man Jesus. At the cross ("the suffering of death") Jesus accomplished a great victory. Today He is enthroned in heaven ("crowned with glory and honor"). There He waits for the day when His enemies will be defeated (cf. Heb. 1:13; 10:13). Then He will reign over "the world to come" (2:5).

There is an interesting use of the verb *to see* in verses 8 and 9. In verse 8 the Greek verb used has the sense "to observe." In verse 9 the author uses another Greek word that means "to glance." His thought seems to be this: if we carefully look at mankind and his world, we shall see that things are not as they should be. Yet just a glance at God's right hand will assure us that man's destiny will be realized by Jesus. He has been "crowned with glory and honor."

To win back man's lost destiny, the Son of God "for a little while was made lower than the angels" (2:9). The same language is used of mankind in general in verse 7. Although the same phrase ("little while lower") is used in the Greek text, there is possibly a change in the author's mind. Man was made "lower than the angels." The Son of God, however, was made "for a little while ... lower than the angels." Verse 9 clearly speaks of two stages in Jesus' career: incarnation and exaltation. Although Jesus became a man forever, He was lower in status to angels only for a while.

We see the cost of man's restoration in the phrase "the suffering of death." Jesus died to bring human beings to their glorious destiny in "the world to come." We must remember that the Bible teaches that death is the punishment for sin. Jesus never sinned (4:15). His death was substitutionary. Jesus died for others. Our author says that He died "for everyone,"— that is, His death has value for all who believe in Him. The reward for man's restoration is expressed by the phrase "crowned with glory and honor." The source of man's restoration is expressed by the phrase "the grace of God." The term *grace* means "God's favor toward those who do not deserve His favor" (D. Guthrie).

> **Jesus died to bring human beings to their glorious destiny in the world to come.**

The author's point, in short, is this: the humanity of Jesus does not mean that He is inferior to angels. He was, for a while, lower in status to them. That is no longer true. Today He is exalted in heaven, and in the future He will rule over "the world to come."

Superior Because of His Suffering (2:10-18)

The word "suffering" in verse 9 serves to introduce the author's subject in the next paragraph (2:10-18). Apparently some of the readers were having trouble with the idea of a suffering Christ. It did not fit with their concept of Messiah or of God. The author now confronts this problem. "It was fitting," he says, for God to make Jesus suffer. The word *fitting* here means worthy, suitable, or appropriate. Christ's suffering was fitting for two reasons. First, it was fitting due to the sovereignty of God ("for whom and by whom all things exist"). He is the cause of every created thing and the goal of every created thing. God created all things for Himself. Whatever God does is "fitting," whether or not we may agree with it. The only way to be sure of what is fitting (worthy or suitable) for God to do is to consider what He has actually done. And, second, it was fitting because of the nature of the problem. Man's problem is suffering and death. To be mankind's Savior and Substitute, Christ must take to Himself a human nature and suffer and die.

In verse 9 the author has implied that Christ became a man in order to die. In more specific terms, however, he suggests that the incarnation and suffering of Christ had a fivefold purpose. Verses 5-9 give the first of these purposes: Christ took human nature to win for human beings their lost destiny. Now, in verses 10-18 he gives four more purposes:

He Became Man and Suffered to Bring Many Sons to Glory (2:10-13)

The term *glory* is one of those rich words with many connotations. It can mean "honor," "praise," "splendor," "radiance," "pomp," "power," or "exaltation." In the present context it speaks of the splendor of our ultimate salvation (see Heb. 9:28). It looks ahead to the "world to come" when the Son of God will receive His inheritance. He will share that time of joy with His "companions" (see Heb. 1:9), that is, with those He saves and makes "sons."

Christians are here called "sons" (2:10). The term *son* suggests status, privilege, and heirship. It was not God's purpose to have just one son in glory. Rather, He determined to have others. There is a difference, of course, between Christ's sonship and ours: Christ is a son by virtue of His divine nature and messiahship; Christians are sons by virtue of their salvation.

Christ is here called "the founder of their salvation." The Greek term translated "founder" in verse 10 can also be translated "captain," "pioneer," or "leader." The context favors one of these instead of "founder." Jesus is the *pioneer* or *leader* of salvation. He endures suffering and leads His people to their promised salvation in the world to come.

> **Jesus is the pioneer or leader of salvation.**

For God to bring many sons to glory, He had to "make the founder of their salvation perfect through suffering." This puzzles some readers of Hebrews. How can Hebrews speak of Jesus being perfected and also speak of Him as being "without sin" (See Heb. 4:15; 7:26)? The Greek verb *to perfect* means "to bring to an end" or "to bring to its goal." In this context it suggests qualification. The sufferings of Jesus qualified Him to be our Savior. The term "suffering" implies a plurality of sufferings. This suggests two things:

1. The suffering of the cross made Him a qualified redeemer. He is the "perfect" Savior in that He died for us (2:9, 17).
2. His sufferings throughout life qualified Him to be our high priest. He is able to understand and sympathize with us in all our sufferings (2:14, 18).

In verse 11 the author says that it was Christ's human nature that made His saving work possible. "He who sanctifies [Jesus] and those who are sanctified [Christians] all have one source." His point is that both Savior and those He saves are all made from the same substance: human nature. It was fitting that the deliverer of mankind should be a man. Jesus was truly human.

Hebrews here describes Christ's work for His people as "sanctification." The NT elsewhere describes sanctification as a process of growth in Christian maturity. This process begins at conversion and is completed at the resurrection. In Hebrews, however, sanctification is not a process. Rather, it is an event that takes place once-for-all at conversion. Hebrews 10:10 says that "we

> **By becoming a man our Lord showed that He was not ashamed to place Himself on the level of our humanity.**

have been sanctified through the offering of the body of Jesus Christ once for all" (see also Heb. 13:12). In Hebrews "to sanctify" means to dedicate people to God, to consecrate them or set them apart to Him as worshiping people. At the moment of his conversion, the believer is "sanctified"—that is, he or she is set apart to worship and serve God.

By becoming a man our Lord showed that He was not ashamed to place Himself on the level of our humanity. "He is not ashamed to call them brothers." He totally identified Himself with us to secure our redemption. What greatness! He had the right to be ashamed. What grace! He was not ashamed (H. A. Kent). The term "brothers" speaks of those who have been sanctified, that is, it speaks of believers.

As is his practice, the author now quotes the OT. His purpose is to show that the Son of God has fully identified with men. In verse 12 he quotes Psalm 22:22. This psalm has two parts. In the first, David is persecuted by Saul. In the second, he comes to the throne rejoicing. The psalm is a prophecy of our Lord. The first part speaks of the horrors of crucifixion. In the second part He comes to the throne rejoicing. Just as David's victory was shared by his followers, so Christ's victory is shared by His followers. The author's point is that the relationship between the Savior and His people is that of brothers. This relationship required that He become a man.

In verse 13 he quotes from Isaiah 8:17-18. In that passage Isaiah rebukes the unbelief of Judah in making an alliance with pagan Syria. The prophet says that his trust and that of his children is in God. In Hebrews 2:13 the author applies the words of Isaiah to Christ. He puts His trust in God; and His companions, the "children" of God, also trust Him. The point of this quotation is that Jesus is closely identified with believers. Such close fellowship demands a common humanity.

He Became Man and Suffered to Bear the Judgment of Sin, Namely Death (2:9, 14)

The Bible clearly teaches that death is a punishment for sin (see Gen. 2:17; Rom. 5:12). God's holy will demands that sin be punished. At the cross, Jesus met these demands. He was Himself without sin. He did not need to die. When He died, He died for others. He tasted "death for everyone."

He Became Man and Suffered to Make the Devil Powerless (2:14-16)

The inspired author of Hebrews believed in the existence of the devil. He states that one of the reasons the Son of God became man was to defeat the devil. The devil keeps people in "slavery" through the "fear of death" (2:15). Death is his weapon. Why do people fear death? They fear death because they are afraid of future misery. In other words, they fear what may come after death, namely, judgment (see Heb. 9:27).

To deliver "the children" (2:14) from the fear of death, Christ had to assume human nature ("flesh and blood"). The problem faced by mankind was death, so God's Son had to assume human nature that was capable of dying. Someone has said that it is fitting that the one who defeated man (Satan) should at the cross be defeated by a man. The man (Jesus) defeated the devil with his own weapon: death. The Savior was punished with death for our sins. Now we need to fear death no longer.

Verse 14 says that the devil had "the power of death." This phrase suggests three things:

1. The devil was the means of bringing death into the world.
2. He is the prince of the state of death—that is, death is his sphere of operation.
3. He uses death to terrify and frighten people.

Christ assumed human nature, our author says, to "destroy" the devil. The translation "destroy" is too strong. The Greek verb has the sense "to make ineffective," "to make powerless," or "to condemn to inactivity." The term does not imply "loss of being, but loss of well being" (W. E. Vine). The work of Christ does not destroy the devil. Rather, it undoes his work and dooms him to the complete loss of power.

In verse 16 the author explains and summarizes Christ's reason for becoming man. "He became man, then, in order to help man" (F. F. Bruce). The original readers of this epistle highly honored angels. The author implies that angels are not to be envied because they are not a part of God's plan of redemption: "For indeed He does not give aid to angels." Some of the readers thought less of Christ because He was a human being and because He suffered. The author reminds them that Christ became a man and died to give them "help." The verb "help" may be literally rendered in this verse, "to grasp by the hand in order to help."

Verse 16 does not say that Christ gives aid to mankind in general, although we may make that application today. It says that He gives aid to "the offspring of Abraham." The first readers of the epistle were Jewish. The author wants to bring his point home to them personally. We may paraphrase the verse in this way: "Christ does not give aid to angels, but to yourselves, my Hebrew brethren." Verses 17-18 further explain the "help" He gives.

> **The work of Christ undoes the work of the devil and dooms him to the complete loss of power.**

He Became Man and Suffered to Be Our High Priest (2:17-18)

Once Christ assumed a true human nature, He was obligated to be made like His brethren "in every respect." The phrase "in every respect" does not refer to the properties of human nature. The author already commented on these in verse 14 ("flesh and blood"). Rather, it speaks of the sufferings, toils, perils, and conflicts that weigh down the life of man (F. Delitzsch). It means that He did not have a phantom or pretend human experience. Rather, He truly went through the ordinary experiences of life. He saw things from the human point of view.

It was necessary that He become man and suffer in order "that he might become a *merciful and faithful* high priest." It was not necessary for God the Son to become man to be "merciful." He has always been a God of mercy. He had to become man to become a merciful High Priest. In verse 17 the author is thinking of the mercy shown by Jesus at the cross. There He offered

Himself for the sins of the people. Jesus was "merciful" in His relationship to men, and "faithful" in His relationship to God (H. Montefiore).

This is the first time the expression *high priest* occurs in Hebrews. A priest is a mediator (middleman) between God and man. He is the "person through whom and through whose ministry people draw near to God" (J. Denney). Universally, people sense the need of a priest. People are sinful, and without some kind of middleman they cannot draw near to God at all. Jesus served as High Priest "in the service of God." This expression suggests that people are responsible or answerable to God for their behavior. They are answerable to God for their sins, and they require the services of a high priest to make matters right.

As High Priest, Christ made "propitiation for the sins of the people." The verb *to propitiate* means "to put away divine wrath." God is holy, and He directs His anger or wrath towards wrongdoing of every kind. At the cross God's holy anger against sin was poured out on Christ. Jesus died as a sacrifice under the divine anger. He died in the place of the people, and God's wrath was satisfied.

Verse 18 says that because Jesus "has suffered," He is "able to help" His people. The Greek tense of the verb "has suffered" suggests a past event with continuing effects. Christ's suffering is a thing of the past, but its effect is permanent. He is a merciful, compassionate, and understanding high priest (see Heb. 4:15-16).

Because of His sufferings Jesus was "tempted." In context the author has in mind the sufferings associated with the cross, probably including those of Gethsemane (see Heb. 5:7-8). There, as earlier in our Lord's ministry, the devil tried to seduce Him into disobedience. The application is clear. The first readers of this epistle had endured sufferings and faced more to come. They were, no doubt, being tempted, due to these sufferings, to be disloyal to God and to abandon their Christian profession. Although Jesus felt the full force of the devil's temptations, He did not sin.[2] Yet the experience of His suffering and temptation has made Him sympathetic as well as human. When His people are tempted and fall, Christ is "able to help" them.

Jesus is a merciful, compassionate and understanding High Priest.

What does the author mean when he says that Jesus is "able to help those who are being tempted"? In the immediate context (2:10-18) it means that He continually applies the benefits of His sacrifice to the sins of His people—that is, He forgives their sins. Other passages in Hebrews suggest that Jesus also gives aid in the following ways: (1) He has sympathy for them in times of temptation (see Heb. 4:15), (2) His life is an example of triumph over temptation (12:2-3), and (3) He empowers them to overcome temptation (4:16 and 13:21).

SUMMARY

In verses 1-4 the author warns his readers about the dangers of drifting in the Christian life. He then continues His argument that Christ is superior to angels. In verses 5-18 he argues that He is superior because of His manhood. In view of the assertion of Psalm 8 (see Heb. 2:7) that man is subordinate to the angels, the author seeks to explain the need for the incarnation. The Son of God became man for these reasons:

1. To restore to man his lost destiny of sovereignty over the world to come, verses 5-9.
2. To bring many sons to glory, verses 10-13.
3. To taste death for everyone, verses 9, 14.
4. To render the devil powerless, verses 14-15.
5. To become a merciful and faithful High Priest, verses 16-18.

Endnotes

[1] The term *Gospel* means "good news." The classic NT summary of the Gospel is 1 Corinthians 15:1-8. There we learn that the Gospel is the good news that Christ died for our sins, was buried, and rose again on the third day.

[2] See Endnote 14 on lesson 3.

LESSON 2 EXAM

Use the exam sheet at the back of the course to complete your exam.

1. **Hebrews 2:1 seems to suggest that**
   A. the author grew up in the mountains.
   B. the author grew up on a farm.
   C. the author grew up by the sea.
   D. the author grew up in a city.

2. **The author's greatest fear about his readers is that**
   A. they are false professors in danger of eternal punishment.
   B. they are weak Christians who will lose their rewards in the kingdom of heaven.
   C. they are Jews who refuse the Gospel message.
   D. they are Gentiles who refuse the Gospel message.

3. **The expression "world to come" in verse 5 refers to**
   A. the future millennial reign of Christ on earth.
   B. the blessing of knowing Christ as Savior.
   C. the future life of the believer in heaven.
   D. the world of angels.

4. **Verses 6-8 are a quotation from**
   A. Psalm 2.   C. Psalm 40.
   B. Psalm 110.   D. Psalm 8.

5. **According to Hebrews 2:9, to become our Savior Christ had to**
   A. become a man.
   B. become a man and suffer and die for our sins.
   C. be crowned with glory in heaven.
   D. become superior to angels.

6. **Jesus is called the "founder" of salvation because**
   A. He wrote the book of Hebrews.
   B. He leads His people to their promised salvation in the world to come.
   C. He was made lower than the angels.
   D. He is superior to angels.

7. **In Hebrews, "sanctification" most often refers to**
   A. propitiation.
   B. a process of renewal and maturity in the Christian life.
   C. justification.
   D. the once-for-all event at conversion when the believer is set apart to worship and serve God.

8. **When verse 14 says that Christ came to "destroy" the work of the devil, it means that**
   A. the devil no longer exists.
   B. the devil will one day cease to exist.
   C. Christ's work dooms the devil to a complete loss of power.
   D. the devil will one day be saved.

9. **The term "propitiation" means**
   A. temptation.
   B. the wiping away of sin.
   C. the redemption of sinners.
   D. the putting away of divine wrath.

10. **Jesus helps His people by**
    A. sympathizing with them in their struggles.
    B. offering them an example of triumph over temptation.
    C. forgiving their sins.
    D. All of the above.

What Do You Say?

Why did God become a man? Or what benefit is that to you?

To be a mediator, experience ordinary human life by temptation and suffering. Take on Him my sins, to be sympathetic, merciful, able to help me. I am now a daughter of God because Christ is my brother.

Hebrews 3 and 4

The original readers of Hebrews were professing Jewish Christians. They were immature and unstable believers, and some of them were wavering in their loyalty to Christ. They were thinking of returning to Judaism, the religion of Moses. They believed Moses was higher in rank than the very angels of heaven. He was a patriot. He was a legislator or law giver (people acknowledge his moral principles even today). He founded a national literature (his writings are read to this very day by men and women in every walk of life). He established the religious institutions of Israel (tabernacle and priesthood).

> **Only those who hold fast to Christ and obtain His help will enter God's rest.**

In their immature state some of the readers of the epistle were beginning to compare Jesus unfavorably to Moses. Jesus had not delivered the Jewish people from Rome as Moses had delivered them from the Egyptians. Jesus had not added any beautiful religious ritual to the life of Israel, but Moses had given the awe-inspiring tabernacle service to the nation.

The author of Hebrews now meets these arguments head on and asserts that Jesus is greater than Moses. By implication He is greater than any religious personality. Moses was God's servant, it is true. But Jesus was God's Son. Furthermore, he will now argue that a return to Judaism would be a departure from the living God. Many Jewish people (even Moses himself) at the time of the exodus had failed to enter the land of Canaan because of disobedience. So today many professing Christians are in danger of not entering God's rest. Only those who hold fast to Christ and obtain His help will enter that rest.

SUPERIOR TO MOSES (3:1-4:16)

Because Christ Is a Son, but Moses Was a Servant (3:1-6)

The word "therefore" (3:1) connects verse 1 with what has gone before. Because of the finality of the revelation given in Jesus,[1] and because of His true deity and victorious humanity, the readers should carefully consider Him.

The Description of the Readers (3:1a)

The terms of address used by the author serve to remind the Christian reader of the dignity with which God has invested them. It is a dignity "which it would be insulting to God for them to treat lightly" (F. F. Bruce). They are "holy," i.e., God has set them apart to worship and serve Him. They are "brothers," i.e., God has made them members of His family. And they are "[those] who share in a heavenly calling," i.e., they have been invited to participate in the blessings of the messianic kingdom to be established in the world to come.

The Designations of the Son (3:1b)

The author assigns two titles to Jesus. First, he calls Him "the apostle." This is the only time in the NT that Jesus is called "apostle." The term *apostle* is from a verb meaning "to send forth." It was used of an ambassador or representative who was sent with authority. Jesus was sent to be God's representative among mankind. This title looks back at all that has been said about Jesus in chapters 1 and 2.

Second, the author calls Jesus "high priest." A priest represents men and women in the presence of God. The Latin word for priest *pontifex*, means a "bridge builder." As High Priest, Jesus builds a bridge between man and God. This title looks forward to what the author will say about Jesus in chapters 5 through 10.

The two titles are joined in the phrase "apostle and high priest of our confession." The term *confession* may refer to the daily testimony Christians bear to Christ. It is more likely, however, that it refers to the content of that testimony. In other words, Jesus and His work are the fundamental doctrines of the body of truth that makes up the Christian faith.

The Faithfulness of the Son (3:2)

In verse 2 the author says that Jesus loyally discharged the duties with which He was entrusted by God. We should note that nothing negative about Moses is said here. The author's point is that Jesus does not come behind Moses in faithfulness to the One who appointed Him.

Moses was faithful "in all God's house." The term *house* may refer to the community of God's people in the OT. It is more likely, however, that the term refers to the tabernacle, i.e., the tent sanctuary where the Israelites worshiped. In the LXX the expression "house of God" or "house of the Lord" is a fixed term for the tabernacle (Ps. 23:6; 26:8, etc.). Furthermore, verse 2 probably contains an allusion to Numbers 12:7. In that passage Miriam and Aaron confront Moses before the tabernacle. The Lord rebukes them there and tells them that Moses had faithfully carried out all that God had told him concerning His house, i.e., the tabernacle.

The Superiority of the Son (3:3-6)

In verses 3-6 the author says that Jesus is "worthy of more glory than Moses." He is worthy of more glory because He has a more exalted relationship to God than did Moses. Moses was God's servant. He was a mere laborer who brought the details of the tabernacle from God to the Israeli artisans (Ex. 25:1-2). Jesus, however, was God's Son. God, the architect or builder of the house, had a Creator-servant relationship to Moses. But He has a Father-Son relationship to Jesus.

Jesus is the Messiah of whom Moses and all the prophets spoke.

Yet Moses was faithful, and his house (namely, the tabernacle) served "to testify to the things that were to be spoken later." In other words, the tabernacle with its priesthood, offerings and ceremonies was typical.[2] It illustrated and predicted the truths to be later revealed in the NT era about the person and work of Christ.

In verse 6 the title *Christ*[3] is ascribed to Jesus for the first time in Hebrews. The term *Christ* is the Greek form of the Hebrew title *Messiah* (see Dan. 9:25, 26). It means "an anointed person or thing." It became a technical term among the Jewish people for the future Davidic king who would be God's deliverer of Israel. The Christ would free Israel and defeat her enemies. By using this title the author is reminding his readers that Jesus is the Messiah of whom Moses and all the prophets spoke (see Luke 24:25-27).

The Lesson for the Readers

In verse 6 the author uses the word *house* to make a shift from the OT tabernacle to the present day. He tells his readers that they, not the tabernacle, are God's dwelling place today (see John 14:17; 1 Cor. 6:19).

The author wishes to inject a godly fear into his readers. He says that we are God's "house" (i.e., His dwelling place or people) "if indeed we hold fast." This is the doctrine of perseverance, i.e., the doctrine that only those who continue in the faith are truly saved. The author does not say that we *become* God's house by continuing; rather we *are* His house if we continue. The sure proof of eternal life is that one holds out to the end.[4]

Because Rejection of Him Is More Serious than Rejection of Moses—A Warning Against Unbelief (3:7-19)

Having quickly demonstrated that Jesus is superior to Moses, the author launches into the second major admonition of his epistle. He bases his warning on Israel's experience in the wilderness as they journeyed from Egypt to Canaan. They did not enter the land of Canaan due to unbelief (which led to rebellion). If Israel's rejection of Moses was serious, the author implies, how much more serious would be the rejection of Christ.

The Quotation of a Psalm (3:7-11)

As is his custom, the author bases his lessons on the exposition of Scripture, which he attributes to the authorship of "the Holy Spirit" (3:7). He quotes Psalm 95:7-11 where the psalmist uses Israel's experience of disobedience as a warning against unbelief. The trip to Canaan should have taken the Israelites about eleven days (Deut. 1:2, 6-8), yet it took forty years (3:9). The delay was due to God's anger at their rebellion and hardness of heart, i.e., their stubbornness, indifference, and callousness toward the Word of God.

The author of Hebrews may have a number of incidents in mind. He is probably thinking of Rephidim (Ex. 17:2-7) when the people grumbled against Moses due to their lack of water. He may have been thinking as well of the time (Num. 20:11-12) when Moses struck the rock in anger. And he certainly must have been thinking of the time at Kadesh-Barnea (Num. 13–14) when the people refused to enter the land due to fear and unbelief.

As a result the Lord swore, "They shall not enter my rest" (3:11). For thirty-eight years Israel was kept in the area of Kadesh-Barnea. The term "rest" refers here to the land of Canaan (Deut. 12:9). Due to God's anger against their unbelief and rebellion they were not allowed into the Promised Land.

The Application of the Psalm (3:12-15)

The need for self-examination, 3:12. The application to the readers (and to us) is obvious. "Take care, brothers," the author warns. The term "take care," or as other versions say, *beware,* speaks of an intent, earnest contemplation. The readers of Hebrews were to examine themselves to see if there was unbelief in their hearts. The expression "an evil, unbelieving heart" tells us something about the nature of sin. Unbelief produces an evil heart. Unbelief is the root of sin that leads to disobedience and transgression.

Apparently some of the readers were thinking of leaving their profession of Christian faith and returning to Judaism. Such a move would be a departure "from the living God." The Greek word translated "fall away" is the word from which we get the English word *apostasy.* The old religion was now obsolete (see Heb. 8:13). If one returned to Judaism, he or she would be falling away from the living God.

The need for mutual exhortation, 3:13. The readers are to "exhort one another every day." There is no such thing as a solitary Christian. Believers need to get together regularly for mutual encouragement. The readers were dull and immature (see Heb. 5:11-12), and a few of them were not truly born again (see John 3:3-16). The congregation needed to exhort the believers to maturity and the unbelievers to faith in Christ. To persist in unbelief would lead to hardness of heart. The term "today"[5] suggests that God is still patiently waiting for the unbelievers among them to come to saving faith in Christ.

The need for steadfast endurance, 3:14. Those who are truly Christians need to stand firmly upon the truth they have believed about Christ. The Greek word translated "confidence" does not refer to their subjective, personal convictions. Rather it speaks of the objective ground or basis ("foundation") upon which they have placed their confidence. In other words, they are to stand firmly upon the foundation of salvation in Christ and not Judaism.

The need for immediate application, 3:15. The author calls upon his readers to come to a decision. They must not stubbornly resist the divine invitation that calls them to faith in Christ.

The Lesson of the Psalm (3:16-19)

In the closing verses of the chapter, the author asks three questions:

1. Who rebelled against God? It was the very people that God had rescued. They rejected Moses, the divinely appointed leader.
2. Who made God angry? It was the people who had sinned against Him. They were punished with death in the wilderness.
3. Who did God say would not enter "rest" (i.e., the land of Canaan)? It was those whose unbelief had led them to disobedience and a refusal to listen to the Lord. The lesson is this: unbelief kept the Israelites out of the land of promise, and unbelief today will keep the reader out of the heavenly city (see Heb. 11:10, 13-16; 13:14).[6]

Because Rest Is Attained Exclusively through Him (4:1-13)

It Is a Rest of Faith (4:1-3a)

The time of the rest. The promise of rest was not fulfilled in OT times due to unbelief. The author now explicitly applies the lesson of the OT account to the readers (and to us). He says, "The promise of entering his rest still stands." What does the author mean by "rest"? It will help us answer this question if we ask another one: when does this rest take place? Many Bible teachers believe that the rest is something in the present experience of the believer. Some say it refers to the experience of conversion. They say that Christian salvation is the rest. Others say that the rest refers to the experience of Christian surrender. When the believing Christian fully dedicates his or her life to God's will, he or she enters the "faith-rest" life.

There is much truth to the view that conversion and surrender bring rest to one's life (see Matt. 11:28-30). However, the author is not speaking of conversion and surrender here. The "rest" of which our author speaks is a yet future experience in the life of the believer. There are three reasons why this is so:

1. In verses 1, 6, and 9 the author says that "a promise still stands" for some to enter rest. It is a promise yet to be fulfilled.
2. In verses 1-16 the expression "let us" occurs four times (4:1, 11, 14, 16). The author uses the expression as an exhortation to enter the rest in the future (4:11).

3. The epistle to the Hebrews portrays the Christian life as a pilgrimage or journey. Christians have not yet arrived at their destination, yet they are on their way to the city that is to come (13:14). Entering "rest," then, is not a present attainment but a promise of something that lies at the end of the Christian journey.

The nature of the rest. What, then, does the author mean by "rest"? Some say that this speaks of the future home of the redeemed in heaven. Others say that the rest is the future home of the redeemed in Christ's millennial kingdom upon the earth.[7] There are at least five reasons for accepting the millennial view:

1. In chapters 3 and 4 the author is basing his remarks on Psalm 95. This psalm is part of a block of psalms (Ps. 93–100) known as enthronement or millennial psalms (W. C. Kaiser).
2. As we have seen, the phrase "a promise still stands" suggests that the rest is yet future.
3. In verse 2 the author says that the same message was given to the OT saints as is given to us. The "good news" preached to them included the promise of "rest," which in Psalm 95 refers to the land of Canaan.
4. In verse 1 the author says, "a promise still stands." The biblical doctrine of promise goes back to Abraham. One of the elements of the promise to Abraham included the land (see Heb. 11:9), and the promises of God are unchangeable (see Heb. 6:17).
5. The identification of the "rest" as the home of God's people in the earthly kingdom of Christ fits the context of the book. The author elsewhere states that "the world to come" (see Heb. 2:5) will be subject to a redeemed humanity.

The participants of the rest. The author is afraid that some of his readers might not meet the entrance requirements for Christ's kingdom. "Let us fear lest any of you should seem to have failed to reach it." God makes a promise of "rest" (entrance into the kingdom) to all who believe in Christ. The OT Israelites did not enter the land because of unbelief. The present day reader will not enter the kingdom of God unless he or she is born again (John 3:3-5). Only those who have trusted Christ to forgive their sins and be their Savior are qualified to enter the kingdom.

It Is the Rest of God (4:3b-8)

At the end of verse 3, the author moves in thought from the future kingdom to the creation story. He wants to prevent an erroneous assumption on the part of the readers. The readers must not assume that because Israel did not enter "rest," God must have abandoned His original intentions for man to rule the world. No, the Sabbath day (4:4) was the pledge of God's ultimate purpose for creation. It was the pledge of a future Sabbath rest, namely the millennial kingdom when the whole universe will be at rest.

In verses 5-7 the author again drives home his lesson. The OT Israelites rebelled against Moses and failed to enter Canaan. Will you, the modern reader, rebel against Christ and fail to enter the kingdom? Many of the original readers (and many readers today) were very immature Christians, and some may not even have been saved.

If the problem is immaturity, then the Christian must confess his or her sins (see 1 John 1:9) and press on in the faith (see Heb. 6:1-3). If the problem is that one has never trusted Christ as Savior, then they must do so "Today"!

> Only those who have trusted Christ to forgive their sins and be their Savior are qualified to enter the kingdom.

Verse 8 has caused many to misunderstand Hebrews 4:1-10.[8] It is reported in Joshua 21:43-45 that Joshua did enter Canaan and did enter "rest." Psalm 95, written 400 years later than Joshua, says the Israelites did not enter "rest." It speaks of a day of "rest" yet future. Some interpreters have therefore concluded that Psalm 95 (and Hebrews 3 and 4) must refer to a different "rest" than the one in Joshua. They argue that Joshua 21 speaks of the "rest" of Canaan while Psalm 95 refers to the "rest" of heaven.

We must remember, however, that Psalm 95 is a millennial psalm. It looks forward to the "rest" of Christ's kingdom. The psalmist based his comments on Israel's failure to enter "rest" on texts such as Exodus 17 and Numbers 13, 14 and 20. He believed that Joshua did not enter "rest" in the fullest sense of the term. Joshua brought the people into Canaan, but he did not bring them into the millennial kingdom. Three short chapters after entering the land of Canaan, Joshua rebukes the people for their idolatry (Josh. 24:14). The years that followed were marked by rebellion, idolatry, and a failure to defeat Israel's enemies (Judg. 2:20-23). Joshua's "rest" was only a foretaste of the glorious kingdom to come when Jesus returns to the earth.[9]

It Is a Rest from Works (4:9-10)

A Sabbath rest. In verse 9 the author introduces a different Greek word for *rest* than the one he has been using. The word *rest* in verse 9 means "a Sabbath rest." He seeks to encourage his readers by pointing them to the future. God sanctified (i.e., "set apart") the seventh day at the creation (Gen. 2:2-3; Ex. 20:8-11). This was a pledge that He will accomplish His purposes for this earth (namely, the royal dominion over the earth by man, Gen. 1:26-28).[10]

A future rest. Verse 10 makes it clear that the believer's "rest" (i.e., entrance into the kingdom) is yet future. Why is it future? If the believer had entered his rest, he would be resting.

The "works" of verse 10 are not to be interpreted as something bad. They parallel the works of God and must therefore be good. The implied message to these discouraged Jewish Christians is this: Now is no time to let down your guard. It is a time for endurance. This is the time for labor on the part of Christians. The time of "rest" awaits us.

It Is a Rest after Endurance (4:11-13)

The imperative of diligence. The author of Hebrews did not view the present age as a time of rest. Rather, it is a time for perseverance. "Let us therefore strive to enter that rest." The verb "strive" expresses the seriousness and concern we owe God's Word. Using the OT Israelites as an illustration, the author sees his readers as pilgrims on their way to the celestial city (see Heb. 11:16; 12:22). Unconcern caused the Israelites to die in the wilderness and miss out on Canaan. A lack of diligence may cause many readers today to be excluded from God's "rest," i.e., the future kingdom.

The role of Scripture. God is not to be trifled with. We cannot ignore His Word.[11] Verse 12 tells us why this is so. The Word of God is "living," i.e., it has the capacity to diligently search the hearts of men and women.[12] It is "active," i.e., it is effective. It never acts without results and those results are inevitable. It will bring a person to either rest or to judgment.

It is "sharper than any two-edged sword." The translation "sword" can be improved. The Greek word means "knife," and a number of writers have found here a reference to a surgeon's knife or scalpel. The Word of God is like a physician's "scalpel" that cuts "pitilessly to disclose the secret thoughts of the heart of man" (W. Michaelis).

The Word of God is so sharp that it can divide "soul and spirit." The "soul" is the whole inner life of man with its powers of will, reason, and emotion. It is that which individualizes and personifies each of us. The "spirit" is the new nature, the newly infused principle of divine life that is fathered in us by God ("the Father of spirits," 12:9) at the new birth. In the inner life of the Christian, the impulses from soul and spirit are often so entwined that we are inclined to confuse them. We cannot tell what is of the flesh and what is of the Spirit. The Word of God can sort these impulses out. The author is suggesting to the readers that some of their recent behavior needs the dissecting work of the Word of God. They may think that a return to Judaism was motivated by spiritual impulses, but the Word would show them that they were acting unfaithfully (Z. C. Hodges).

The Word even affects our physical being. It divides "joints and marrow." Christian counselors have long observed that many bodily ailments such as ulcers, paralysis, diarrhea, and obesity can result from spiritual difficulties. Sin can cause bodily sickness (see 1 Cor. 11:29-31; 1 John 5:16). A believer may seek to rationalize guilt, rebellion and bitterness against God. The Word of God can cut through the cover-up and expose what is at the heart of our problem.

In short, the Word of God "[is] discerning the thoughts and intentions of the heart." As a person reads Scripture and hears it proclaimed from the pulpit they find that it scrutinizes every thought and action.

The certainty of judgment. In verse 13 the subject changes from God's Word to God Himself. He is omniscient (all-knowing). He knows the true motives behind our behavior. All will one day give an account for their lives. The Christian will give an account at the judgment seat of Christ (2 Cor. 5:10). The unbeliever will give an account at the great white throne of judgment (Rev. 20:11-15).

Because He Has Better Resources than Moses (4:14-16)

The author closes this section on a positive note.[13] "After terrifying us, the (author) now comforts us" (M. Luther). The readers, he says, should "hold fast," mindful that they have a high priest whose greatness does not alienate them from Him. Due to His true humanity He fully understands their human struggles and is able to strengthen those who draw near.

The Dignity of Our High Priest (4:14)

His title. Jesus has resources that Moses never had. He is "a great high priest." This title is never used in the OT, not even of Aaron, the brother of Moses and the high priest of Israel. It suggests that Jesus is greater than the priests of OT times.

His abode. His greatness is seen in the author's statement that Jesus "passed through the heavens." Once a year Aaron was allowed to go through the court of the tabernacle and into the inner sanctuary ("the Most Holy Place," 9:3). But Jesus has ascended through space and has gone into the very presence of God (see Heb. 7:26; 8:1).

His names. No name is more precious to Christian ears than the name "Jesus." It is the human name of the Savior. It tells us that today there is a man in heaven serving as our priest. He is also called "the Son of God." This name or title looks at His deity. Our priest is God and man.

His doctrine. The readers (and we today) are exhorted to "hold fast our confession." The term "confession" here refers to the doctrines or teachings we hold about Christ (e.g., His deity, His humanity, His atoning sacrifice). They are to hold fast to the body of revealed truth that has been entrusted to them.

> **Christ feels for us in our trials and temptations.**

The verb "hold fast" was sometimes used as a nautical (sailor's) term meaning "to steer towards, to land at." If you are not saved, the author seems to say, steer for Christ who can save you. If you are a professing believer, check your lines. Make sure you are tied securely to the dock of salvation.

The Sympathy of Our High Priest (4:15)

His weaknesses. Does Jesus' ascension into heaven mean that there is a barrier between Him and His people? No, due to His true human nature He is able to "sympathize with our weaknesses." He had human weaknesses, too. By "weaknesses" our author simply means those qualities of human nature such as hunger, thirst, weariness, disappointment, capacity for pain and loneliness. The devil uses these "weaknesses," innocent in themselves, to tempt men and women. Because of these "weaknesses" Jesus is able "to sympathize." The verb "to sympathize" denotes the disposition of fellow-feeling. He feels for us in our trials and temptations.

His sinlessness. His sympathy is not a sympathy that condones everything. His "weaknesses" did not involve a moral weakening. He sympathizes with our weaknesses, not our sins. In His encounters with Satan, Jesus was tempted, but He did not sin.[14] Had He sinned, He would have needed a Savior for Himself.

Sympathy with the sinner does not depend upon Jesus having experienced sin. It depends rather on the strength of the temptation to sin that only a sinless person can know in its full intensity (B. F. Westcott). To sympathize it is not necessary to have fallen but to have endured it. Jesus felt the full force of temptation while we never have (for we too readily give in). Not the tree that falls, but the one that stands, feels the full force of a hurricane.

The Sufficiency of Our High Priest (4:16)

He is available. The author now exhorts readers to "with confidence draw near to the throne of grace," i.e., the throne of God in heaven. Jesus Christ, our High Priest, is present at this throne (see Heb. 1:3). The term "confidence" is not a good translation. The Greek word in this context means "freedom of speech" or "freedom of access." If you are a Christian, you have full authority to come right into the Lord's presence in prayer and tell Him all that is on your heart.

> **Jesus felt the full force of temptation, while we never have.**

He is helpful. At the throne of grace help is available. There we may obtain "grace." The term "grace" refers to divine favor. It implies divine assistance in present and future needs. The term "mercy" refers to pardon for sins that are past. In time of need, the believer should flee to the throne of grace for well-timed help.

SUMMARY

In Hebrews 3:1-6 the author argues that Jesus is superior to Moses in that He is the Son of God while Moses is God's servant. In verses 7-19 he warns his readers of the danger of apostasy. He uses the wilderness generation of OT Israelites and Psalm 95 to illustrate his point. The Israelites failed to enter Canaan because of unbelief. Some of the readers of this epistle may not enter the kingdom of heaven ("rest") for the same reason. There is still time for the readers to embrace Christ in faith. In Hebrews 4:1-10 the author assures them that the promise of rest remains. They must not trifle with God, for He knows the true condition of their hearts. His Word sifts a person's heart and reveals whether he or she embraces the good news of rest or shrinks from it (4:11-13). The readers should hold fast to the truth they know about Jesus as the Great High Priest (4:14-16).

Endnotes

[1] The NKJV and AV of Hebrews 3:1 both read "Christ Jesus." The Greek mss. favored by most modern translations read "Jesus" (NASB, NIV, etc.).

[2] Typology is the study of the spiritual correspondences between persons, events, and things in the OT and similar persons, events, and things in the NT.

[3] The title *Christ* occurs nine times in Hebrews (3:6, 14; 5:5; 6:1; 9:11, 14, 24, 28; 11:26).

[4] The NT adopts a dual approach. On the one hand it teaches the doctrine of eternal security, i.e., "once a Christian, always a Christian" (Rom. 8:28-30; 1 Peter 1:5; John 10:28-29; 1 John 5:13; Jude 24). On the other hand it teaches that continuance in the Christian life is the test of reality (1 John 2:19). There is such a thing as temporary faith, i.e., a faith that is not genuine (Luke 8:13). The NT exhorts those who profess faith in Christ to persevere in that faith (Matt. 24:12-13; 26:41; 1 Cor. 10:12).

[5] The Jewish Rabbis interpreted the "today" of Psalm 95 as a reference to the age of Messiah (F. Delitzsch). That day is now here, the author seems to say. It began when Jesus sat in the synagogue and read from Isaiah. He said, "Today this Scripture has been fulfilled in your hearing" (Luke 4:21).

[6] An important question has divided interpreters of Hebrews at this point: what was the spiritual condition of the original readers? Some say they were unbelievers. This is undermined by the fact that the author calls them "holy brothers" (3:1). Others say they were all believers. This is undermined by the author's use of "if indeed" in 3:6 and 14, by his warning of apostasy in 3:12, and by his threat of fiery judgment in 10:26-30. Most likely they were a mixed group. Most were believers, but a few were unbelievers.

[7] The Bible looks ahead to a time when Israel will be restored to the land of Palestine (Isa. 14:1-2; Ez. 36:6-12; Acts 1:6), and Christ will rule from the throne of His father David (Luke 1:31-33). This kingdom will last "forever" (1:33), yet the first phase of that kingdom will last 1000 years (Rev. 20:4-6). The terms *millennium* and *millennial* are from the Latin expression meaning one thousand years.

[8] A legitimate translation of verse 8 is, "For if Joshua had given them rest, but he did not, then he would not afterward have spoken of another day."

[9] "As long as there is a problem unsettled... as long as God's enemies are permitted to destroy the earth... God's 'rest' will not, cannot be completed" (William R. Newell).

[10] "The rest of God... will have its Sabbath... in the millennium" (J. N. Darby).

[11] The expression "Word of God" refers to the proclaimed message that was ignored in the wilderness and which was proclaimed in NT times by the apostles. This message is now preserved in Scripture.

[12] The NT points to other aspects of this "living" quality of the Word of God. It witnesses to Christ (Rom. 10:17). It brings spiritual life to people (1 Peter 1:23), it cleanses them (Eph. 5:26), it nourishes them (1 Peter 2:20) and it causes them to grow (John 17:17-19).

[13] Verses 14-16 form a transitional paragraph. They conclude the preceding section, and they serve as an introduction to the author's next topic, namely, the high priesthood of Christ.

[14] The author of Hebrews supports the doctrine of impeccability, i.e., the doctrine that Jesus could not have sinned. We should remember the following truths about Christ: (1) He is a divine person (Heb. 1:8). (2) In history He took a human nature as an additional nature (10:5). (3) He is one person, not two. (4) He is as mighty to overcome Satan as is His mightiest nature, i.e., His divine nature (W. G. T. Shedd).

LESSON 3 EXAM

Use the exam sheet at the back of the course to complete your exam.

1. **The author's argument in chapters 3 and 4 is that**
    A. Christ is superior to prophets.
    B. Christ is superior to angels.
    C. Christ is superior to Moses.
    D. Christ is superior to Aaron.

2. **Chapter 3 refers to Christ as**
    A. apostle.   C. Son.
    B. High Priest.   D. All of the above.

3. **In Hebrews 3:2, the term *house* refers to**
    A. the household of Israel.
    B. the universe.
    C. heaven.
    D. the tabernacle.

4. **In 3:6, the term *house* refers to**
    A. heaven.
    B. Christian believers (the Church) as God's dwelling place.
    C. church buildings.
    D. None of the above.

5. **The root of sin is**
    A. unbelief.   C. an evil heart.
    B. disobedience.   D. lawlessness.

6. **In 3:7-15, the author's concern seems to be that**
    A. some of his readers are not saved and may be in danger of apostasy.
    B. some of his readers are disobedient and will miss out on rewards in the kingdom.
    C. some of his readers are in danger of church discipline.
    D. some of his readers lack self confidence.

7. **By the term *rest* the author of Hebrews refers to**
   A. Christian conversion.
   B. Christian dedication.
   C. the Christian's home in heaven.
   D. the Christian's entrance into the millennial kingdom.

8. **Joshua 21:44 and Psalm 95:11 both speak of "rest." How may the two passages be compared?**
   A. Joshua refers to Canaan and Psalm 95 speaks of heaven.
   B. Both passages speak of heaven.
   C. Joshua speaks of Canaan and Psalm 95 speaks of the millennium.
   D. The two passages contradict each other.

9. **When the author speaks of "our weaknesses" (4:15), he means**
   A. the sins of our human nature.
   B. our human capacity to sympathize.
   C. the capacity of our human nature to experience hunger, thirst, weariness, disappointment, pain, loneliness, etc.
   D. the physical defects of our bodies.

10. **What is true about the "throne of grace" (4:16)?**
    A. It is God's throne in heaven.
    B. Jesus, the High Priest, is present at this throne.
    C. Help is available there for the believer.
    D. All of the above.

What Do You Say?

Hebrews 4:12 describes the Word of God as "living and active, sharper than any two-edged sword." No one can hide their life from God. Does this comfort or worry you? Explain.

My flesh may fear the needed pain of surgical removal of sin but my Spirit desires to communion with God that's pure. This is an assurance of His presence. I use His word to prevent deception and draw closer to Him.

Hebrews 5

At the end of chapter 4, the author tells his readers, "We have a great high priest." This leads him to the next major contrast between Christianity and Judaism. He has argued that Christ is superior in His person to the OT prophets (1:1-3), to the angels (1:4–2:18) and to Moses (3:1–4:16). Now he will argue that Christ is superior in His person to Aaron, the first high priest of Israel (5:1–7:28). Some of the readers were longing to return to Judaism with its ancient and visible priesthood. The author of Hebrews will argue that the priesthood of Jesus Christ is superior to that of Aaron.

SUPERIOR TO AARON (5:1–7:28)

The Functions of the High Priest (5:1)

Representation

What is a high priest according to the author of Hebrews? He answers that question in 5:1.[1] The primary idea of the biblical concept of priesthood is that of mediation. A high priest is a middleman between man and God. The idea of mediation has three facets, each of which is found in Hebrews (J. L. Houlden). First, the high priest represents others before God (see also 2:17). In 5:1 the author says that the high priest "is appointed to act on behalf

> **A high priest is a middleman between man and God.**

of men in relation to God." In other words the high priest represented men in the whole range of things having to do with God. People are sinful and need mediation, and in the person of the high priest they have a mediator.

Sacrifice

Second, the high priest is specifically appointed "to offer gifts and sacrifices for sins." In other words, the high priest's function is connected with sin, i.e., with guilt and its removal.

Two things make it clear that the particular sin offerings that the author has in mind are those presented once a year on the Day of Atonement. First, he mentions the high priest and not just a priest. Second, his discussion later in the epistle (see Heb. 9:1-14; 10:10-14) focuses on the annual sacrifices of the Day of Atonement.

Access

The third facet of the high priest's mediatorial work (not specifically mentioned in 5:1) is entering into the presence of God. Once a year, the author says in 9:7, the high priest went ("enters," NASB) into the Most Holy Place to offer blood for the sins of the people. The high priest has special access to God and wins this access for others.

The author will later argue that the priesthood of Aaron was a failure for it did not cleanse the conscience (9:9; 10:2). The high priesthood of Christ is a success, however, for two reasons:

1. He entered the actual presence of God and not the inner sanctuary of an earthly tent (8:2, 5; 9:11).
2. His sacrifice does cleanse the conscience and secure redemption (9:12-14). Because of Christ's priesthood, therefore, the forgiven sinner is granted access to God's presence (4:14-16; 10:19-21).

The Qualifications of the High Priest (5:1-10)

In the opening paragraph of chapter 5 (verses 1-10), the author does two things. First, he lists three qualifications for high priesthood (humanity, human compassion, and divine appointment). Then he proves that Christ has met the qualifications.

The Requirements of the Office (5:1-4)

Human nature, 5:1. The author uses the conjunction "for" to make the connection between chapters 4 and 5. Christians are to come boldly to the throne of grace "for" every high priest has been appointed for this very purpose, i.e., to secure free access into God's presence.

What are the requirements of the office of high priest? As the author considers the OT priesthood of Aaron, he finds three. First, he must be human. He is "chosen from among men." He must be human because he is to represent human beings before God.

> **Because of Christ's priesthood, the forgiven sinner is granted access to God's presence.**

Human compassion, 5:2-3. The high priest's human nature would help him to "deal gently" with sinners. Such "gentleness" is the second requirement of the office. The Greek verb translated "deal gently" speaks of someone who can moderate his passions. The high priest might see or hear of the sins of the people and be filled with displeasure and anger. The thought of his own weaknesses and sins would moderate his displeasure. The high priest was to be neither too severe nor too lenient.

Verse 3 highlights the problem of the OT high priest. He was sinful. He was not only required to offer sacrifices for the sins of the people but also "for his own sins." What the original readers needed (and what we need) "was not a fellow loser but a winner" (P. E. Hughes). We need a high priest who is sinless.

Divine appointment, 5:4. The high priesthood of Israel was not an office open to volunteers. It was a position one entered only when he was "called by God." Aaron did not take the dignity to himself.[2] He was high priest by divine appointment.

The Qualifications of Christ (5:5-10)

Divine appointment, 5:5-6. In verses 5-10 the author shows that Christ[3] meets the qualifications for the high priesthood. First, he points out that Christ was divinely appointed ("did not exalt himself"). He supports his contention by citing two passages from the Book of Psalms.

The first passage he quotes is Psalm 2:7 ("you are my son; today I have begotten you"). This passage refers to Christ's appointment and proclamation as messianic Son or Davidic heir. In the author's mind the messianic dignity (sonship) involves priesthood. The one worthy to be appointed as God's Son must certainly be worthy to be High Priest. Sonship is the foundation of priesthood.

The time of Christ's proclamation as Son is indicated by the use of Psalm 2:7 in Acts 13:33. That passage associates the psalm with Christ's resurrection. This would indicate that the messianic title *Son* was given to Christ at the time of His exaltation to God's right hand. At the time of His resurrection-ascension Christ was "begotten," as it were, as God's Son.

In verse 6 the author quotes Psalm 110:4. In that psalm it is God who speaks, and He says to Christ, "You are a priest forever after the order of Melchizedek." The author will say more about Melchizedek in chapter 7. The only point he wants to make here is this: since God said to Christ, "You are a priest," evidently our Lord is High Priest by divine appointment.

Human compassion, 5:7-8. Not only is Christ qualified to be our High Priest because of divine appointment, He is also qualified because He is a man and has experienced the deepest of human sufferings. The author draws our attention to a particular event in the life of Christ upon earth ("in the days of his flesh"). In the garden of Gethsemane, Jesus "offered up prayers and supplications, with loud cries and tears, to him who was able to save him from death." The events of Gethsemane assure us that Christ is One who has understanding of our human sorrows, for He has experienced them there Himself.

> **True prayer—the prayer that God always answers—is the personal recognition and acceptance of God's will.**

The author of Hebrews (5:7) says that in Gethsemane Christ cried out in "reverence" ("piety," NASB) to the One who was "able to save Him from death." In view of the Gospel accounts that portray Jesus steadfastly facing His death (see Matt. 16:21-23; 17:22-23; 20:17-19), it is inadequate to say that He sought to be delivered from physical death. Rather, Christ asked His Father, "Remove this cup from me" (Mark 14:36). The term *cup* is clearly a reference to the wrath of God against sin (Isa. 51:17-23; Jer. 25:15-16, 27-29; Matt. 26:27-28). In the Garden Jesus began to anticipate all that was involved when "the Father would put into His hand the cup our sins had mingled" (J. Denney). He recoiled in horror at the thought of tasting death for everyone, of identifying Himself with human iniquity and enduring divine condemnation for sin.

The author of Hebrews (5:7) says that Christ's prayer in Gethsemane "was heard." "But how?" we may ask. After all, He died upon the cross bearing our sins. The answer to our question is found in the phrase "from death." We may translate the Greek phrase either as "from death" or "out of death." Our Lord's prayer was answered with an answer different from the request. He was not saved "from death," but He was saved "out of death," i.e., at the resurrection.

There is a lesson here for all who pray. True prayer—the prayer that God always answers—is the personal recognition and acceptance of God's will. Jesus prayed (Mark 14:36) for the will of God to be done, and His prayer "was heard."

In verse 8 the author draws his lesson. Our Lord's sufferings were a learning experience that gave Him human compassion. He says, "Although he was a son, he learned obedience." It might appear strange, yet the Son of God with His attribute of omniscience "learned." How did He learn? The answer is that He learned in His manhood.

Our author does not say that Christ learned to obey as if He learned through trial and error, through disobedience and punishment. That is the way we learn. Being sinless, however, He did not learn that way. Yet "he learned." In His sufferings He learned just what obedience to God involved in practice. He did it in the only way possible, namely by submitting to the revealed will of God.

Human nature. It is also required of a high priest that he be human ("chosen from among men") so that he might be a representative of men to God. We can see that Christ was truly human in the phrase "in the days of his flesh" (5:7) and in the human emotions and actions ascribed to Him in verses 7-8.

In verse 9 the author says that the result of His human experiences is that Christ has "[been] made perfect." One writer calls this the "grand paradox" (C. Spicq). How can One who is truly God and sinless be perfected? It will help us to solve this apparent difficulty if we do two things:

1. Remember that he is speaking of Christ's human nature, and
2. Understand his usage of the verb *to perfect*. The verb *to perfect* is related to a noun meaning "the goal" or "the end." The verb means "to complete, bring to an end, finish, accomplish, bring to its goal or to accomplishment." By being "made perfect," then, Christ was brought to His divinely intended end or goal.

The author of Hebrews probably has three things in mind in his use of the verb "to perfect":

1. *The ceremonial aspect.* The LXX (Ex. 29:9, 29, 33) uses the verb in a phrase meaning "to consecrate" or "to install." In this sense the verb *to perfect* means that Christ was installed as High Priest.

2. *The inner, personal aspect.* Because of the experiences of life, there was a process of inward training and human moral development (Luke 2:52). This process is implied in the expression "through suffering" (2:10) and when he says that the Son "learned obedience" (5:8). In life, Jesus went through a process of obedience and suffering so that He Himself might learn what it is like to carry out the task of a servant of the Lord to its end. When the author of Hebrews suggests that there was development or growth in Jesus, He is not alone. Luke, for example, says that Jesus "grew and became strong" and that He "increased in wisdom and in stature" (Luke 2:40, 52). Such comments in no way imply prior imperfection. Nor do they imply that He morally progressed from less to greater obedience. He was perfect from birth and at each stage of His existence. "At each stage He was perfect for that stage" (A. Plummer).[4] Nevertheless, the author of Hebrews emphasizes Jesus' genuine humanity, and genuine human nature involves the element of personal development.

   > **Jesus is One who fully understands the deepest needs of His people.**

3. *The official or vocational aspect.* Not only was the process of perfection significant for Jesus Himself. It was also significant for those who benefit from His saving work. The experiences of obedience and suffering qualified Him to be High Priest for His people. In Hebrews 5:9 we may translate the phrase "being made perfect" as "having been qualified." This official or vocational qualification has two elements. First, through the sufferings of the cross, Christ becomes "the source of (i.e., the ground of or the cause of) eternal salvation." Second, through the process of sufferings that He has endured in life, He has become qualified to be a compassionate High Priest. He is One who fully understands the deepest needs of His people (2:17-18; 4:15-16).

The term "salvation" in verse 9 means "deliverance." In the NT there are three aspects to Christ's saving work. First, there is deliverance from the penalty of sin (Eph. 2:5, 8). The Christian can say that he or she has been saved. Then there is deliverance from the power of sin in the believer's life (2 Cor. 1:6; 7:10). The believer is in a lifelong process of being delivered from indwelling sin. Finally, there is future deliverance from the very presence of sin at the final consummation (Rom. 13:11). In Hebrews the term *salvation* does not refer so much to the present acquisition of eternal life (John 3:16). Rather, it refers to the final deliverance of God's people from all their enemies and their enjoyment of future glory (see Heb. 1:14; 2:10; 9:28).

This salvation is for "all who obey Him." In Hebrews 4:2-3 clearly the one condition for entering God's rest is belief in Christ. Is the author of Hebrews here suggesting that obedience is an additional condition of initial salvation? If he does suggest this, then he is in disagreement with the apostle Paul who taught that people were not saved by obedience or works (Eph. 2:8-9; Rom. 4:1-5; Gal. 3:2-3). The author is not telling unbelievers that they are saved by works. He is again teaching the doctrine of perseverance to professing believers. Those who are genuine Christians are those who continue in the faith. Obedience marks their lives. Those who persevere are those who shall be delivered into the kingdom at the second coming of Christ (see Heb. 9:28).

Divine approval, 5:10. Now the scene shifts to heaven. After He had been perfectly equipped by the sufferings and trials of life to be our High Priest, the Son ascended into heaven. There He was "designated by God a high priest." The Greek verb here translated "designated" means "to call, name, designate." The thought is that when the Son ascended and appeared in the sanctuary on high, the Father saluted Him or addressed Him as a High Priest after the order of Melchizedek (A. B. Davidson). At that moment Jesus Christ was formally installed as High Priest.

The Consequences of Spiritual Immaturity (5:11–6:20)

In verse 11 there is a transition from exposition to the author's third exhortation (5:11–6:20). No sooner has he begun his exposition of the high priesthood of Christ than he remembers the spiritual condition of his readers. They are dull and sluggish Christians who have gone back to the most elementary teaching.

The Presentation of the Problem (5:11)

The difficulty of the subject. In verse 10 the author says that Christ is a "high priest after the order of Melchizedek." We might expect him now to develop this theme. After all, he says that he has "much to say" about Melchizedek. However, the author does not say more about Melchizedek at this point. The priesthood of Melchizedek is a subject that is "hard to explain."

The sluggishness of the readers. The problem is not only with the subject. Admittedly, the high priesthood of Melchizedek is complex and profound. It is "solid food" (5:12, 14). The major problem,

> **God expects His people to make progress in spiritual things.**

however, is with the readers. The author says, "You have become dull of hearing." The Greek verb tense ("have become") suggests that the readers were not always like this. The problem is not constitutional, i.e., it is not what they are by nature. Rather, it is dispositional. They are spiritually sluggish or *lazy* ("dull of hearing"). Their capacity to understand spiritual truth has been blunted and dulled. They are responsible for their present condition, and the author blames them.

The Evidence of the Problem (5:12-13)

They do not act like adults. It is a tragedy to see a full-grown adult acting like a child. It is even more tragic to see someone who has been a believer for a long time still acting like a spiritual infant. The original readers of the epistle ought to have been mature believers, but they were spiritually childish.

The author says to them, "By this time you ought to be teachers." The phrase "by this time" means the period that had passed since they became Christians. He is saying that a sufficient interval of time had passed since their conversion for them to have become well-grounded in the faith. Yet they were not mature. The author is here telling us two very important lessons of the Christian life:

1. God expects His people to make progress in spiritual things.
2. Time alone does not produce spiritual maturity! There are many believers who have been converted to Christ for a considerable period of time. Yet they are spiritually immature.

The readers "ought to be teachers," but they are not. The author does not mean that every mature Christian is to be a public teacher or expositor of the Word. He is using the term *teacher* in a non-technical sense. He simply means that every Christian should advance in his or her comprehension of the faith to the point where he or she can informally instruct or edify others. One evidence that someone is a mature believer is that he or she can explain his or her faith to others (see 1 Peter 3:15).

Instead of being able to share the truth with others, the readers again "need someone" to teach them "the basic principles of the oracles of God." The Greek word translated "basic principles" refers to things in a series like the letters of the alphabet. The readers need to be taught "the ABCs of God's oracles" (cf. NEB). They need someone to review with them "the elementary truths" (NIV) of the faith.

In the context of Hebrews, the phrase "oracles of God"[5] does not refer to the OT as a whole. Rather it refers to those passages of the OT that are fulfilled in the ministry of Jesus Christ (E. C. Selwyn). The author of Hebrews, however, does not distinguish between the authority of the oracles and the authority of the Scriptures as a whole. The authority that he attributes to the part ("the oracles") he also attributes to the whole (the OT Scriptures). The readers have not matured and still need basic teaching on the rudiments of the Word.

> **Doctrine and correct behavior go together.**

They do not eat like adults. For the author of Hebrews, the Christian life revolves around the Scriptures. He measures spiritual growth in relation to the written Word of God. We may diagram his equation for spiritual growth this way:

Knowledge of Scripture + Time + Application of Scripture = Growth

The Scriptures provide two kinds of food, "milk" and "solid food." The term *milk* refers to the kind of elementary instruction in the Scriptures that is suitable for the new believer (see 1 Peter 2:2). The term *solid food* suggests the nourishment of adults that is not readily digested by infants. For babies, lighter, fluid food is appropriate. In Hebrews the "milk" of the Word is outlined in 6:1-2. The "solid food" of the Word is the author's teaching on the high priesthood of Jesus Christ.[6]

The readers were weaklings in the faith. Their diet was one that indicated arrested development. They have relapsed into a state of spiritual infancy (P. E. Hughes). By this time they ought to be adults, yet their spiritual diet shows them to be children in the faith.

They do not function like adults. The readers were "unskilled in the word of righteousness" (5:13). They were inexperienced in the Bible's teaching about righteousness, i.e., righteousness of life. They were like babies who do not know the difference between right and wrong. The readers did not know how to apply the Bible to the moral choices of life.

Of course, the problem of the readers went beyond their lack of skill in moral understanding. The author's real concern was their doctrinal backwardness. This is clear from his comment in verses 10-11 that they were unprepared to appreciate the meaning of Melchizedek and Christ's high priestly work. There is an important lesson to be learned here; doctrine and correct behavior go together. Theological maturity and moral discernment cannot be separated. Doctrinal stagnation always has serious moral consequences.

The Remedy for the Problem (5:14)

The way to grow up. The dull, apathetic state of the readers is not a hopeless problem. How are they to grow up? The author suggests that the way to grow is to exercise their spiritual faculties. Grown-up Christians are mature in the faith "by constant practice" of their spiritual senses. They have practice in the application of the Scriptures to life. In short, they grow by the use and frequent study of Holy Scripture (Alcuin, quoted by P. E. Hughes).

> The Lord opens up to the spiritually mature the deeper riches of God's Word.

The Greek verb (participial form) translated "trained" is the verb from which we get our word *gymnasium*. The readers of the epistle need to get involved in a spiritual training program. Such a training program will involve serious Bible study (involving observation, interpretation, and application of the text) and a steady exposure to a solid preaching ministry.

The need to grow up. They need to grow up to develop discrimination in doctrinal matters and in the moral choices of life. An immature Christian is not discriminating. Such believers cannot "distinguish good from evil." They cannot choose between true and false doctrine. And they cannot choose between what is right and wrong, or what is wholesome or injurious, in moral areas. "When a Christian so saturates himself with the Word that a pertinent verse of Scripture flashes into his mind in any situation, he is in the process of growing out of infancy into maturity" (J. D. Pentecost).

The motive to grow up. For the spiritually mature there is a reward. The Lord opens up to them the deeper riches of God's Word. Our author writes,

"Solid food is for the mature." The "solid food" of the book of Hebrews, as we have learned, is the doctrine of the high priesthood of Christ.

We should note that there are three stages of spiritual growth mentioned in Hebrews 5:12-14 (H. P. Owen). First, there is infancy. The new believer feeds on the "milk" ("elementary doctrine," 6:1) of the Word. For a healthy Christian this stage must be only temporary. Second, there is the stage of ethical and doctrinal growth. The believer becomes increasingly adept at using Scripture. He or she learns to determine what is "good from evil," what is true and false, what is right and wrong, what is worthwhile and not worthwhile, what is profitable and unprofitable. Third, there is the stage of spiritual maturity. The mature are skilled in the "word of righteousness." They are able to feed on the "solid food" of the Word.

SUMMARY

In Hebrews 5:1 the author of Hebrews begins a discussion (which will take him through chapter 7) proving that Christ is superior in His person to Aaron, the high priest of Israel. In 4:14–5:1 he briefly touches on the functions of a high priest (representation, sacrifice, entering in). Then, in verses 1-10 he lists the qualifications for the high priesthood (human nature, human compassion, divine appointment) and shows how the Son of God met those qualifications. In verses 11-14 the author addresses the spiritual immaturity of his readers. He shows that maturity is linked to skill in the use of Holy Scripture.

Endnotes

[1] The ideas of priesthood found in Hebrews are biblical, i.e., they are derived from the OT.

[2] During Aaron's lifetime Korah, Datham and Abiram were destroyed for burning incense (a priestly duty) without God's call (see Num. 16:1-35). In the NT era Herod and the Romans arbitrarily installed and deposed twenty-eight high priests. Twenty-five of these came from non-legitimate families.

3   The author shifts from the use of the name Jesus (4:14) to the use of the title Christ. He is deeply "impressed by the thought that the anointed one, the Messiah, in his office did not exalt himself as he might well have done" (D. Guthrie).

4   "The bud may be perfect, but there is a difference between its perfection and that of the [full-grown] flower" (L. Morris).

5   In classical Greek the term oracle was used of short sayings that originated from a deity. In the LXX it is used of individual sayings of God. In the NT the primary force is "saying."

6   Some students of the Bible misunderstand the nature of "milk" and "solid food." They erroneously believe that particular subjects of Christian doctrine (e.g., salvation, the inspiration of Scripture) are "milk," while others (the doctrine of the Holy Spirit, prophecy) are "solid food." Actually there are "milk" truths and "solid food" truths in every division of Christian doctrine. There is teaching about the Holy Spirit that is "milk," and there is teaching about the Holy Spirit that is "solid food." There is teaching about prophecy that is "milk," and there is teaching about prophecy that is "solid food." The author of Hebrews says that there is teaching about Christ that is "milk" (see Heb. 6:1-2), and there is teaching about Christ that is "solid food."

LESSON 4 EXAM

Use the exam sheet at the back of the course to complete your exam.

1. **In Hebrews 5:1-7:28, the author argues that Christ is**
   A. superior to Aaron.   C. superior to prophets.
   B. superior to angels.   D. superior to Moses.

2. **The expression "on behalf of men" in Hebrews 5:1 highlights**
   A. the high priest's work of intercession.
   B. the high priest's work of representation.
   C. the high priest's work of sacrifice.
   D. the high priest's work of entering in.

3. **By *sacrifices* (5:1), the author has in mind the sacrifices of**
   A. Passover.   C. the Day of Atonement.
   B. the Day of Pentecost.   D. daily sin offerings.

4. **In Psalm 2:7 God the Father says to Christ, "Today I have begotten you" (see Hebrews 5:5). To what event in the experience of Christ does this specific text refer?**
   A. His physical birth.   C. His death on the cross.
   B. His baptism.   D. His resurrection-ascension.

5. **When the author of Hebrews says that our Lord was "made perfect," He means that Christ**
   A. was at one time imperfect.
   B. morally progressed from lesser to greater obedience.
   C. learned by trial and error.
   D. was qualified to be our High Priest.

6. **The term *salvation* means "deliverance." In the epistle to the Hebrews, salvation refers to**
   A. our past deliverance from the penalty of sin.
   B. our present deliverance from the power of indwelling sin.
   C. our future deliverance from our enemies, and the enjoyment of future glory.
   D. All of the above.

EXAM 4

7. **In Hebrews 5:11 the author hesitates to teach about Melchizedek. He hesitates primarily because**
   A. the subject matter is just too difficult.
   B. he feels inadequate to teach it.
   C. the subject is "milk," and the readers need "solid" food.
   D. they are dull and backslidden Christians.

8. **The "oracles of God" in Hebrews 5:12 are**
   A. specific OT sayings or passages that find their fulfillment in the person and work of Christ.
   B. the entire Old Testament.
   C. sayings of a pagan deity.
   D. the book of Psalms.

9. **The expression "word of righteousness" refers to**
   A. the doctrine of justification by faith.
   B. the biblical teaching about righteousness, i.e., ethical behavior.
   C. the teaching about legalistic doctrine.
   D. Both B and C.

10. **A Christian who is growing from infancy to maturity**
    A. uses their spiritual senses.
    B. is able to discern between true and false doctrine.
    C. is able to make moral decisions in accordance with the Word of God.
    D. All of the above.

What Do You Say?

Why is Christ perfectly qualified to be our High Priest?

He is the son of God, appointed. He became a man, going through our experiences, learning how it is to serve the Lord to the end. He felt our sorrows + pains. He suffered and endured,

Hebrews 6

As we learned in Lesson 4, the author of the epistle to the Hebrews teaches that there are three stages in Christian growth (H. P. Owen):

1. Spiritual infancy
2. Moral development through practice in applying the word of righteousness to the doctrinal and ethical questions of life
3. Maturity, when the believer is able to appreciate the "solid food" of the Word of God, namely the doctrine of the high priesthood of Christ

The problem with the original readers of the epistle (and with many modern readers) is that they were stuck in stage one. At one time they had known the joy of believing in Christ as Savior. Now they have become dull and apathetic and do not want to hear the kind of Bible teaching that will require growth and progress. They lack skill in the use of the Word of God and are unable to teach others. This is true of every backslidden Christian.[1]

In view of the spiritual state of the readers, we might expect the author to review the elementary doctrines of the faith ("milk," 5:12-13) with his readers. His readers would have been happy to do

> **Backslidden Christians lack skill in the use of the Word of God and are unable to teach others.**

that. When we are lazy and backslidden, it is comfortable to go over the basic principles (the "A-B-Cs"). However, the author refuses to feed them more "milk." Instead, he is determined to put his readers on an accelerated spiritual bodybuilding course. He is going to force feed them on a high spiritual protein diet of high priesthood truth. He proposes to lead them away from stage one (spiritual infancy) and on to stage three (mature appreciation of the doctrine of Christ's high priesthood). Normally one would have to go through stage two (ethical maturity) to appreciate the "solid food" of stage three. In 6:1 the author seems to assume that ingesting the "solid food" of Christ's high priesthood will confer the maturity of stage two.

The Need for Progress in the Christian Life (6:1-3)

The author's objective stated positively, 6:1a. The author declares his intentions in the statement, "Let us ... go on to maturity." By "maturity" the author may mean his teaching ("a higher course of lessons," J. Moffatt). On the other hand, he may refer to the readers' condition ("maturity," B. F. Westcott). In either case the author's intentions are clear. He intends to lead them on to the mature mental grasp of the truth about Christ as High Priest.

The author's objective stated negatively, 6:1-2. He is intent on "leaving the elementary doctrine of Christ." The "elementary doctrine of Christ" has to do with the foundational principles of the OT that revealed the doctrine of a coming Messiah (A. Nairne).[2] When the original readers had first become Christians, they had been taught that the great messianic promises and principles of the OT were fulfilled in Jesus of Nazareth.

> **"Repentance" refers to a change of mind about something.**

Now they are to "leave" this "elementary doctrine." The author does not mean that these are doctrines his readers were to abandon. When a child finally learns to form words and read, he does not forget the alphabet. No, the "elementary doctrine" is a foundation. It is basic to every stage of growth. The author's point is that it is a stepping stone, not a stopping place (P. E. Hughes).

The author specifically mentions six OT doctrines that make up the "elementary doctrine" or the "foundation":

1. "Repentance from dead works." Most scholars assume that this phrase refers to conversion. The term "repentance" refers to a change of mind about something. Some understand the phrase to refer to the act of turning from sinful practices ("dead works"). In view of Hebrews 9:14, however, it is more likely that the expression "dead works" refers to the Levitical rituals of the

OT.[3] At conversion the readers abandoned all attempts to obtain salvation by following the rituals of Judaism.

2. "Faith toward God." The essential ingredient to a true relationship with God was explained in the OT (see Gen. 15:6; Isa. 7:9). It is faith (belief or trust). These readers have already been told the dangers of unbelief (3:7-11). At their conversion they had ceased their attempts at self-righteousness ("dead works"). They had cast themselves upon the mercy of God, receiving salvation through Christ by faith (H. A. Kent).

3. "Instruction about washings." The term translated "washings" is not the usual one for baptism, and in 9:10 it clearly refers to OT washings. The many washing or cleansing rituals of the OT[4] were all typical or illustrative of the true cleansing provided by the blood of Christ.

4. "Laying on of hands." Here the author may have in mind the annual sacrificial ritual of the OT Day of Atonement. The high priest would put his hands on the sacrificial animal and confess the sins of the people, thereby laying their sins on the sacrifice. When first converted to Christianity, the readers would have learned that this action of the priest typified or illustrated the sacrifice of Jesus Christ who bore the sins of His people.

5. "The resurrection of the dead." The OT prophets (see Isa. 26:19; Dan. 12:2) foresaw that God's people would one day rise bodily from the dead and enter the kingdom of God. As new converts the readers learned that the OT promise would be realized because of the resurrection of Christ.

6. "Eternal judgment." The OT looked forward to a great end-time judgment to be carried out by the Son of Man (Dan. 7:9-14). The NT identifies the Son of Man as Jesus Christ who shall one day render His judgments (see John 5:22-27; Acts 17:31). The Greek term here translated "judgment" usually has the sense of an unfavorable decision, i.e., condemnation (F. Buchsel).

The author's objective stated conditionally, 6:3. The readers knew these basic OT principles and their fulfillment in Christ. Now they (some of them, at least) were flirting with the thought of returning to Judaism. They felt they could abandon those things that were distinctive of Christianity and still hold on to the fundamentals of the truth. The author was determined, however, to correct their thinking and to prevent their defection.

He says that he intends to lead his readers on to maturity in Christ. This he will do "if God permits." He is conscious that his success in bringing his readers to maturity depends wholly on God's will. His use of the conditional word "if" implies that some of his readers may be so hard of heart that it will not be possible.

The Danger of Apostasy in the Christian Life (6:4-8)

In Hebrews 5:11 the readers are described as "dull of hearing." They appear to be sluggish and lazy. They are negligent in their spiritual responsibilities and unreceptive to the Word of God. There are two possible explanations for this condition:

1. They are at heart unbelievers who are drifting toward a repudiation of Christ.
2. They are genuine believers in a backslidden state. They have been converted to Christ, but after initial growth they have returned to an immature state.

The author of the epistle picks the second solution. He is persuaded of the genuineness of their faith (6:9-10). He believes that they are true Christians. However, the first alternative (they are at heart unbelievers) remains an individual possibility for some in the congregation. It is those individuals that he describes in verses 4-8.[5]

A dreadful possibility, 6:4-6. The word "for" in verse 4 introduces an explanation of verse 3. In verse 1 he encourages his readers to follow him as he leads them on to maturity. However, in verse 3 he suggests that there may be some who will not press on. God will not permit it. What kind of people will not go on to maturity? The author will now describe them, and he will state a fact about them and explain the cause of that fact (M. Dods).

The author describes a class of people. The author uses a series of six phrases[6] to describe the kind of person God will not permit to go on to maturity:

1. They had "once been enlightened." The LXX (e.g., Judg. 13:8; 2 Kings 17:27) uses this expression in the sense of "teaching" or "giving instruction." The same term is used in 10:32 (NKJV has "illuminated") where it seems to mean the same thing as the phrase "receiving the knowledge of the truth" (see Heb.

10:26). The people described in verse 4 had heard the Gospel. They had also been instructed in the basic principle that Jesus Christ had fulfilled the great OT promise of a coming Messiah. It should be noted here that the verb *to enlighten* is not one of the author's terms for true salvation (cleansing, sanctification, perfection, salvation).

2. They "have tasted the heavenly gift." The term "gift" refers to all the salvation blessings God confers in Christ (see Rom. 5:15, 17; 2 Cor. 9:15). The Greek verb "to taste" can mean "to eat fully" (see Heb. 2:9). However, the common meaning is "to taste," i.e., to take a small amount of food to see if it is suitable or pleasing. These people had received instruction about Christ, and they had learned enough to know that salvation was a gift.

3. They "have shared in the Holy Spirit." He does not say that they have become possessors of the Holy Spirit, nor does he use any of the terms associated with the Holy Spirit's work in believers (regeneration, sealing, indwelling, baptizing, anointing nor filling). This phrase means nothing more than that they had become part of a local church. There they had been exposed to the benefits that come to a congregation because of the Spirit's presence (R. Nicole).

4. They "have tasted the goodness of the word of God." In the meetings of the church they had heard the Word of God expounded. The expression "goodness of the word" (or "beautiful word") is used in the LXX to describe the glorious future (see Josh. 21:43; Zech. 1:13). They had heard the divine promises of a blessed future in "the land of promise" (11:9).

5. They have tasted "the powers of the age to come." This expression is closely tied in the Greek text to the preceding phrase. The expression "age to come" means the same thing as the phrase "the world to come" in 2:5. It refers to the future 1,000-year reign of Jesus Christ upon the earth (Rev. 20:4-6). The OT prophets foretold that "the age to come" would be characterized by miraculous signs and wonders (see Isa. 35:1-6). During the earthly ministry of Jesus and His apostles many of these miraculous powers were seen. Such miracles proved that Christ was the One who would one day usher in the "age to come." In 2:4 the author says that his readers had seen such miracles.

6. They have "fallen away." The reading of the NKJV ("if they fall away") is incorrect in that the Greek text does not allow an "if." The people described in verses 4-6 do fall away. The same thought is found in 3:12 where the author warns of "falling away from the living God." This class of people leaves the outward profession of Christianity. They completely and finally repudiate the Lord Jesus Christ (see Heb. 10:26). They are like stillborn children. For a while there appears to be spiritual life. But they were never truly born again (R. Stedman). The Holy Spirit has brought them to conviction of sin (see John 16:8-11). They were brought to the doorstep of faith, and we may even think for a while that they are converted. However, their apostasy (falling away) reveals that they were never truly Christians at all (see 1 John 2:19). "There is a quickening short of regeneration" (R. A. Torrey, quoted by W. R. Newell).

> **Fruitfulness or continuance in the faith is the evidence of the genuineness of faith.**

The author states a fact about this class of people. He says, "It is impossible … to restore them again to repentance." The word "impossible" is emphatic. It is the first word in the Greek text of verse 4. The term should not be watered down. It does not mean "difficult" or "impossible for man." It means "absolutely impossible." The same word is used in verse 18 where it says that "it is impossible for God to lie." Such people have become so hardened to the truth that they cannot be brought to "repentance." They will never believe in Christ for cleansing and forgiveness.

The author explains the cause of this fact. Such people are "crucifying once again the Son of God to their own harm." When they completely break with Christianity, they align themselves with those who crucified the Lord. They ultimately agree with the crucifixion of the Savior and stand with those who ridiculed Him at Golgotha (Luke 23:35-36). They are "holding him up to contempt." The use of the title "Son of God" emphasizes the greatness of their crime.

A dreadful illustration, 6:7-8. The author now illustrates his point with a test of a plot of ground ("land"). On the one hand it may bear vegetables ("crop"). In that case it is good soil. Such soil pictures the reception given the Gospel by a believing heart. On the other hand it may bear "thorns and thistles." Such soil is "worthless." It is ultimately "burned" by its owner. The burning does not refer to the practice of burning the stubble off a field to allow it to be fruitful. The picture is of destruction as by a volcano (B. F. Westcott). The burning is a reference to eternal judgment (see Heb. 10:26-27, 39).

The lesson is clear. Fruitfulness or continuance in the faith is the evidence of the genuineness of faith. Apostasy is evidence that their faith was never genuine (see Luke 8:13).

The Encouragement to Persevere in the Christian Life (6:9-12)

The Author's Confidence in the Readers, 6:9-10

The nature of his confidence: their salvation, 6:9. In spite of the severe warning in verses 4-8, the author is convinced that his readers are, for the most part, true Christians. The words "Yet in your case, beloved" introduce a contrast with what has gone before. Although a few of his readers may be drifting toward apostasy, the author is "sure of better things" concerning his readers as a whole. After carefully considering their condition, he has become convinced that, at the future coming of Christ, they will enjoy "salvation," i.e., deliverance into the kingdom (1:14; 9:28).[7]

The basis of his confidence: their love, 6:10. In verse 9 the author has indicated that in the lives of his readers he has seen "things that belong to salvation." These "things" are described in verse 10. The author of Hebrews, like James, the Lord's brother (James 2:14-17), believed that a living faith produced good works. As he considers the lives of his readers, he sees just the kind of "love" and service toward their fellow Christians ("the saints")[8] that would indicate that their profession of faith in Christ was real. Not only have they shown such love and service in the past, but they continue "serving." The virtue of perseverance, of "sticking with it," is a virtue that suggests reality.

The Author's Desire for the Readers, 6:11-12

The nature of his desire: the full development of their hope, 6:11. The readers have shown a true loving concern for their brethren. The author now encourages them to show "the same earnestness to have the full assurance of hope." The readers are in the midst of an inner struggle. They have professed to be Christians, yet they bitterly feel the separation between themselves and their Jewish brethren. The author wants them to come to an unwavering confidence in Christ. A person has made real progress toward maturity when his or her heart is fully persuaded that the Christian hope is a certainty (H. Kent).

The term *hope* does not refer to wishful thinking. We may define it as a patient, confident expectation of the future fulfillment of the "promises" (6:12) of God in Scripture. How may we come to the "full assurance" or "full development" (Westcott) of hope? It may be developed through the exercise of spiritual "earnestness." We have already learned (see Heb. 5:13-14) that such diligence involves gaining skill in the use of Holy Scripture. By devoting oneself to the study and application of Scripture the believer will find his or her beliefs developing into assured convictions. Christians cannot let up in their "earnestness." They must keep it up "until the end," i.e., throughout their lives on earth.

> **Believers who devote themselves to the study and application of Scripture will find their beliefs developing into assured convictions.**

The fulfillment of his desire: the final inheritance of the promises, 6:12. In Hebrews 5:11 the author tells his readers that they "have become dull of hearing." Here, in 6:12, he longs that they might "not be sluggish."[9] He is afraid that their lack of understanding will lead to a despair affecting the whole of life. The way to avoid this, he suggests, is to follow the inspiring example of others (see Heb. 11). Like the OT heroes they are to believe ("faith") God's "promises." They are to live in patient expectation ("patience") that those promises will be fulfilled. If they (and we today) have such enduring faith, the author's desire will be fulfilled. We, like the faithful of old, will inherit the promises. We shall enter the "land of promise" (11:9). We shall reach the heavenly country (11:16).

The Promise of God and the Christian Life (6:13-20)

Such enduring faith in the promises of God is not only necessary but also reasonable. Though their fulfillment be delayed they are certain. In verses 13-15 the author gives the three grounds for his certainty that they will be fulfilled (Westcott): the example of Abraham (6:13-15), the oath of God (6:16-18) and the exaltation of Jesus (6:19-20).

The example of Abraham, 6:13-15. In verse 12 the author encourages his readers to "imitate" faithful men and women. As an example of such faithful people the author refers to "Abraham." He uses Abraham as his example for three reasons (Westcott and F. F. Bruce). First, by using him he takes his readers back before the giving of the Mosaic Law. This was necessary in that the religion of Moses (Judaism) was such a fixation to his readers. Second, Abraham's faith is a wonderful example of persevering faith. Third, he played a significant part in the OT story of Melchizedek to which the author will soon return (7:1-3).

In verses 13-15 the author refers to the event recorded in Genesis 22:16-17[10] when Abraham offered his son Isaac in obedience to God's command. Several years earlier (Gen. 12:2-3) God promised to bless Abraham[11] and make him a great nation. At that time he was childless and old. The promise was reaffirmed in Genesis 15:5 and 17:5-8. A child was at last born to Abraham. On that child's well-being hung every hope that the other promises would be fulfilled. God then commanded that Abraham offer his son Isaac as a sacrifice. Abraham showed his faith and obedience by his readiness to offer his son.

God then gave Isaac back and reaffirmed the promises, this time with an oath. Genesis 22:16-18 (22:17 is quoted in Heb. 6:14) is the first time in history that God is said to have taken an oath. Why did He do it? His promise should have been enough. He did it for Abraham's sake. The Lord condescended to human custom and swore that the promise would come true.

When men or women take an oath, they generally swear to God. They appeal to a power higher than themselves. When God took an oath He could not swear to a higher power. Therefore, "he swore by himself." The author says in verse 15 that Abraham "patiently waited" and then "obtained the promise." At first glance this appears to conflict with Hebrews 11:13 and 39, which says that Abraham and the OT saints did not see the promises fulfilled. There is no conflict between these two passages. It is clear from Hebrews 11:13-16, 9:28 and 13:14 that the complete fulfillment of the promises awaits the second coming of Christ. Nevertheless, Abraham lived to see partial fulfillment of the promise in the birth of Jacob.[12]

The oath of God, 6:16-18. In verse 16 the author speaks of human oaths generally. In OT times the most common oath was, "As the LORD lives" (Judg. 8:19; 1 Sam. 14:39, 45). Abraham himself swore by God and insisted upon others doing the same (Gen. 14:22; 21:23-24; 24:3). Such oaths had two results (Westcott):

1. An oath confirmed what was said. The Greek term here translated "confirmation" is a word that was used with the sense of a guarantee. An oath guaranteed a statement. It placed God's integrity behind a statement or promise.
2. An oath stopped all contradiction. It ended "all their disputes." When a person said, "I swear that such and such is so," nothing more could be said.

In verse 17 the subject changes from human oaths to the oath of God. God swore His oath to demonstrate "the unchangeable character of His purpose." This means that God's purpose to fulfill His promises is unbreakable and unchangeable. The objects of His oath were "the heirs of the promise." This includes Abraham and the patriarchs, OT believers, Christian Jews of the NT era, and all believers in Jesus Christ (see Rom. 4:11; Gal. 3:29).[13]

> **God's purpose to fulfill His promises is unbreakable and unchangeable.**

These two unchangeable things—God's promise and His oath—testify to the strong encouragement of the Christian message. The author grounds his argument in the very character of God. It is "impossible" for Him to lie. He is free from all deceit. He is truthful and trustworthy.

In verse 18 the author describes believers as those "who have fled for refuge" to Christ (see 6:20). The Greek verb tense here suggests an event in the life of his readers, viz., the time of their conversion to Christ. This expression "who have fled for refuge" is taken from the OT regulations guiding the cities of refuge (Num. 35:6-32). These six cities provided a safe haven for anyone who had accidentally killed a person. The author's allusion to this OT practice expresses the urgency and despair that drive a sinner to Christ for forgiveness. It also suggests the safe refuge that the Savior gives to all who flee to Him for forgiveness of their sins.

To flee to Christ for safety is "to hold fast to the hope set before us." The term "hope" can refer to an attitude (confident expectation). It can also refer to the object of hope, the thing hoped for. It has the latter meaning here. The "hope set before us" is the fulfillment of the "promise" in the "world to come" (2:5).

The exaltation of Jesus, 6:19-20: the certainty of our hope. The Christian hope—the truth that Christ shall one day return and deliver us into the heavenly country—is an "anchor of the soul." The author of Hebrews has had much to say about Christian endurance. Now, however, his attention has turned to the security of the Christian's future salvation. Christians are like a ship that has anchored in a safe harbor. Our security does not rest on our own feelings, experiences, religious systems, or circumstances. Rather, we are safe because of the High Priest we have in heaven.

The place of our hope. The phrase "behind the curtain" (6:19) is an allusion to the veil that was the door to the innermost room of the OT tabernacle. That room was called the Most Holy Place or the Holy of Holies. It was a symbol of the actual dwelling place ("the inner place") of God in heaven, the true Holy of Holies (see Heb. 8:1-2). Sailors cast their anchors down into the depths of the sea. The anchor of the Christian is thrown upwards into the depths of heaven. It finds its "sure and steadfast" mooring there. We are anchored to an immovable object, namely, the throne of God (A. B. Davidson).

The person of our hope. It is because of the work of Jesus that the believer is secure. The OT high priest went behind the veil of the earthly tabernacle once a year. Jesus, however, after His death and resurrection, ascended into heaven. There He entered the very "inner place" of God. He is there "as a forerunner on our behalf." The OT priest went into the Holy of Holies, but the people waited outside and kept their distance. Jesus, however, is a different kind of priest. He is of a different order ("the order of Melchizedek"). He has gone to heaven to open up the way for His people to follow Him (P. E. Hughes). Today He is there "on our behalf," i.e., as our representative. "Christ stands in God's presence representing us." He exhibits "in His own person what He guarantees *we* shall be" (J. Denney). His presence in heaven today is a "pledge that He, as our Head, will also take us, His members, up to Himself" (Heidelberg Catechism).

> **We are anchored to an immovable object, namely, the throne of God.**

SUMMARY

In Hebrews 6:1-3 the author announces his intention to lead his readers beyond their immature state. He is determined to help them gain a deeper appreciation of Christ and His work. In verses 4-8 he warns them that some of their number may be heading toward apostasy. The people he describes in these verses have never truly been converted. If they continue to resist the truth they will gradually become so hardened that they will fall away from Christianity. Such hardened apostates are impossible to rescue.

In verses 9-12 he tells them that the love and concern they have for one another have led him to the conclusion that the congregation is, for the most part, truly converted. Yet they need to show diligence in getting a deeper grasp of what is involved in their faith. Only this will shake off their sluggishness. To inspire them he tells them to imitate the heroes of the past, and he points them to their future inheritance of the promises.

> **Jesus' presence in heaven is a pledge that the "heirs of the promise" will one day be with God.**

In verses 13-16 he provides them with an illustration of perseverance, viz., Abraham. The chapter closes on a note of encouragement (6:17-20). Those who have "fled for refuge" to Christ have a promise from God that their future destiny is secure. Jesus' presence in heaven is a pledge that the "heirs of the promise" will one day be with God.

Endnotes

[1] There are many reasons why Christians refuse to grow. In the case of the original readers, it was probably their historical circumstances. They were converts to Christianity from Judaism. They were probably being pressured by their Jewish neighbors, family, and friends to give up their new Christian ideas and return to the religion of their fathers. They were beginning to give up more and more of those features of doctrine that were distinctive of Christianity. They only wanted to hear the doctrines that were shared by Christians and Jews alike (F. F. Bruce).

[2] Bible commentators have differed in their understanding of the phrase "the elementary doctrine of Christ." There are three interpretations: (1) The original teaching of Jesus during His earthly ministry. (2) The first simple presentation of the Gospel that the readers had heard. (3) The fundamental explanation of the fulfillment of the messianic promises in Jesus Christ.

[3] The OT priests all came from the tribe of Levi. The expression *Levitical ritual* refers to the various religious activities and sacrifices carried on by the priests at the tabernacle.

⁴ Examples of OT washings include the cleansing of the priest at the laver (Ex. 30:18-21), the cleansing of the priest at the red heifer ceremony (Num. 19:7-8), and the cleansing of the leper (Lev. 14:8).

⁵ As we approach this difficult passage, we need to apply three important rules of biblical interpretation. First, interpret the passage in light of the immediate context, i.e., the verses that immediately precede it and follow it. Second, interpret in view of the context of the book of Hebrews. Third, interpret in view of the context of the NT as a whole. If an interpretation contradicts what is taught elsewhere in the NT, it is wrong (B. Ramm). Bible teachers have offered several explanations of the problem addressed by the author in verses 4-8. The following four are very common: (1) The danger described is that of a true Christian losing his or her salvation. However, these people are not true Christians. The author contrasts them with true believers in the immediate context (6:9). Furthermore, the NT elsewhere teaches that a true Christian cannot lose their salvation (Rom. 8:28; John 10:27-30; 14:16-17; 1 Peter 1:5). (2) The danger is that of a true believer falling from his or her Christian profession and suffering not the loss of salvation but disqualification from further service and future reward. However, the punishment threatened elsewhere in the epistle is not loss of reward but eternal judgment (10:26-29). (3) The danger is only hypothetical. It describes what would happen if a believer could fall away. However, a believer cannot fall away, so they must press on. The problem with this view is that the Greek text of verse 6 does not say, "If they fall away." These verses describe people who *do* fall away. (4) The danger is that of falling from a public profession of faith, a faith that proves to be temporary, i.e., not genuine. The fourth view is to be preferred.

⁶ The six phrases represent five participles in the Greek text.

⁷ The term *salvation* may refer to a present possession, namely, the forgiveness of sin and deliverance from its penalty (see Heb. 2:10). In Hebrews, however, the emphasis is not on salvation as a present possession but as a future inheritance in the "world to come" (1:14; 2:5; 9:28).

⁸ The term *saint* is related to the Greek word *to sanctify*. It means one who is set apart to worship and serve God. In the NT every Christian is considered a saint.

[9] The same Greek word is translated "dull of hearing" in 5:11 that is translated "sluggish" in 6:12. The author gives the word a different nuance in each passage.

[10] We know that the author is referring to Genesis 22 because he quotes Genesis 22:17 in verse 14.

[11] In the OT the promise consists of three elements: (1) An "offspring" or a line of heirs culminating in a chief heir, namely Christ. This promise was made to Eve, Abraham, Isaac and Jacob (Gen. 3:15; 12:3, 7; 15:4-5; 26:24; 28:14; Gal. 3:16). (2) The land of Canaan, which is given to the patriarchs and their descendants forever as an inheritance (Gen. 12:1, 7; 13:15, 17; 26:2-3; 28:13). (3) Through this heritage all the peoples of the earth will be blessed (12:3; 18:18; 26:4; 28:14). The apostle Paul calls this third item the "Gospel" in Galatians 3:8 (W. C. Kaiser). The theme of promise is very important in Hebrews. The noun "promise" occurs fourteen times (4:1; 6:12, 15, 17; 7:6; 8:6; 9:15; 10:36; 11:9 (twice); 11:13, 17, 33, 39). The verb "to promise" occurs four times (6:13; 10:23; 11:11; 12:26). Promises were given to Abraham (6:12-15; 7:6), Isaac and Jacob (11:9), Sarah (11:11), the patriarchs and prophets (11:33), and the Jewish people (4:1-3). These were assured of the land of Canaan (11:9), of rest (4:1), of a posterity (6:14; 11:11), and of an eternal inheritance (9:15; Schniewind and Friedrich).

[12] Abraham saw partial fulfillment of the promise of Genesis 12:2-3 in the birth of Isaac. In Genesis 22:17 Isaac is already alive when the promise of an "offspring" is given. Abraham lived to see a partial fulfillment of the Genesis 22 promise in the birth of Jacob.

[13] In this epistle the author of Hebrews was appealing to a congregation on the basis of their Jewishness. It is therefore likely that in this context "heirs of the promise" refers primarily to Jews (Acts 2:39; 3:25; J. Calvin).

LESSON 5 EXAM

Use the exam sheet at the back of the course to complete your exam.

1. **By the phrase "the elementary doctrine of Christ" the author means**
   A. the original teaching of Jesus during His earthly ministry.
   B. the basic teaching of the Apostles that the foundational doctrines of the OT were fulfilled in Christ.
   C. the Sunday School lessons the readers had heard as children.
   D. doctrines that the readers were to abandon.

2. **In verses 4-8 the author describes a class of people. According to lesson 5, these people are**
   A. true Christians who lose their salvation.
   B. true Christians who are disqualified from further service and future reward.
   C. a hypothetical (imaginary) group who fall away. Since it is impossible to fall away, the readers are urged to press on.
   D. people who abandon a profession of Christian faith that was not genuine.

3. **The author's basic terms for true salvation are:**
   A. cleansing, sanctification, perfection, and salvation.
   B. justification and reconciliation.
   C. enlightenment, partaking of the Holy Spirit, tasting the Word of God.
   D. fellowship, friendship, and a happy life.

4. **The illustration of verses 7-8 is intended to prove that**
   A. divine chastisement comes upon believers to make them fruitful.
   B. divine retribution will come upon those who finally reject Christ.
   C. even if one is saved he or she can still go to hell.
   D. the fruitful ground is an illustration of apostasy.

5. **From verses 9 and 10, we learn that the author of Hebrews considered good works and love toward fellow Christians as**
   A. a requirement of someone before he or she can become Christian.
   B. an evidence that the readers are truly Christians.
   C. an evidence that the readers are close to becoming Christians.
   D. a requirement if one wishes to receive rewards in heaven.

6. **In chapter 6, the author speaks of "hope" (6:11, 18-19). By "hope" he means**
   A. an attitude (wishful thinking) and the object of hope (a home in heaven).
   B. diligent endurance in the study of Scripture.
   C. an attitude (confident expectation) and the object of hope (namely, the fulfillment of the promises).
   D. the earnest desire to please the Lord.

7. **The author's confidence that God's promises will be fulfilled is based on**
   A. the example of Abraham.   C. the exaltation of Christ.
   B. God's oath.   D. All of the above.

8. **How did God reaffirm His promises to Abraham?**
   A. With a sacrifice.   C. With fire from heaven.
   B. With immense wealth.   D. With an oath.

9. **According to some Bible translations, God's promise and oath (6:17-18) are immutable because God is immutable. When we say that God is immutable, we mean that He is**
   A. unchangeable.   C. holy.
   B. eternal.   D. all powerful.

10. **When the author calls Jesus "the forerunner" (v. 20), he means that**
    A. Jesus is the first to enter the Most Holy Place in heaven.
    B. Jesus has entered heaven as our representative.
    C. Jesus' entrance into heaven assures that we also shall go there.
    D. All of the above.

What Do You Say?

According to Hebrews 6:10-12, what is the remedy for a spiritual life that is dull and sluggish?

Diligence to persue full assurance of hope by imitating those who've already inherited promises through faith and Patience, This hope is of future glory in heaven.

Hebrews 7

The author of Hebrews had a pastor's heart. He was aware of the pressures that his readers have experienced and are experiencing (see Heb. 10:32-34; 12:3-4). He knows that the Christian's real resource is the high priesthood of Jesus Christ. If his readers—both in the first century and today—are to persevere in the faith, in spite of the pressures of life, they need a correct conception of the High Priest who can help them. In chapter 7 he begins to expound at length the high priesthood of Jesus Christ. This is the central theme of the epistle.

In Hebrews 5:1-10 the author demonstrated that Jesus is qualified to be our High Priest. He now turns to an exposition of those qualities that prove Him to be a High Priest who is superior to Aaron (compare Heb. 5:11 and 7:1-28) These qualities are summed up by the author when he says that Jesus is a High Priest "after the order of Melchizedek" (5:10). It is evident from 7:15, where he substitutes the phrase "in the likeness of" for the phrase "after the order of," that the term "order" has the sense of "nature, quality or manner" (F. Delitzsch). In short, Christ is superior to Aaron because He is "the same sort" of high priest as Melchizedek. He is like Melchizedek.

SUPERIOR TO AARON (CONTINUED) (5:1–7:28)

The Order of the Priesthood of the Son of God (7:1-28)

The author first mentioned Melchizedek in Hebrews 5:10. He hesitated to elaborate on the subject in view of the spiritual condition of the readers. After pausing to admonish them (5:11-14), warn them of the dangers of apostasy (6:4-8), and encourage them (6:9-20), he again returns to the subject of Melchizedek.

The Characteristics of the Melchizedekian Priesthood (7:1-3)

The story of Melchizedek, 7:1-2a. In these verses the author presents a brief summary of the facts of Melchizedek's encounter with Abraham in Genesis 14:18-20. Abraham (then called Abram) gathered a force of 318 men and defeated a group of four kings who had invaded the area of Sodom (Gen. 14:1-16). They had taken booty and hostages, Abram's nephew Lot among them. As Abram's force returned home they were met by Melchizedek, "priest of the Most High God." Melchizedek fed bread and wine to Abram's troops, and he blessed him. Abram then gave the priest one tenth of the spoils of his victory.

> The title "Most High God" speaks of the supreme sovereignty of Yahweh.

The typology of Melchizedek, 7:2b-3. The author now interprets the Melchizedek story typologically.[1] He says that Melchizedek is typical of Christ ("resembling the Son of God") in four ways:

1. *His name and title.* The name of the historical king of Salem was "Melchizedek," which means "king of righteousness." He was dedicated to righteousness and ruled in righteousness. In his name Melchizedek prefigured Christ whose person and ministry are characterized by righteousness. The author understands Melchizedek's domain, namely the city of Salem (ancient Jerusalem, Ps. 76:2), to prefigure Christ's kingdom which is to be characterized by peace (see Zech. 9:9-10). The word *Salem* means "peace." The fact that Melchizedek was a king pointed ahead to Christ who would unite in His person the dual offices of royalty and priesthood.[2]

2. *His office.* Melchizedek was "priest of the Most High God." He was a priest in Canaan, yet he was a priest of Jehovah (=Yahweh),[3] the God of the Bible (see Gen. 14:22). The title "Most High God" speaks of the supreme sovereignty of Yahweh. The Lord is exalted above all creaturely existence (F. Delitzsch). In his office as priest Melchizedek prefigured Christ, who is also "priest of the Most High God."

3. *His lack of priestly ancestry.* The OT Law required the Levitical priests to be of Aaronic descent (Ex. 28:1; Num. 3:10; 18:1). Melchizedek, however, was "without ... genealogy" (7:3), i.e., he had no priestly ancestors. Because of this he prefigured "our Lord" who was descended from the non-priestly tribe of Judah and was therefore without priestly genealogy (7:14).

4. *The absence of any record of his birth or death.* The OT is silent about Melchizedek's parents as well as about his birth and death. We might well ask the author, "Did Melchizedek have parents?" "Was he born?" "Did he die?" The answer to all three questions is, "Of course!" "You see," our author would tell us, "the similarity is not between Christ and Melchizedek, but between Christ and the *portrait* of Melchizedek in Genesis 14." Just as a portrait may omit parts of its subject's body (you may only see the face), so the OT portrait of Melchizedek has omitted many details. Yet the silences of Genesis 14 are just as typical as the explicit statements. In the OT picture Melchizedek is "without father or mother." His lack of father and mother typifies the deity of Christ who, as the divine Son, had no human father or mother. Melchizedek had "neither beginning of days nor end of life." This typifies the eternality of the Son of God and insures us that He shall remain a priest forever.

The Greatness of the Melchizedekian Priesthood (7:4-10)

Continuing his observations on Genesis 14, the author moves to the next stage of his argument. He now establishes the greatness of Melchizedek. The argument in verses 4-10 is fourfold. Melchizedek is great because:

1. Abraham gave him a tithe.
2. He blessed Abraham.
3. He eternally lives on, while the Levitical priests were dying men.
4. Levi paid him a tithe.

Greater than Abraham, 7:4-7. "See how great this man was," the author writes. This is a subject, he implies, that merits detailed study. He is even greater than Abraham who gave him "a tenth of the spoils" of war. The Greek term here translated "spoils" means "firstfruits." This, the finest portion of the spoils of war, was generally dedicated to the deity. To pay a tithe ("tenth") to a priest was to acknowledge the divine character and dignity of his priesthood.

At first the readers might have said, "Surely the author means another Abraham. He cannot mean Abraham who was the father of the nation of Israel and the friend of God (James 2:23; Isa. 41:8). Surely the biblical Abraham did not give the choicest spoils to this insignificant Gentile priest." The author, however, leaves no room for confusion. It was "the patriarch" (lit. head of the clan or tribe) Abraham who paid the tithe to Melchizedek. Melchizedek's greatness is demonstrated by the tithe he received and the importance of the one who gave it.

> Melchizedek's greatness is demonstrated by the tithe he received and the importance of the one who gave it.

In verses 5-6a the author mentions "Levi," Abraham's great-grandson. He says that the Levites were "descended from Abraham." It was the tribe of Levi in ancient Israel, "in the law," that was the priestly tribe. Tithing (giving a tenth to God) was to be done through the Levites. Yet the patriarch paid a tithe to Melchizedek, a priest with no priestly genealogy.

Melchizedek is great not only because he received a tithe from Abraham but also because he "blessed him" (7:6). When we bless people today we are commending them to the care of the Lord. Many times in the Bible, however, a blessing was an official and prophetic announcement of God's purpose for a person. Blessings come down from those above someone— from a patriarch, a king, a prophet, or a priest. Surely, if "the inferior is blessed by the superior," then Melchizedek should have been blessed by Abraham, "who had the promises." But, no. Melchizedek blessed Abraham. Melchizedek was greater than Abraham!

Greater than Levi, 7:8-10. The author argues that Melchizedek was greater than the priests of Israel (the Levitical priests) for two reasons. First, Melchizedek is greater in that "he lives" forever (7:8). The Levitical priests, however, were "mortal men," (lit. "men that die," AV).[4] Evidently a priest who lives forever would be better than a priesthood made up of priests who have to be replaced every few years because of death.

Second, Melchizedek's priesthood is greater than Levi's, because Levi paid a tithe to Melchizedek (7:9-10). In ancient Israel one family of the tribe of Levi (Aaron's family) functioned as priests. The other Levitical families assisted the priests in their religious functions and in maintaining the tabernacle. "In the law" all the other tribes were to give a tenth (a tithe) of their crops and livestock to the Levites (7:5). The Levites in turn gave a tenth to the priests (Num. 3:5-7; 18:1-3, 25-27; Neh. 10:37-39).

When the tribes paid a tithe to the Levites, they were acknowledging the special dignity of their calling. When Levi paid a tithe to Melchizedek, he was acknowledging that Melchizedek's priesthood was superior to his own.

The author's argument in verses 9 and 10 seems strange to modern readers. It may have seemed a bit strange to the original readers. The author recognized this and added the phrase "one might even say" (7:9) to alert us that he was not speaking in a literal sense. We must remember, however, that the author, under the inspiration of the Holy Spirit, is using a typological argument. In the Bible there is a unity to the human race and to families. Abraham was the great-grandfather of Levi. When Abraham paid a tithe to Melchizedek, he acted "one might even say," as a representative for all his children, including Levi. Abraham really paid a tithe to Melchizedek. Levi did so in a relative or typical sense.[5]

What is the author trying to prove in verses 4-10? He is pressing his argument that the readers have more in Christ than they had in Judaism and the Levitical priesthood.[6] Why should they return to a religion and priesthood that was inferior to the priesthood of Christ? Christ's priesthood was the same kind as Melchizedek's. Both Abraham, "who had the promises," and Levi, the father of Aaron and Israel's priesthood, acknowledged that Melchizedek's priesthood was of a superior kind.

The Significance of the Melchizedekian Priesthood (7:11-19)

In verses 11-19 the author continues his discussion of Melchizedek, but he changes his text. In verses 1-10 his comments have been based on the historical account of Melchizedek in Genesis 14. Now he turns his attention to Psalm 110[7] which was written by King David.

The failure of the Aaronic priesthood, 7:11-14. Apparently some of the readers were reasoning that Aaron's priesthood was better than Melchizedek's priesthood. After all, they may have thought, Aaron's priesthood was instituted 600 years after Melchizedek's. To the readers this seemed to suggest that Aaron's priesthood had replaced Melchizedek's. The author quotes Psalm 110:4 (see Heb. 7:17, 21) to disprove that line of thinking. Aaron's priesthood had not brought in the age of "perfection." If it had brought "perfection," why did God prophesy a different priesthood for the future? The fact that God calls for this new priesthood in David's day shows that Aaron's priesthood was not all it should be. David wrote of the future Melchizedekian priesthood 400 years after the beginning of Aaron's priesthood.

The "Levitical priesthood" did not bring "perfection" (7:11). When the author uses the term *perfection* he is not speaking of moral perfection. The Greek word means "to complete, bring to its goal, consummate." The precise sense must be determined by usage, and a clue to the author's usage is found in 7:19. In contrasting the old and new priesthoods, he says, "The Law [the Aaronic priesthood in particular] made nothing perfect," but under the Melchizedekian priesthood we may "draw near to God." Through the new priesthood of Melchizedek, believers reach perfection (i.e., their goal) in a direct and lasting personal relationship with God. The Law (the old priesthood of Aaron) failed to remove the obstacle to free access to God, namely sin. The priesthood of Melchizedek is "better" (7:22) because it gives the believer the freedom to approach God through the sacrifice of Christ (F. F. Bruce, D. Peterson).

> **Christ's priesthood was the same kind as Melchizedek's.**

If the Levitical priesthood had removed sin and given people access to God, there would be no need of another kind of priest (7:11). However, the Levitical priesthood had failed. This proves that the Melchizedekian priesthood was necessary.

An important result issues from the fact that Christ has become a high priest like Melchizedek. The Levitical priesthood and the Mosaic law have been set aside (7:11-12, 18). The author says that the law was received on the basis of the priesthood. The Levitical priesthood was "the pillar upon which the Mosaic system rests" (Hewitt). Of necessity, then, when the Levitical priesthood was set aside, the Mosaic Law must also have been set aside.

Verses 13 and 14 show how radical the change is. In verse 13 the author reminds his readers that Jesus ("the One of whom these things are spoken") belonged to "another tribe" (Judah). No man from Judah had ever been in the priesthood ("served at the altar"). The law of Moses made no provision for a priest from the tribe of Judah (7:14). The fact that Jesus (a non-Levite) has been appointed as a priest proves that the Law has been set aside.

The success of the Melchizedekian priesthood, 7:15-19. The Melchizedekian priesthood has succeeded where the Aaronic priesthood failed because of a better priest (7:15-17) who has provided a better access to God (7:18-19). In verse 15 the author continues to argue that the Levitical priesthood was ineffective and needed to be set aside. This is even "more evident," he says, because there has arisen "another priest" (lit. "another kind of priest" or "a different kind of priest").

The contrast between the new priesthood and the old is twofold:

1. *The negative contrast.* Christ did not become a priest "on the basis of a legal requirement concerning bodily descent" (7:16). What the author means is that the Law established "a system of earth-bound rules" (NEB) for entrance into the Levitical priesthood. One had to have a definite ancestry (family of Aaron). When ordained, a priest had to be clothed with special garments, anointed with oil and anointed with blood on the right ear, the right thumb, and the right big toe (Lev. 8). Christ's priesthood does not depend on such material, external things.

2. *The positive contrast.* Jesus' qualifications for the office of priest are not external and official. They are internal and personal. The ground of His priesthood is "the power of an indestructible life." It suggests two things. First, Christ's priesthood is based on His essential divine nature which death could not destroy. Second, Christ's priesthood is also based on His resurrection life, i.e., the new quality of life with which He was empowered in His human nature at His exaltation and glorification.

In verse 17 the author adds the testimony of God (from Ps. 110) to prove his argument. In Psalm 110:4 God the Father said to His Son, "You are a priest forever after the order of Melchizedek." The key word here is "forever." The Levitical system was temporary. Individual priests died and were succeeded by new priests, but Christ will never die. His priesthood will never change. It is "forever."

The implications of God's statement to Christ in Psalm 110:4 are spelled out in verses 18-19. "On the one hand," the Law that established the Aaronic priesthood is annulled or set aside. It "made nothing perfect." It failed to achieve true access to God. "On the other hand," the believer in Jesus Christ has "a better hope." The author explains this "better hope" later in 10:19-22. The essential point is that through the new Melchizedekian priesthood of Christ there has been the removal of sin which kept men and women at a distance from God.

We have access into God's very presence in heaven through the blood of Christ.

The author's point is that we are better off than the OT saint. The author of Hebrews does not mean that believers in OT times did not have a sense of forgiveness and God's nearness; they did (see Ps. 32:1-2; 73:28). The OT saints could know God, pray to God, and love God, yet our hope and access to God are better. Why? Because Christ has come. We have access into God's very presence in heaven through the blood of Christ.

The Law had failed: the OT saint could not keep all the commandments, and the sacrificed animals could not really wash sin away (see Heb. 10:1-4). The OT saint had to look ahead and hope for the Messiah (the Christ). It is Christ's sacrifice that has really put sins away (see Heb. 10:11-18).

The Superiority of the Melchizedekian Priesthood (7:20-27)

Continuing to use Psalm 110:4 as his text, the author goes on in verses 20-27 to list several ways in which the Melchizedekian priesthood of God's Son is superior to Aaron's:

1. It was confirmed by an oath.
2. It is permanent because of Christ's eternality.
3. It is better in character because of Jesus' sinlessness.
4. It is efficacious (effective).

Superior because of a divine oath, 7:20-22. The very way that the new priesthood (the priesthood of Christ) was inaugurated declares that it is better. In Moses' day the priesthood of Aaron was based on a commandment from God (Ex. 28:1).

There was no divine oath. Jesus' priesthood, however, was confirmed by God's oath. At the time of Christ's installation as priest, namely at His exaltation which took place at the time of His ascension into heaven, God the Father ("the Lord") swore that the Son would be "a priest forever."

The difference that God's oath makes is this: it makes Jesus the "guarantor of a better covenant." The Aaronic priesthood was the basis of the Mosaic Law (7:11-12). The Melchizedekian priesthood is the basis of a new covenant. The new covenant is better because of the oath of God. The oath of God confirms the superior dignity of the Melchizedekian priest.

In verse 22, we should note, the author introduces the word *covenant* which will play a significant part in his argument in chapters 8–10.[8] The term refers to a binding contract, treaty, or agreement. The author will argue in detail in chapter 8 that the priesthood of Christ is the basis of a better covenant than the priesthood of Aaron.

The author here calls Jesus the "guarantor of a better covenant." A guarantor was the person who accepted the legal obligation for payment in a bond or contract. The old covenant (the Law) had a mediator (Gal. 3:19), i.e., a middleman (Moses) who brought the parties (God and Israel) together. However, the old covenant did not have a guarantor. The Israelites pledged to abide by the terms of the Law (Ex. 24:7), but they failed. The new covenant has a guarantor. With His death and exaltation Jesus guarantees that the provisions of the covenant (the forgiveness of sins, Heb. 8:12) will be accomplished.

Superior because of a permanent priest, 7:23-25. Over the years "former priests" served. One historian (Josephus) estimated that between the death of Aaron and the destruction of the Temple in AD 70 there were 83 high priests. Each priest's occupation of the office was interrupted by death. Because Christ "continues forever" His priesthood is "permanent." Because of the eternality of Christ He cannot step out of His priesthood nor can another step into it. His occupation of the office will not be interrupted. The office is His alone.

> A guarantor was the person who accepted the legal obligation for payment in a bond or contract.

Today believers in Jesus Christ ("those who draw near to God through him") have a priest who "always lives to make intercession for them." The verb "to make intercession" means "to appeal to, to entreat, to make petition." In heaven today the Christian has a high priest who prays to God for him or her. His intercession insures the final salvation of believers. The phrase "to the uttermost" suggests two ideas: Christ will save His people completely, and He will save them forever. The verb "to save" is related to the word *salvation* which elsewhere in Hebrews (1:14; 9:28) refers to the yet future, final deliverance into the promised blessings of the kingdom.

Those who benefit from Christ's intercession are described as "those who draw near to God through him." They are Christian believers who should be continually,[9] day by day, drawing near to "the throne of grace" (4:16) in faith. The phrase "through him" reminds us that it is through the priestly office of Christ that we have access to God's throne.

Superior because of a sinless priest, 7:26-27a. The kind of priest the author has described in verses 1-25 is "indeed fitting." He is just what we need. His assets exactly satisfy our needs. We are sinners, but His moral qualifications more than offset our liabilities. Three words describe our Lord's character:

1. *Holy.* This term describes Jesus in relation to God. The basic sense of the word is loyalty to covenant obligations. Christ was faithful in all His duties to God.
2. *Innocent.* This term describes the Savior in relation to other people. The sense of the word is brought out by the translation "guileless" (NEB). Jesus' life was not soiled by false motives or unworthy deeds. He was without guile, without malice and without unkindness.
3. *Unstained.* This term describes our Lord in relation to Himself and the world. The sense of the word is freedom from blemish or spot. Jesus was morally and spiritually flawless (H. Montefiore).

Some scholars take the phrase "separated from sinners" with the one that follows it ("exalted above the heavens"). They say that the author is referring to spatial separation. Jesus is now in heaven where He is free from the contagion and hostility of sinners (J. Moffatt). However, that is not the author's point here. The phrase "separated from sinners" is a summary of the three words that precede it. The author is referring to moral separation. Jesus was "holy, innocent, unstained" and, as a result, "separated from sinners." He spent all His time on earth with sinners—some notorious (see Matt. 9:11-12; Luke 7:39)—yet He never acquired their depravity.

> **Today the Christian's priest is in heaven.**

Today the Christian's priest is in heaven. The author's observation that Jesus "[is] exalted above the heavens" speaks of the triumph of His resurrection, ascension, and glorification (P. E. Hughes).

The sinlessness of Christ is contrasted in verse 27 with the weaknesses[10] and failures of the Levitical priests. The Aaronic high priest was a sinner who before he offered a sacrifice for the sins of the people offered one for himself. This was especially true on the annual Day of Atonement when Aaron offered a young bull in sacrifice "for his own sins" (see Lev. 16:6). It was also true of occasional or "daily" sins of the high priest (see Lev. 4:3).[11] However, Christ, the Melchizedekian priest, did not offer a sacrifice "for His own sins," because He was sinless. His sinless character makes Him a better high priest than Aaron.

Superior because of an effective sacrifice, 7:27b. When the author says that the Son of God "offered up himself," he anticipates a fuller discussion of Christ's sacrifice in Hebrews 10:1-18. The sacrifice of Jesus was better than the sacrifices of Aaron for two reasons:

1. *The finality of the sacrifice.* Christ offered a sacrifice for the sins of the people that was "once for all" (see Heb. 10:12, 14). Unlike the sacrifices of Aaron, which were "daily" and annual, Jesus offered one sacrifice, and it never needs to be repeated.

2. *The nature of the sacrifice.* Jesus "offered up himself." The Levitical priests offered animal sacrifices that could not take away sin (10:4). Jesus, the perfect priest, offered the perfect sacrifice ("himself") which does "put away sin" (9:26).

The Perfection of the Melchizedekian Priesthood (7:28)

The Mosaic "law appoints men in their weakness as high priests." They were men who died and needed to be replaced. They were sinners who needed divine forgiveness themselves. They offered sacrifices that were not effective. As a result of these failures, God has appointed a new high priesthood, under oath, which replaces the old. That the new priesthood replaces the old is proven by the fact that the oath "came later than the law." The oath was sworn at the time of Christ's exaltation and installation as High Priest. Because of His perfect work on earth, He "has been made perfect" (qualified and consecrated)[12] as High Priest.

Unlike the OT priests who were merely "men," the Melchizedekian priest is the Son of God. He has a divine nature. Because of His deity, His sinlessness and His once-for-all perfect sacrifice, He is qualified to serve "forever."

SUMMARY

The author's argument in chapter 7 is that the Son of God is a high priest who is superior to Aaron. He is superior because He is a high priest of the same sort as Melchizedek. The key elements of his argument are as follows:

1. Christ unites the offices of priest and king (7:1-2).
2. He is an eternal priest (7:3, 17, 21, 24).
3. He is superior to the patriarchs (7:4-10).

4. He is an effective high priest in that His one sacrifice dealt with sin and made His people "perfect" (7:11, 19, 27).
5. He is a divine priest with an endless life (7:16).
6. His priesthood was confirmed by divine oath (7:20-22, 28).
7. His priesthood is "permanent" (7:24).
8. He is a sinless priest. In short, the Son of God is a qualified ("made perfect," 7:28) high priest, and His priesthood is superior to Aaron's.

COMPARISON OF MELCHIZEDEK AND JESUS CHRIST

MELCHIZEDEK	JESUS CHRIST
1. A King-Priest, 7:1.	1. A King-Priest.
2. He is "King of Righteousness," 7:2.	2. He is "our Righteousness," Jer. 23:6.
3. He is "King of Salem" (i.e., "King of Peace"), 7:2.	3. He is King of Peace (see Rom. 5:1) and will be King of Jerusalem (Psalm 110:2).
4. He is without [recorded] father or mother, 7:3.	4. He is, in His divine nature, without earthly father or mother.
5. He is without [recorded] genealogy (i.e., without priestly ancestry), 7:3.	5. He is without priestly ancestry, 7:13-14.
6. He has no [recorded] birth or end of life, 7:3.	6. In His divine nature, He has no birth or end of life.
7. His priesthood is therefore uninterrupted by death, 7:3	7. His priesthood is eternal, 7:3, 17, 21, 24.
8. He blessed Abraham, 7:6-7.	8. He blesses all "who draw near to God through him," 7:25.
9. He fed Abraham bread and wine, i.e., he sustained him (not discussed in Hebrews).	9. He feeds His people, and they enjoy His fellowship in the symbols of a finished work, namely bread and wine.

THE CONTRASTS BETWEEN THE PRIESTHOODS OF AARON AND CHRIST

	AARON *(Levitical Priesthood)*	**CHRIST** *(Melchizedekian Priesthood)*
1. Order	Aaron.	Melchizedek.
2. Office	High Priest.	High Priest and King.
3. Effect	Did not accomplish "perfection."	Accomplishes "perfection," 7:11, 18, 19, 25.
4. Function	Basis of the old covenant, which was weak and useless and had no guarantor, 7:11, 18.	Basis of the new covenant, which has a guarantor, 7:22.
5. Basis	On the basis of their ancestry 7:16 (NIV).	The "power of an indestructible life" 7:16.
6. Inauguration	By appointment only, 7:20-21.	By appointment and God's oath, 7:21.
7. Duration	Transitory with many successors, 7:23.	Unchangeable and without succession, 7:23-24.
8. Character	Sinful. High Priest offered sacrifices for himself, 7:27.	Sinless, 7:26. His only sacrifice was for others, 7:27.
9. Offering	Animal sacrifices offered repeatedly, 9:12.	Himself and once-for-all, 7:27.
10. Nature	Weak men with no divine strength to help, 7:28.	The Son of God is divine in nature with divine resources to help in time of need, 7:28.
11. Location	On earth, in an earthly sanctuary, 9:1.	In heaven, in the true tabernacle, 7:28; 8:1-2.

Endnotes

[1] Typology is the study of the types of Scripture. The word *type* is derived from the Greek word *typos* which means "the mark or impression left by a blow." The basic ideas expressed by the word are "resemblance, likeness and similarity." By the term *type* Bible scholars mean a person, thing, event or institution in the OT which symbolically represents, illustrates and prefigures a person, concept or event in the NT. For example, in John 3:14-15 we learn that the serpent in the wilderness was a type of Christ. It prefigured the life-giving effects of Jesus being lifted up and hanged upon a cross.

[2] In ancient Israel the two offices of king and priest were divided between two tribes. The kings came from the tribe of Judah, and the priests came from the tribe of Levi.

[3] The divine name *Yahweh* is generally translated LORD in modern English translations of the OT.

[4] Like all human beings, Melchizedek died. Yet there is no record of his death in Genesis. We must remember that the author is here speaking typologically. In a literary sense, i.e., in the portrait in Genesis 14, Melchizedek lives on. In this deathless photograph in Genesis 14, Melchizedek is a picture of Jesus Christ, the eternal Son of God who never dies.

[5] Some students of Hebrews have understood verses 9-10 in a realistic sense. They say that when Abraham paid the tithe to Melchizedek, his great-grandson (Levi) was in him ("in the loins") in seed form. I do not believe this is true.

"Abraham *really* paid tithes to Melchizedek, but Levi did *not really* do so … The tithing of Levi in Abraham was no more real than Melchizedek was *really* the Son of God. The relationships were typical" (S. L. Johnson).

[6] The expression *Levitical priesthood* means the same thing as the expression *Aaronic priesthood*. Levi was the priestly tribe. Aaron, the brother of Moses, was the first high priest.

[7] Melchizedek is mentioned in three chapters of the Bible. He is described *historically* in Genesis 14, *prophetically* in Psalm 110, and *typologically* in Hebrews 7.

[8] We shall consider the term *covenant* in Chapter 8. The Hebrew term has the sense of a binding settlement, compact, agreement, contract or alliance. The OT phrase "to make a covenant" literally means "to cut a covenant," in that covenants were solemnized or inaugurated by a sacrifice (Gen. 15:18). This element of sacrifice has led one writer (O. P. Robertson) to describe a covenant as "a bond in blood." The old covenant is the compact or binding settlement that God made with Israel at Mt. Sinai (Ex. 24:8). It is "the law" (Heb. 7:11, 19). The new covenant is the better arrangement that was inaugurated by the sacrifice of Jesus Christ (see Luke 22:20).

[9] The phrase "those who draw near" is a present participle in the Greek text. The present tense of the participle suggests a habitual drawing near.

[10] The term *weakness* can have a neutral sense as in 4:15 (hunger, thirst, fatigue, sorrow, etc.) It can also have a moral sense as in 5:2 and 7:28 where it suggests sinful failures.

[11] The OT does not contain an explicit command for the high priest to offer a daily sacrifice for himself. By *daily* the author of Hebrews means the occasional sins of the high priest spoken of in Leviticus 4:3 (F. F. Bruce).

[12] Christ's eternal sonship and His messianic sonship almost merge in texts like Hebrews 1:8 and 7:28.

LESSON 6 EXAM

Use the exam sheet at the back of the course to complete your exam.

1. **Christ is High Priest "after the order of Melchizedek." By the term *order* the author of Hebrews means**
   A. that Jesus is in the succession of Melchizedekian priests.
   B. that Jesus has the same rank as Melchizedek.
   C. that Jesus is like Melchizedek.
   D. that Jesus has the right to issue commands.

2. **The term *Salem* means**
   A. righteousness.　　　　C. peace.
   B. joy.　　　　　　　　　D. long-suffering.

3. **In 7:3 the author says that Melchizedek was "without … genealogy." This typically prefigures**
   A. Christ's lack of a true human nature.
   B. Christ's lack of priestly ancestry.
   C. Christ's lack of sin.
   D. Christ's failure to offer animal sacrifices.

4. **Both Abraham and Levi paid tithes to Melchizedek. The author points to this fact as proof that Melchizedek was**
   A. entitled to a tenth because he was a priest.
   B. a king-priest.
   C. righteous and peace loving.
   D. superior to Abraham and Levi.

5. **The author precisely explains the relationship of priesthood to the old and new covenants, saying that**
   A. the old and new covenants are the basis of their respective priesthoods.
   B. priesthood is the basis or foundation of the covenants.
   C. priesthood is not important to the covenants.
   D. the covenants are the rule books of the priest.

6. **The Levitical priesthood did not bring "perfection," therefore**
   A. the Law as a whole would have to be set aside.
   B. only the laws concerning the priesthood would have to be changed.
   C. there would have to be revisions in the Mosaic covenant.
   D. the tribe of Levi would have to be annulled.

7. **When the author says that "the law made nothing perfect" (7:19), he means that**
   A. men were not made morally perfect by the Law.
   B. Christians on earth today are morally perfect because of the new covenant.
   C. the Law failed to remove the obstacle to free access to God, namely sin.
   D. the new covenant does not make people morally perfect.

8. **God the Father swore an oath installing Jesus as High Priest at the time of His**
   A. birth.
   B. agony in the Garden of Gethsemane.
   C. death on the cross.
   D. ascension into heaven.

9. **The Lord today makes intercession in heaven for His people (7:25). This means that He**
   A. offers an eternal sacrifice for them in heaven.
   B. prays for them in heaven.
   C. represents them in heaven.
   D. makes sure their prayers are heard in heaven.

10. **A high priest like Jesus Christ "was indeed fitting" (7:26). This means that**
   A. a priest who offers a once-for-all sacrifice is just the kind we need.
   B. an eternal, permanent priest is just the kind we needed.
   C. a sinless priest is just the kind we sinners needed.
   D. All of the above.

What Do You Say?

What is the significance of the fact that Christ is a High Priest after the order of Melchizedek?

Jesus is divine, eternal, needing no ancestry, fulfilled the law, removed sin, superior to Levitical priesthood. His priesthood never changes. By Him, we have access to God's presence.

Hebrews 8

In chapter 8 the author continues his exposition of the high priesthood of Christ. He continues to prove that Christ is a better high priest than Aaron. Beginning in chapter 8, however, he changes his approach. In chapters 5-7 he has demonstrated that Christ is superior to Aaron in His person. In chapters 8–10 he will argue that Christ is superior to Aaron in His functions.

It is vitally important, because of his readers, that the author prove the functional superiority of Christ. His readers were Hebrews by birth. They believed that the basic idea of religion was access to God (W. Barclay).[1] They believed that access to God was possible through the institutions of Judaism. These institutions included the priesthood, the sanctuary, the Mosaic covenant, the tabernacle ritual, and the sacrifices. In chapters 8–10 the author will show that Jesus Christ is superior to these institutions.

II. Christ as High Priest: Superior in His Functions (8:1 - 10:18)

HE SERVES A BETTER SANCTUARY (8:1-6)

The Centrality of the High Priesthood of Christ (8:1-2)

The Dignity of His Office (8:1)

In 7:26 the author has told his readers that they need a certain kind of priest. Now, in 8:1 he says, "We have such a high priest." He is just the kind we need. In fact, the author says, "Now [this is] the point in what we are saying." In other words, the fact that Christians have a High Priest in heaven is the central theme ("the point") of the epistle.

The High Priest of the Christian "is seated at the right hand of the throne of the Majesty in heaven." The divine title "Majesty" draws our attention to the greatness and supremacy of God. Our High Priest is seated at "the right hand" of God. The right hand of a king was considered the place of honor in the kingdom (1 Kings 2:19). Isaiah (48:13) says that God created the world with His right hand. With His right hand He saves the oppressed (Ps. 17:7). In Exodus (15:6, 12) we learn that the Lord redeemed Israel from Egypt with His right hand. The psalmist (48:10) says that God does what is righteous with His right hand. To be at God's right hand, then, is to be at the place of dignity and honor.

Jesus is just the kind of High Priest we need.

The verb "is seated" in verse 1 should be translated "has taken His seat" (NASB). It draws our attention to the moment of His exaltation when God invited Him to take this place of honor. Not only does Christ's seat at God's right hand speak of honor and glory; it also says something about His sacrificial work. There were no chairs in the OT tabernacle. The OT high priests were always standing because their sacrificial work was never completed (10:11). Christ sat down because His work of purification of sins was completed (1:3; 10:12).

The Nature of His Work (8:2)

Jesus Christ is today "a Minister in the holy places." The LXX uses the verb form of the word *minister* as a technical term. It refers to the service or work of priests and Levites in the tabernacle (Ex. 28:35; 35:19; Num. 8:22; 16:9). In verse 1 the author says that Jesus "is seated" in heaven. His work of sacrifice is completed. The term *minister* draws attention to the fact that although His sacrificial work is finished there is a work that continues. What does our Lord do in heaven today? The author of Hebrews will give us more details later (9:24; 10:20; 13:15, 21). He has already told his readers in 7:25 of one thing that Jesus is doing today. He is interceding for them, i.e., He is praying for their perseverance and final deliverance into the kingdom. Because of His intercession we may be assured they will persevere.

The OT tabernacle was a tent-like structure where the sacrifices of the people of Israel were offered to God. The innermost room of the tabernacle was called the Holy of Holies or the Most Holy Place. The word translated "holy places" is the word which everywhere in Hebrews means the Most Holy Place (9:2-3, 8, 12, 24-25; 10:19; 13:11).[2] Jesus today serves in the "true tent." It is evident from 8:1 and 9:24 that the "true tent" is the abode of God, i.e., the Holy of Holies in heaven itself. We might translate verse 2 in this way: "a minister in the Holy of Holies, in the true tent." The true tabernacle was erected by the Lord, not by man.

The Function of the High Priesthood of Jesus Christ (8:3)

The word "for" in verse 3 introduces the first part of the author's explanation of his "point" (8:1). The "high priest" of Israel was appointed by God to offer sacrifices. Jesus Christ is the High Priest of His people. As such it is necessary that He make an offering to God. This is His central function in Hebrews.[3]

There is an important distinction in the two uses of the verb "to offer" in verse 3. In the Greek text the first use is in the present tense which suggests repeated offerings. The OT high priest regularly came to the tabernacle to offer animal sacrifices. The second use of the verb "to offer" is in a different Greek tense. The immediate context (see Heb. 7:27) suggests that we should understand the offering of Jesus to be "once for all." The offering of Jesus Christ is, of course, His offering of Himself upon the cross (9:12, 14).

> **The offering of Jesus Christ is His offering of Himself upon the cross.**

The Scene of the High Priesthood of Jesus Christ (8:4-6)

The Sphere of Aaron (8:4-5)

When the author says that a high priest must have an offering, he implies that he must also have a sanctuary. Some of the readers may have thought that if Jesus was a high priest, He should be serving the temple in Jerusalem.[4] The author now tells his readers that Jesus cannot perform His ministry on earth for three reasons:

1. *First, the old sanctuary was earthly, 8:4.* Under the old dispensation there was a clergy-laity distinction. Jesus was from the tribe of Judah and not from the priestly tribe of Levi. According to the Law, therefore, He could not be a priest on earth and enter the earthly Holy of Holies. The author's unwritten practical application is this: If Jesus Christ is barred from the earthly sanctuary and cannot exercise His priesthood there, then why are the readers clinging to that sanctuary and its rituals (D. Gooding)?

2. *Second, the old sanctuary was typical, 8:5.* The Levitical priests served in a tabernacle that was a "copy and shadow" of the "true tent" in heaven. The Greek word translated "copy" is used in various contexts with the meaning "example, model, pattern, sketch, outline or imitation." A modern illustration would be the drawing, plan or model of a building. The word "shadow" suggests something that is unreal. A tree or rock is real, but its shadow is insubstantial. In Hebrews 10:1 the author says that the tabernacle service of the OT Law foreshadowed Christ. The person and work of Christ cast their shadow back over the OT. Here in 8:5 the author suggests that the tabernacle had no independent life of its own. It was merely a sketch or outline of the "true tabernacle" in heaven.

3. The OT tabernacle was built by Moses according to divine instructions. According to Exodus 25:40 (quoted in 8:5) Moses was given instructions for the building of the tabernacle while on Mt. Sinai. Some scholars say that Moses was shown a scale model of the tabernacle.[5] Others say he saw a vision of the true tabernacle, the dwelling place of God. In one way or another, "he [Moses] was instructed by God" in how to build the tabernacle, its furnishings, and utensils. There is no attempt by the author to demean the tabernacle. In its time it served the divine purpose.

4. *Third, the old sanctuary was inferior, 8:6.* The author's statement that Jesus "has obtained a ministry that is as much more excellent than the old" implies that the ministry associated with the tabernacle was inferior. As we have already learned in our study of 7:11-12, the OT system could not provide sinners with access to God.

The Sphere of Jesus (8:1-6)

Clearly, Jesus Christ must perform His priestly work in heaven. Because He was not of the tribe of Levi, He could not serve in the temple in Jerusalem. This does not make His work inferior. It is "more excellent" than the work of Aaron for three reasons.

1. *First, it is heavenly, 8:1, 5.* The OT high priest entered an earthly sanctuary that was but a symbol of the throne room of God (Ps.

99:1). Our High Priest has entered the actual throne room of God in heaven.

2. *Second, it is real, 8:2.* In verse 2 heaven is called "the true tent." This does not mean that the earthly tabernacle was false. There are two Greek words for *true.* One means "true as opposed to false." That word is not used in Hebrews. The other word means "real as opposed to apparent." That is the word used here. The OT tabernacle was a sketch or model of the actual tabernacle in heaven.

3. *Third, it is superior, 8:6.* The work of Christ is "more excellent" than that of Aaron. It is superior in that it is associated with a "covenant [that] … is better" than the one given at Mt. Sinai. This "new covenant" (8:8) is "better" because it is established on "better promises." The author explains in verses 7-13 why the promises are better. The main reason is that the better promises include the absolute forgiveness of sins (8:12).

In 7:22 Jesus is called the "guarantor of a better covenant." Here in 8:6 He is referred to as the One who mediates to a better covenant.[6] The two terms, guarantor and mediator, are different. The old covenant had a mediator, but no surety or guarantor. In NT times the word mediator was a common business term meaning "arbitrator" or "go-between." In the NT itself it is used of Moses as the "middleman" of the old covenant (Gal. 3:19-20). In 1 Timothy 2:5 Jesus is the Mediator, that is, "the One who represents God to men and men to God, and brings them together" (A. Oepke). In Hebrews He is the Mediator par excellence. He mediates or negotiates a new covenant, and in doing so He protects the interests of both parties for whom He acts. He is zealous for God's honor, and with equal zeal He seeks the sinner's rescue (E. K. Simpson).

Verses 3-4 raise an interesting question. In verse 3 the author suggests that Jesus Christ offered a sacrifice to God as High Priest. In 10:10-12 he clearly states that Jesus offered His body in death as a sacrifice. In 8:4, however, he says that our Lord does not serve as a High Priest on earth. Did Jesus, or did He not, offer a priestly sacrifice of Himself while on earth?

In answer to this question, I would suggest that we ask the wrong question when we ask, "Where did Christ die?" The proper question is: "In connection with which sanctuary did He die?" Our Lord's death must be understood not in terms of physical geography but in terms of ritual geography. If Christ's self-sacrifice is a true sacrifice, then it belongs to the "true tent." The author of Hebrews teaches that Christ's high priesthood, and therefore His sacrifice, is linked with "the greater and more perfect tent" (9:11), that is, the "true tent" in heaven.[7] From the divine standpoint, even though Jesus died at Calvary, His sacrifice belongs to the heavenly world (A. B. Bruce).

HE MEDIATED A BETTER COVENANT (8:7-13)

In verse 6 the author says that the "covenant he [Jesus] mediates is better." The "covenant [that] ... is better" is the new covenant established as a result of the death of Christ (see Luke 22:20). With Jeremiah 31:31-34 as his text the author will now demonstrate (in chapters 8 and 9) that the new covenant is better than the "first covenant"[8] (8:7) made with Israel at Sinai. Careful attention needs to be paid to his comments on the terminology, the institution, the mediator, the need, the provisions, and the finality of the new covenant.

The Terminology of the New Covenant

It will be helpful if we briefly review what we learned in Lesson 6 about the word *covenant*. It is one of the great doctrinal words of the Bible. Some think it is the unifying theme of all of Scripture. The Hebrew word translated "covenant" has the idea of a binding settlement, compact, agreement, contract or alliance. The most common expression in the OT for establishing a covenant is the phrase "to cut a covenant." This expression is derived from the practice of sacrificing animals at covenant-making ceremonies (see Gen. 15:9-17; Ex. 24:5-8).

The Greek word for covenant used in the NT is not the word that means a compact or agreement between two parties who are equal in status. Rather, it is a term which suggests that one party of the covenant is

> **The new covenant is better than the "first covenant" made with Israel at Sinai.**

sovereign over or superior to the other. This dominant party lays down the provisions and conditions of the compact or agreement for another. The other party must either accept or reject the covenant. In the Bible God and man are not equal parties in the covenants. God is sovereign and supreme.

In mercy and kindness He made the biblical covenants for the benefit and blessing of mankind. The people of the covenant must by faith receive the blessings of the covenant and abide by its provisions.

In verse 7 the author speaks of the "first covenant." The Mosaic covenant ("the law," 7:11, 12) was the first covenant in the Bible that provided for a priesthood to represent men before God. We have already learned in Lesson 6 that the "first covenant" failed to achieve access to God and forgiveness of sins for the people. A "new covenant" (8:8) was therefore needed. The death of Jesus Christ was the sacrifice that inaugurated this new covenant.

> **The death of Jesus Christ was the sacrifice that inaugurated this new covenant.**

Two different Greek words for "new" are used in Hebrews to describe the new covenant. One of the words means "new in time, recent" (12:24). The new covenant is more recent than the Mosaic covenant. The other word means "new in quality, new in kind" (8:8; 9:15). The new covenant is not only new in time, but also new in kind. It is different from the first covenant.

The Institution of the New Covenant

In verse 6 the author says that the new covenant "was enacted."[9] The time of its enactment is implied in 9:15-18. Covenants, the author implies, are inaugurated by blood. The new covenant, then, was instituted at the time of Christ's death (13:20).

The Mediator of the New Covenant

As we noted earlier in this lesson, the author says that Jesus is the "[one who] mediates" the new covenant. He is the arbitrator, go-between, or middleman who has established good relations between God and man in this "covenant [that] … is better." As Mediator He is the One through whom the terms of the new covenant are carried out. He is the One who has negotiated and ratified the new covenant.

The Need of the New Covenant (8:7-8)

The Faultiness of the Old Covenant (8:7-8a)

The new covenant would not have been needed, says the author, if the Mosaic covenant had been faultless. But the "first covenant" was not faultless. The author does not mean to suggest that it was sinful (see Rom. 7:7, 12). He means that it failed to provide a relationship of full and free access into God's presence. The old covenant perfectly revealed man's sin and inability, but it did not provide full forgiveness and pardon for sin. And it did not give sinners a new redeemed nature.

The Promise of the New Covenant (8:8b)

The setting of the promise. The author bases his comments in verses 7-13 on Jeremiah 31:31-34. The prophecy of Jeremiah was written at a time of almost continuous disobedience on the part of the people.[10] The promise of a new covenant is set in the context of the nation's violation of the covenant of Exodus 24:1-8 ("my covenant that they broke," Jer. 31:32). The new covenant was foretold at Judah's midnight hour when the Babylonian army was at the gates of Jerusalem. At that grim time Jeremiah wrote his "book of consolation" (Jer. 30–33) with its message of hope. Although the nation would go through a period of divine chastening, it would eventually be restored with a new covenant. This new covenant contained the promise, "I will forgive their iniquity, and I will remember their sin no more" (31:34).

The people of the promise. Quoting Jeremiah 31:31, the author says that the new covenant will be made "with the house of Israel and the house of Judah" (8:8). It was made with the same people as the first covenant, namely the people of Israel. Elsewhere in the NT we are told that unbelieving Israel has been cut off from divine blessing during the present age (Rom. 11:20). Nevertheless, today there is also a remnant of believing Jewish people (11:3-4) that the apostle Paul calls the "Israel of God" (Gal. 6:16). The earliest Christians, namely the apostles and their associates, were all Jewish, and the new covenant was made with them. Gentile believers were later grafted into the stock of Abraham (Rom. 11:16-24) and were made fellow heirs with Israel of the blessings of the new covenant (Eph. 1:11-13; 3:6).[11] Unlike Paul, however, the author of Hebrews is not concerned in his epistle with Gentile believers. His concern is to tell his Hebrew readers that the new covenant, promised by Jeremiah, has now been enacted.

The time of the promise. Looking ahead into the future Jeremiah said, "Behold, the days are coming, declares the Lord, when I will establish a new covenant" (8:8). The new covenant was future in Jeremiah's day, but it was already instituted when Hebrews was written. In short, the new covenant is in force today.[12]

The Provisions of the New Covenant (8:9-12)

The Negative Description (8:9)

The new covenant is not like the covenant made with the nation of Israel at the time of the exodus. The word "fathers" refers to the generation of Jewish people in Moses' time. The author pinpoints the problem of the Mosaic covenant: "They did not continue in My covenant." The old covenant was a conditional covenant. The benefits of the covenant depended on Israel's obedience. The Israelites promised to keep the covenant. They said, "All that the LORD has spoken we will do" (Ex. 19:8). Yet from the beginning they fell into idolatry and disobedience (32:1-4). They "did not continue" in the covenant. In Jeremiah 31:32 the Lord says, "they broke" it. As a result the Lord "showed no concern for them." He revoked the covenant and abandoned them.

The Positive Description (8:10-12)

Jeremiah looked on to a future time ("After those days") when a new covenant would be enacted and take the place of the old. That future time arrived when our Lord was crucified. The new covenant was inaugurated by Jesus Christ at the cross (1 Cor. 11:25; Luke 22:20). It has four provisions that make it different from and superior to the covenant made at Sinai:

1. *An internal inclination to obey.* The Lord promised Jeremiah and the people that the new covenant would be different. It would be an internal rather than an external covenant. Under the Mosaic covenant God's law was engraved on tablets of stone (Ex. 19:3-8; 2 Cor. 3:3). Under the new covenant God's "laws"[13] would be put within the minds of His people and inscribed on their hearts (Heb. 8:10). In the parallel promise in Ezekiel 36:25-27, God's people are promised a new heart and spirit as well as the gift of the indwelling Spirit of God. These promises of the prophets describe more than mere Scripture memorization. Scripture memorization was encouraged under the old covenant (Deut. 6:6-9; 10:12; 30:6). Two things were promised by the prophets:

- A new nature that knows and loves God's will for the believer[14]
- The indwelling Spirit of God who would enable the believer to do God's will

2. *An unconditional relationship to God.* The old covenant was a covenant of works. Blessing was conditioned on the obedience of the people. Israel "did not continue" in the covenant (8:9). She failed to meet its demands. The new covenant is different. It is an unconditional covenant of grace. The emphasis throughout this passage is on the initiative of God. He says, "I will establish" (8:8, 10), "I made" (8:9), "I will put" (8:10), "I will … write" (8:10), "I will be" (8:10, 12), "I will remember … no more" (8:12). He accomplishes all that needs to be done. Our High Priest Jesus Christ is the "guarantor" of the new covenant (7:22). His work at the cross, not our obedience and works, guarantees that all the demands of the covenant will be met.

3. *A personal knowledge of God.* Another superior feature of the new covenant is found in the promise, "They shall all know me" (8:11). Under the old covenant only the educated scribes knew the details of the Law. Furthermore, access to the Lord was denied to individuals, and His grace was obtained through the mediation of faulty Levitical priests (Ex. 20:15, 19). Under the new covenant, however, there is no privileged class of mediators between God and man. There is access to God for all believers through Christ, their faultless and perfect High Priest (Heb. 4:16; 10:19-22). Each believer has an absolute, inborn, and direct acquaintance with God[15] that is not dependent on any kind of external instruction.[16]

> **There is access to God for all believers through Christ.**

4. *A merciful forgiveness of sins.* The word "for" at the beginning of verse 12 introduces the ground of all the promises in verses 8-11 (W. E. Vine). The ground or basis of these promises is the mercy of God. The animal sacrifices of the old covenant did not bring forgiveness of sins. In fact, they brought sins to remembrance (see Heb. 10:3-4). Because of the sacrifice of the new covenant (10:12-18), however, God no longer remembers sin. He forgives them.[17] The true and final and complete forgiveness of sins makes the new covenant superior to the old.[18]

The Finality of the New Covenant (8:13)

Some of the original readers wanted to go back to the old covenant. The author turns to the OT (Jer. 31) and shows that the prophets themselves predicted the end of the old covenant. As soon as Jeremiah predicted a new covenant, the old covenant began to grow "obsolete." Now, the author says, it is expiring of old age (A. B. Davidson). The author is no doubt thinking of Jerusalem as he writes. In two or three short years the city would be defeated and the temple destroyed. "The cross fulfilled and annulled the legal covenant; the destruction of Jerusalem and of its temple was its grave" (W. Kelly).

SUMMARY

In Hebrews 8:1 the author says that his primary theme is that believers have a seated High Priest in heaven. This High Priest ministers there in the true tabernacle (8:2). He could not have been a High Priest on earth because there already was a high priest serving there. Christ's service is better, however, in that the OT tabernacle with its ceremonies was only a copy and shadow of the true tabernacle that is related to a better covenant (8:3-6).

The fact that Jeremiah (31:31-34) spoke of a new covenant, the author notes, proves that the Mosaic covenant was not without fault. What was needed was an internal covenant that actually dealt with mankind's sin problem. The announcement of this new covenant makes the earlier covenant obsolete.

Endnotes

[1]   In Hebrews 7:11, you will remember, the author implied that the Levitical priesthood did not accomplish *perfection*. We learned in lesson 6 that *perfection* in that context means free access to God.

[2]   As we shall learn later (Lesson 8), the tabernacle was typical, i.e., it was an OT illustration of NT teaching.

[3]   According to Delitzsch, verse 3 consists of a syllogism (logical argument) with three parts: (1) A high priest's function is to offer sacrifice. (2) Christ is a high priest. (3) Therefore, Christ must have something to offer.

[4]   Hebrews was probably written about 2-3 years before the temple in Jerusalem was destroyed (AD 70).

[5]   Some of the Jewish rabbis believed that models of the tabernacle and all its fixtures descended from heaven. Then Gabriel appeared in a worker's apron and showed Moses how to build them (M. Dods).

[6] The author refers to Jesus three times as the One who mediates a new covenant (8:6; 9:15; 12:24).

[7] We may translate Hebrews 9:11 as follows: "But when Christ appeared as a high priest of the good things that have come, in connection with the greater and more perfect tent (not made with hands, that is, not of this creation)."

[8] The "first covenant" of 8:7 is the Mosaic covenant made by God with Israel at Sinai (Ex. 24:8). The author does not mention the earlier Noahic (Gen. 9:9-17) and Abrahamic (15:18) covenants. In that he is concerned with covenants made with Israel, his omission of the Noahic covenant, a universal covenant, is easy to understand. The author's decision not to describe the promises made to Abraham as a covenant is startling, however, because these promises receive significant attention in the epistle (6:13-18; 7:6; 11:8-16). The reason the author of Hebrews does not call the Abrahamic promises a covenant is, nevertheless, easy to understand. He reserves the term covenant for his contrast between the two great high priestly systems of worship and forgiveness, namely, Judaism and Christianity.

[9] The Greek verb translated "enacted" in 8:6 is a perfect passive. The verb in the passive voice has the sense "to settle or institute legally." The perfect tense suggests that the new covenant was already enacted when the author wrote his epistle.

[10] Jeremiah served as a prophet for about 40 years, from the 13th year of King Josiah (626 BC) to the fall of Jerusalem to the Babylonians (586 BC).

[11] The people of God today, namely the church, is made up of believing Gentiles and believing Jews. Paul calls believing Jews "the Israel of God" (Gal. 6:16).

[12] In the larger context of Jeremiah, the promise of the new covenant includes the regathering of the Jewish people (Jer. 30:1-3), the reunion of Israel and Judah (31:31) and Israel's restoration to the land of Palestine (30:18-22; 31:38-40; 33:14-17). This part of the new covenant promise awaits the second coming of Christ. Hebrews 11:13 and 39 speak of aspects of the new covenant promise that yet await fulfillment.

[13] The LXX of Jeremiah 31:33 uses the plural "laws" instead of the singular "law" found in the Hebrew. Nowhere else in the LXX is the plural "laws" substituted for the Hebrew singular "law." The new covenant is not a legal covenant conditioned on the obedience of the believer. F. F. Bruce

suggests that the term *laws* in Hebrews 8:10 be translated "guidance, direction or instruction."

[14] All Christians agree that OT believers were truly converted and justified. Bible students have differed, however, over whether the promises in Ezekiel and Jeremiah of a radical change in the inner man imply that believers under the old covenant were or were not regenerate. I lean toward the view that the new regenerate nature and the universal indwelling of the Spirit in believers are blessings known only to believers under the new covenant.

[15] Complete fulfillment of the promise in verse 11 (Jer. 31:34) awaits the future. Only at the second advent of Christ, when His earthly kingdom is inaugurated, will there be perfect fulfillment. Yet there has been a limited fulfillment of the promise today. There is a real sense in which the Holy Spirit has brought a knowledge of God to the heart of all who know Christ as Savior.

[16] We should not misunderstand verse 11. It does not mean that gifted teachers are unnecessary under the new covenant (see 1 Cor. 12:28-29; Eph. 4:11-12). The promise in Jeremiah ("they shall all know me") speaks of the knowledge of divine grace based upon the inward experience of the heart. It is that knowledge which the Holy Spirit gives to the heart when a sinner hears the Gospel, is convinced that it is true, and is assured that Jesus died in their place. Once a person has this inner knowledge they will still need instruction in the Scriptures.

[17] Suppose a Christian fails. Will God treat him or her like Israel and put them aside? No! The promise of verse 12 is absolute: "I will be merciful toward their iniquities, and I will remember their sins no more." What God expects under the new covenant is not sinless perfection but progress. He has guaranteed the ultimate righteousness of every believer. This is provided in Christ. We are to grasp this truth, and we are to count on it. We are not to struggle to keep an external Law. Rather, we are to saturate ourselves with the written Word of God. The Lord has implanted within us a new nature. His Spirit dwells in our hearts. These wonderful gifts will prompt us to obedient response to Scripture. We are to expect God to do His work within and progressively reshape us until we share the holiness of Jesus (L. Richards).

[18] "The law demands what it cannot give. Grace gives what it demands" (Pascal, *Pensées*).

LESSON 7 EXAM

Use the exam sheet at the back of the course to complete your exam.

1. **The central theme of the Letter to the Hebrews is that**
   A. Christianity is superior to Judaism.
   B. Christians are pilgrims on their way to the kingdom.
   C. Jesus Christ is High Priest.
   D. Jesus Christ is God and man.

2. **When the author tells his readers that Christ "is seated" (8:1) in heaven, he wants them to know that**
   A. Jesus' sacrificial work is completed.
   B. Jesus now occupies a place of great honor.
   C. Jesus is in the very presence of God.
   D. All of the above.

3. **The "true tent" (8:2) is**
   A. the physical body of Christ.
   B. the church.
   C. the visible heavens.
   D. the Most Holy Place in heaven itself.

4. **Jesus "mediates" the new covenant. This means that**
   A. He only watches out for God's interests in the covenant.
   B. He guarantees the new covenant.
   C. He serves as middleman and negotiates the covenant.
   D. He only watches out for the sinner's interests in the covenant.

5. **Verses 1-5 teach that**
   A. Christ died as a sacrifice on earth, but that sacrifice was connected with the true tabernacle in heaven.
   B. the sacrifice of Christ was made in heaven.
   C. the death of Christ on earth was not a sacrifice.
   D. Christ was not allowed to make a sacrifice because He was from the wrong tribe.

6. **When the author of Hebrews speaks of the Mosaic covenant as the "first covenant" (8:7), he seems to ignore the earlier Noahic and Abrahamic covenants.**
   A. This means that the Mosaic covenant actually came before the Noahic and Abrahamic covenants.
   B. This means that the Mosaic covenant was the first covenant that had anything to do with Israel.
   C. This means that he was ignorant of those earlier covenants.
   D. This means that the Mosaic covenant was the first covenant with a priesthood.

7. **The new covenant was instituted with**
   A. the remnant of Israel.
   B. the church made up of Jews and gentiles.
   C. the church which is now called "Israel."
   D. None of the above.

8. **In Hebrews 8:7-13, the author quotes**
   A. Ezekiel 36:22-28.   C. Psalm 2:7-12.
   B. Psalm 110:1-7.   D. Jeremiah 31:31-34.

9. **The Mosaic covenant was faulty because**
   A. it was instituted without the use of blood.
   B. it was not demanding enough of people.
   C. it made no provision for the Gentiles.
   D. it failed to provide full forgiveness of sins and access to God.

10. **In verse 13, the author alludes to which event when he says that the old covenant is "ready to vanish away"?**
    A. The destruction of Jerusalem in 586 BC.
    B. The destruction of Jerusalem in the future tribulation.
    C. The sin of Jerusalem in AD 30 or 33.
    D. The destruction of Jerusalem in AD 70.

What Do You Say?

How is the new covenant better than the old?

The NC is unconditional. God's Spirit renews and indwells the man. _a new creature_ _blessings_
Sins are all forgiven, remembered no more. Not on man's
obedience to laws but God's _gift of_ grace. God will teach + enable men
to keep the spirit of the law, NC is for Jews + Gentiles.

LESSON 8

Hebrews 9

The author of Hebrews is seeking to show that at the heart of every person's need is access to and communion with God. Before their conversion to Christ, the original readers of this epistle had been taught that access to God was possible only through the institutions of Judaism. These institutions included the priesthood of Aaron, the sanctuary or tabernacle, the covenant made with Moses at Sinai, and the animal sacrifices.

As we learned in the last lesson, the author is seeking to prove in chapters 8 through 10 that Jesus Christ is superior to the institutions of Judaism. In chapter 8 the author explained the superiority of the heavenly sanctuary over the earthly tabernacle, and he demonstrated that the new covenant is superior to the old. Now, in chapter 9 he will argue that the ministry performed by Christ is superior to that performed by the high priest on the Day of Atonement. The whole purpose of his argument is to show that the new covenant ministry insures access into the presence of God while the old covenant tabernacle rituals did not.

HE PERFORMED A BETTER MINISTRY (9:1-28)

The Earthly Sanctuary of the Old Covenant (9:1-5)

Its Divine Appointment (9:1)

Under the old covenant God did lay down ordinances for worship and sacrifice. These worship ordinances or regulations took place in the tabernacle, a tent-like structure established by the Lord. He established it as His dwelling place and the meeting place between Himself and His people

(Ex. 25:8; 40:2). The tabernacle with its rituals and sacrifices was established by regulations or ordinances of God ("regulations for worship"). The author of Hebrews does not ridicule the tabernacle, nor does he denounce the old system of approaching God.

Although the tabernacle was divinely appointed, the author also implies that it was inadequate. He says it was "earthly." Like everything else in this world it was a temporary and passing thing (1:11).

Its Two Chambers (9:2-5)

After acknowledging the tabernacle's divine appointment, the author goes on to comment on the parts and furniture of the tabernacle. The tabernacle had two rooms. The first room, called the Holy Place, was entered through a veiled doorway from the east. It contained two pieces of furniture, a gold lampstand, which stood to the priest's left as he entered, and a table upon which sacred bread was placed. The "table and the bread" were to the priest's right as he entered.

The west wall of the Holy Place was a veil, which served as a barrier to the second room of the tabernacle, called

> **At the heart of every person's need is access to and communion with God.**

"the Most Holy Place." In the Most Holy Place, our author says, there were two pieces of furniture, "the golden altar of incense and the ark of the covenant." Many scholars have accused the author of Hebrews of making a mistake by placing the altar of incense in the Most Holy Place. The OT (Ex. 30:1-8), they point out, places the altar of incense in the first room (Holy Place), not the second (the Most Holy Place).

The author of Hebrews has not made a mistake. We must remember that in chapter 9 he is expounding the events of the great Day of Atonement (Lev. 16). On that one day the veil was opened, and the altar of incense was considered a part of the ritual that went on in the Most Holy Place. In other words, the author is not speaking of the physical location of the altar of incense; rather, he is speaking of its ritual relationship to the Most Holy Place on the annual Day of Atonement.

"The ark of the covenant" was also in the Most Holy Place. This wooden box was covered with gold and contained three things:

1. "A golden urn holding the manna," the bread-like substance that God had sent to feed the Israelites in the wilderness (Ex. 16).

2. "Aaron's staff that budded," a wooden rod that the Lord had used to prove that Aaron was truly God's priest (Num. 17).
3. "The tablets of the covenant," the two stone tablets upon which God had written the ten commandments (Ex. 32).

These three items are all significant in that they are all reminders of Israel's sin, her idolatry, complaining, and jealousy. They are all evidence of the failure of the old covenant.

On top of the ark was a golden cover called "the mercy seat."[1] On top of the mercy seat were two gold figures of cherubs. Cherubs were angelic beings who proclaimed and protected God's glorious presence. The word "glory" links the cherubs to God's presence, for the mercy seat was viewed in the OT as the throne of God (see Ps. 99:1).

The tabernacle, its compartments, its furnishings, and its rituals all have a rich typological or symbolical value. Yet the author of Hebrews does not take the time here to expound upon this symbolism. The lessons he seeks to draw here do not concern the abiding typological value of the tabernacle. Rather, he wants to emphasize the fleeting and impermanent value of the tabernacle rituals and sacrifices.

The Temporary Rituals of the Old Covenant (9:6-10)

A Description of the Priestly Service (9:6)

In verses 6-10 the author seeks to show the limitations, not the beauty, of the tabernacle (Westcott). Verse 6 suggests one of its limitations. Only priests, not the people as a whole, were allowed to enter. The priests went in and out of "the first section [of the tabernacle]" (the Holy Place) daily to trim the lampstand (Ex. 27:20-21), offer incense on the altar of incense (30:7-8), and change the loaves on the table of showbread (Lev. 24:8-9).

The Restrictions of the Priestly Service (9:7-10)

The lesson of the holy place, 9:7-9a. The "Holy Spirit" (9:8) was teaching a very significant lesson in His division of the tabernacle into two chambers. He was showing, first (as we noted in verse 6), that the people could not approach God directly. He was also showing that the priests, the representatives of the people, could only approach part of the way. They were barred by the veil from entering the second chamber, "the holy places" (9:8).

"Once a year" (9:7) the high priest could enter the second room, but only with the blood of sacrifices, offered for his own sins and those of the people. The author speaks in verse 7 of "unintentional sins." The OT distinguished between apostasy (defiant rebellion against and rejection of the truth) and all other sin (see Num. 15:27-29; 16:30). All sin (including murder and adultery) could be forgiven except the sin of totally rejecting the truth.

The author's main point in verses 7-8 does not concern the blood sacrifices, however. Rather, he wants to draw attention to the fact that under the old covenant access into God's presence was hampered. The "first section" (i.e., Holy Place) was "symbolic" (9:9), i.e., it had a lesson to teach those living in OT times ("symbolic for the present age").

The existence of the first room with the veil on the west wall barring access to the Most Holy Place taught two things (A. B. Davidson):

1. The old religion with its daily rituals was only an imperfect advance toward God's presence.
2. The west wall of the Holy Place (the veil) was in fact an obstacle to God's presence. In short, the outer chamber was designed to stimulate a longing for a more effective sacrifice that would provide perfect access to God (P. E. Hughes).

The lessons of the rituals, 9:9b-10. The rituals of the OT were ultimately a failure for three reasons:

1. They were external. The laws dealt with all phases of life—food and drink laws, washing laws, laws relating to clothing and beards, etc. (9:10a). Such regulations had nothing to do with the spiritual condition of a person's heart.
2. They were ineffective. They did not "perfect the conscience " of a sinner or their priest (9:9a), i.e., they did not erase a person's sin and make them qualified to enter God's presence.
3. They were temporary. The old rituals were imposed only "until the time of reformation" (9:10b). The Greek term translated *reformation* was used in ancient times of the setting of a bone, the repairing of roads, and the paying of debts. It means "to put things right." It refers here to the time of the new order when Christ appeared and did what the old covenant could not do.

The Superior Ministry of the New Covenant (9:11-14)

Because of a Better Priesthood (9:11a)

The old tabernacle was "earthly" (9:1) and "symbolic" (9:9). The rituals associated with it were external, ineffective, and temporary (9:9-10). In verses 11-12 the author of Hebrews tells us why the ministry of Christ is superior to that of Aaron's. There are four reasons (A. B. Bruce):

First, His ministry is superior because He possessed a better priesthood. The Greek text of verse 11 begins, "But when Christ …" When Christ appeared all was changed. The "time of reformation" (9:10) had begun.

As we learned in lesson 3, the title *Christ* comes from the verb meaning "to anoint." The Jewish people had waited centuries for the Christ or the Messiah (i.e., God's Anointed One).[2] He would be a descendent of King David and would deliver Israel from her enemies and rule as king. What the Jewish people had not expected was that this coming Christ would also be a priest.

> **Christ is High Priest of the good things to come.**

Here in verse 11 the author of Hebrews for the first time explicitly relates the title *Christ* to the office of High Priest.

The Greek verb translated "appeared" (9:11) was often used when writers wanted to suggest the majestic arrival of a great person. It is the kind of word that often suggests the roll of drums and the flurry of trumpets. The author seems to be saying, "Now the Christ has stepped forward onto the stage of the world, and He has come as High Priest!"

He is "high priest of the good things that have come." Some Bible teachers understand these "good things" to be the things that came at the time of Christ's death. Others say (and I agree) that the "good things" are yet to come at Christ's second advent (see 9:28). Elsewhere in the epistle (2:5; 6:5; 13:14) the author uses the phrase "to come" of the fulfillment of the promises in the future kingdom upon the earth.

Because of a Better Sanctuary (9:11b)

The imagery behind verses 11 and 12 is that of the annual Day of Atonement held in the fall on the 10th day of Tishri (overlapping our September–October). Leviticus 16 gives the guidelines for this feast. Two goats were selected to represent the people, and a bullock (male calf) was selected to represent the high priest and his family. One of the goats and the bullock were sacrificed as sin offerings. The deaths of the animals were substitutionary payments for the sins of the high priest and the people. On that one day of the year, the high priest was permitted to enter the inner compartment (the Most Holy Place) of the tabernacle to sprinkle the blood of the victims on the mercy seat.

All of this was in contrast with the work of Christ. He performed His priestly work in connection with the "more perfect tent," i.e., the abode of God in heaven. It is the sanctuary in heaven, not the earthly tabernacle, that is the true tabernacle (see Heb. 8:1-2).

Because of a Better Sacrifice (9:12a-b)

Christ did not offer animal blood. He offered "His own blood." The term *blood* is a metaphor meaning loss of life. More specifically it means death by violence. Christ died as a sacrifice.

The author of Hebrews does not intend us to believe that Christ entered heaven literally bringing His blood with Him. It is unlikely, furthermore, that verse 12 speaks of the ascension at all. Rather, verse 12 describes the cross from start to finish. Just as the goat and calf were sacrificed at the altar in the tabernacle, so Christ was sacrificed at the cross. And just as the animal blood was taken behind the veil on the Day of Atonement, so Christ, while hanging on the cross, was, in a spiritual sense, in the "holy places" appearing before the Judge of all mankind.[3]

The OT high priest entered "the holy places" every year. Christ entered "once for all." This means that the sacrifice of Christ, unlike the OT sacrifices, does not need to be repeated and that it cannot be repeated.

Because of an Eternal Redemption (9:12c-14)

At the cross Christ secured "an eternal redemption." The word *redemption* has the idea of deliverance by the payment of a ransom. Christ gave His blood as the ransom price to deliver sinners from the guilt and punishment of their sins. Unlike the animal sacrifices, the sacrifice of Christ was of infinite value. God is therefore eternally satisfied with the ransom price, and it need never be paid again.

Christ's ransom payment was inward, not outward. The word "for" at the beginning of verse 13 introduces a reason or proof. In verses 13 and 14 the author will explain what he has just said. He will justify his remark that Christ has obtained "eternal redemption." His first reason is that Christ's death operated in the realm of spirit.

In verse 13 he mentions two OT rituals: the Day of Atonement sacrifices ("goats and bulls") and the red heifer ceremony. The author has no interest at this point in the typical significance of these rituals. He is only interested in the effect of the rituals in their OT setting.[4]

Their only benefit was ceremonial ("purification of the flesh"). They enabled the Israelite to maintain full, uninterrupted citizenship in the camp, but they did not remove sin from a person's heart.

The sacrifice ("blood") of Christ was different in a number of ways:

1. It was a human and rational sacrifice. If someone is to die in the place of human beings, he must be a man.
2. It was voluntary. Unlike young animals that were forced to the altar, Christ voluntarily "offered Himself" (9:14).
3. It was moral. The OT animal sacrifices were physically without defect, but Christ was morally sinless ("without blemish").
4. It was spiritual and eternal. The phrase "through the eternal Spirit" refers to Christ's divine nature. How could the death of Christ bring about an "eternal redemption"? The answer is that the One who made the sacrifice was endowed with an eternal Spirit.

Christ's ransom payment was radical, not superficial. The problem people face is their guilt. The conscience accuses the human heart of guilt, and until the heart is cleansed, it feels the pain of an accusing conscience. Christ's death deals with the radical problem of man's guilt.

Christ's ransom payment was liberating, not binding. The conscience of the sinner cries out for relief. The tendency of many people (including the original readers of the epistle) is to try to relieve the pain of conscience by doing good deeds, by performing religious rituals. Such activities are "dead works," i.e., they come from an unforgiven heart and cannot remove guilt. Christ's sacrifice truly removes guilt and quiets the conscience. It liberates a person from their guilt. It does not enslave people in an endless grind of "dead works."

> **The sacrifice of Christ was of infinite value.**

The Perfect Mediator of the New Covenant (9:15-22)

The Benefits of the New Covenant (9:15)

Verse 15 begins with the word "Therefore." The word looks back at everything the author has said from 8:6 through 9:14. Because of the total failure of the Mosaic system, a new[5] covenant was needed. The new covenant is effective because of its "mediator" and the death He died. He is the perfect Mediator because He is God and man and seeks to protect the interests of both God and man. He is zealous for God's holy honor, and He is zealous to free sinners from punishment. His death "redeems ... from the transgressions committed." This means that the death of Christ was a ransom price that delivers men and women from the penalty due their transgressions.[6]

The Jewish Christians who first read Hebrews would very naturally ask about their ancestors (parents, grandparents, etc.). They lived in the era of the old covenant. Are all believers who lived under the OT Law lost? No, says the author of Hebrews. The "transgressions committed under the first covenant" are forgiven on the same basis as transgressions today, namely, the death of Christ.[7]

> **Christ's sacrifice liberates a person from their guilt.**

The author refers to those who benefit from redemption as "those who are called." The "called" are God's chosen ones (see Rom. 8:29-30). God summons men and women by His Word and lays hold of them by His power to play a part in and enjoy the benefits of His redemptive purpose.[8]

God's redemptive purpose is that believers will one day receive a promised "inheritance." In Hebrews the inheritance of believers includes: salvation (Heb. 1:14), the promises given to Abraham (6:12), forgiveness (9:15-22), blessing (12:17), and righteousness (11:7) in the land (11:8-9), i.e., in the millennial kingdom.

An Illustration of the New Covenant (9:16-17)

Apparently some of the original readers were embarrassed over the death of Christ. Their Jewish families and friends were appealing to them to forsake Christ on the basis that He had been executed like a criminal. The author turns this argument around. He demonstrates that the death of Christ is not a reason to abandon Christianity; it is, rather, a reason to hold on.

In verses 16-17 the author uses the illustration of a "will"[9] to prove the necessity of Christ's death. The death of Christ was necessary because it makes active God's last "will." The new covenant, he says, is like a will. It is inoperative until the testator (will maker) dies. The new covenant is like a will, the last will and testament of the God-man, bequeathing an inheritance to His people.[10]

A Reminder from the Old Covenant (9:18-22)

Perhaps one of the original readers might object that the idea of a dying Christ is still offensive. The author now seeks to show that the necessity of death follows the pattern laid down under the old covenant. "The first covenant," he says, was dedicated with the use of blood (9:18). In Exodus 24 Moses took the blood of sacrificed "calves and goats" and sprinkled the book of God's laws (representing God) and the people (9:19). Both parties were bound to the agreement by blood. The author's one concern in verses 18-20 is to remind his readers that the Mosaic covenant supports the notion that covenants need to be ratified by blood.

"In the same way," he writes in verse 21, Moses "sprinkled with the blood both the tent and all the vessels used in worship." Thus the tabernacle also serves as an illustration of the demand for blood in the OT.

It is therefore faulty reasoning for the readers to object to the idea that the Mediator of the new covenant must shed blood. It is an established principle of the Mosaic system ("under the law," 9:22) that there is no forgiveness of sins without the shedding of blood.[11]

The author does add the phrase "almost everything." There were exceptions, of course. Metal articles captured in war were cleansed by fire and water (Num. 31:21-24). And poor people were allowed to offer flour in the place of sacrifices (Lev. 5:11). This was a concession of God's grace. The norm was that blood had to be shed.

> **There is no forgiveness of sins without the shedding of blood.**

The word *forgiveness* comes from a verb that means "to send off." It means to release someone from a legal obligation or debt. When we are forgiven our sins, it means that God lets their penalty pass. He releases us from their debt. This can only take place if someone else pays the debt by sacrifice.

The Better Ministry of the New Covenant (9:23-28)

In verses 23-28 the author summarizes why the ministry of Christ is better than the ministry of the OT high priest on the annual Day of Atonement. He cites three reasons, and they all revolve around the idea of Christ's "appearing": His present appearance in heaven for us, His past appearance upon earth to put away sin by the sacrifice of Himself, and His future appearance upon earth to deliver His people into the kingdom.

The New Ministry Is Better Because Christ Appears in Heaven for Us (9:23-24)

The word "thus" (9:23) connects this final paragraph of the chapter to the preceding verses. In verses 16-22 the author has set forth the importance of blood in the OT religion. The biblical norm, then, is that blood is God's agent for consecration, cleansing, and forgiveness. When the OT tabernacle and its furnishings ("copies of the heavenly things") were consecrated, sacrifices were offered. Christ has inaugurated a new ministry and He has dedicated a new tabernacle, the true tabernacle in heaven. This new tabernacle ("the heavenly things") was consecrated with a better sacrifice,[12] namely, the sacrifice of Christ.

There have been many explanations of the author's comment that the "heavenly things" had to be "purified." We are helped in our interpretation when we learn that the word translated "purified" incorporates the ideas of purification and consecration (F. Delitzsch). In this verse both thoughts are present.[13] First, there is the thought of consecration. The author is comparing the consecration, inauguration, or dedication of the old and new tabernacles. The "better sacrifice" of Christ has dedicated the new tabernacle ministry. His death has opened up access to the new sanctuary in heaven.

Second, there is the thought of purification, or cleansing. On the annual Day of Atonement the tabernacle needed to be cleansed because of its contact with sinful people (Lev. 16:16). So it is with God's people under the new covenant. Although we have been cleansed at conversion, we still sin—and yet we approach God in His heavenly sanctuary. As Bengel put it, "The heavenly things are pure in themselves, but we need to be pure to enjoy them." Therefore, our Lord continually applies His blood to keep us clean. This does not mean a literal re-shedding of His blood. Rather it means that His one redeeming death is ever effective—ever available to us (P. E. Hughes).

We are accepted because of our representative.

The word "for" which begins verse 24 gives the reason a better sacrifice was necessary. A better sacrifice was necessary to inaugurate the new tabernacle because it is a better tabernacle than the old one. Christ has not entered the "holy places" of the earthly tabernacle; He has entered the "holy places"[14] in "heaven itself."

At His ascension Christ entered the Most Holy Place in heaven and He appears there even today ("now"). The author's thought is not that Christ looks at God, but that God looks at Him and accepts Him. The purpose of Christ's appearance in heaven is clarified by the phrase "on our behalf." He appeared in heaven as the representative of His people. As God favorably regards His Son, He favorably regards us, for He is our representative. As Christians fail they are often tempted to doubt their acceptance with God. Jesus Christ has been accepted in heaven for about 2,000 years, and He appears there "on our behalf" (D. Gooding)! We are accepted, not because of our own merits, but because of our representative.

The New Ministry Is Better Because Christ Appeared to Put Away Sin by His Once-for-all Sacrifice (9:25-26)

The author now shows that our Lord's present work does not require many sacrifices. To be sure, many sacrifices were offered "every year" under the old covenant (9:25). If Christ's sacrifice was only a temporary provision, then He would have to have been sacrificed repeatedly. But Christ's sacrifice was absolute and final. It was offered "once" and does not need to be repeated.

The death of Christ was the most significant event of all time. He appeared upon earth and died "at the end of the ages." All the ages (epochs) of OT history led up to this central event. His sacrifice was "independent of time," says A. B. Davidson. It was made at one point in history, yet the benefits of it extend back to Adam's time and forward into eternity. It works as well in the 21st century as it did in the first (Ray Stedman).

His sacrifice "put away sin." This expression has the idea of elimination or cancellation. When a person embraces Christ as their Savior, they are saved from the penalty of their sins.

The New Ministry Is Better Because Christ Will Appear to Deliver His People from Judgment (9:27-28)

In verse 27 the author continues his argument that Christ could only die once. The reason that Christ's sacrifice of Himself cannot be repeated is found in His true humanity. Human beings die once and they enter a new existence. They do not die repeatedly. The author says, "it is appointed for man to die once." Death is a certain thing. It is an appointment established on the calendar of God.

After death comes "judgment." The Greek word used here for *judgment* (*krisis*) is one that is used elsewhere in Hebrews (10:27) of future condemnation and punishment. The author is speaking of the lot of all mankind had there been no provision made by God (W. E. Vine).

When Christ was "offered" as a sacrifice He met the double appointment (W. R. Newell). He died physically, and He died under the judgment of God.

Christ was a true man and subject to the laws of human life. Therefore, He died once. However, His death is different from other deaths. The Bible views death as a penalty for sin. Men are "appointed" to die in punishment for their sin. Christ, however, was "without sin" (4:15). He did not need to die at all. He died and was judged for others. He bore the sins "of many."[15]

To believers this death and judgment have been met by Christ in their place (J. N. Darby). They no longer cringe in fear of death (2:15). Instead they are "eagerly waiting for Him." Christ "will appear a second time" to this earth. This time He will appear "not to deal with sin," i.e., there will be no further need for Him to repeat His sacrifice for sins.

> **When Christ returns His people will be saved. They will be delivered from judgment and the presence of sin.**

The term *salvation* means "deliverance" or "preservation." When Christ returns, it will be to save His people. They will be delivered from judgment and the presence of sin. They will enter God's rest (4:9), the land of promise (11:9), and have peace and prosperity while living there.

SUMMARY

The Hebrew Christians, like many in our day, were not happy with the simplicity of the Christian faith. They were attracted to the beautiful rituals—with their sensuous appeal—of the Jewish religion. They were having doubts about the work of Christ and were looking with nostalgia at the trumpets, incense, priests, candles, sanctuaries, and sacrifices of religious ritual.

In chapter 9 the author of Hebrews has argued that the ministry of Christ is better than all of that. He serves the true tabernacle of God in heaven, not an earthly sanctuary. His one sacrifice, unlike the annual sacrifices of the Day of Atonement, is truly effective and provides the forgiveness of sins. His people are truly delivered from the judgment of God.

Endnotes

[1] The Greek word translated "mercy seat" is *hilastérion,* which is translated "propitiation" in Romans 3:25. When blood was sprinkled on the mercy seat, God was propitiated, i.e., His holy wrath was satisfied.

[2] The Greek word *Christ* is a synonym for the Hebrew word *Messiah.* Both mean "anointed."

[3] There have been many interpretations of Hebrews 9:12. In my opinion either of two interpretations is possible here: (1) The preposition *by means* may be translated "by" or "through" (AV, NASB). In that case the author is saying that Christ ascended into the Most Holy Place in heaven "by virtue of" His blood. He ascended "thus securing an eternal redemption" at the cross. (2) The preposition may be translated "with." In that case the entrance of the High Priest into the Most Holy Place with the blood may be considered as taking place at the moment of Christ's death. The important point is that Christ's blood was offered in connection with the tabernacle in heaven. As He offered Himself, He was in a sense both on earth and in heaven at the same time (G. Smeaton).

[4] Numbers 19 explains the red heifer ceremony. A young red cow that had never been bred was taken outside the Israelites' camp and slaughtered. A few drops of its blood were sprinkled in the direction of the tabernacle. The entire cow was set on fire, and as it burned, one of Aaron's sons threw in pieces of cedar, hyssop, and scarlet wool. The ashes were then gathered and stored outside the camp. If an Israelite became ceremonially defiled, some of the ashes were placed in water and sprinkled upon him. He was then free to resume communion with his people and his God. Typically, the Day of Atonement ritual illustrates initial cleansing at conversion and the removal of the sinner's guilt. The sprinkling of the red heifer's ashes pictures the need for daily cleansing in the life of the believer.

[5] The Greek word (*kainé*) translated "new" in 9:15 means "new in kind."

[6] The term *transgression* speaks of a willful act of disobedience against the divine law.

[7] If "the blood of calves and goats" cannot redeem people, how were sinners in OT times redeemed? The answer is given in verse 15. They were redeemed on the basis of the death of Christ. In the era of the old covenant animal sacrifices were allowed to represent for a time the

sacrifice of Christ. We may illustrate this with modern credit cards. Such cards are in themselves worthless. Yet they are backed by the actual payment that is made at the end of the month. The "credit" atonement of the OT has now been replaced by the actual payment of Christ's atoning blood.

[8] Baker's Dictionary of Theology, s.v. "Call," by J. I. Packer, p. 108.

[9] In the Greek text there is a play on words that is not obvious in English. The Greek word (*diathéké*) translated "will" in 9:16-17 is the same word that is translated "covenant" in the rest of the chapter. In the first century the Greek term had these two meanings, and the readers would know them well. When they read the Bible, it had the old fashioned meaning of "covenant." Then, in their day-to-day lives outside the church meetings, it meant "will" or "testament."

[10] *Zondervan Pictorial Encyclopedia of the Bible,* s.v. "Covenant," by J. B. Payne, 1:1003.

[11] In verses 16-22 we learn three things about blood: (1) It consecrates, i.e., it sets things and people apart for divine use (9:18-19, 21). (2) It purifies, i.e., cleanses. (3) It propitiates, i.e., satisfies God's justice and purchases the forgiveness of sins.

[12] The author says "better sacrifices" (plural). This is a plural of accommodation, i.e., the single sacrifice of Christ fulfills perfectly the ideas suggested by all the various OT offerings.

[13] There are Bible scholars who prefer the notion of purification or cleansing in their understanding of this word. Some of these scholars argue that heaven had to be cleansed in that it was the scene of Satan's rebellion. Others argue that the effects of man's sin have extended throughout the universe, and heaven itself has been touched. All of these scholars agree that only the sacrifice of Christ can cleanse these cosmic effects of sin.

[14] The ESV has the translation "holy places." However, the author of Hebrews consistently uses this Greek word (*hagia*) to refer to the Most Holy Place or Holy of Holies, i.e., the inner chamber.

[15] The phrase *"to bear the sins of many"* (9:28) may be understood in two ways: (1) He took sins away, i.e., He removed them. (2) He took upon Himself the consequences (i.e., punishment) and responsibility of sins.

LESSON 8 EXAM

Use the exam sheet at the back of the course to complete your exam.

1. **The argument of Hebrews 9 is that Christ**
    A. serves in a better tabernacle than the one on earth.
    B. inaugurated a better covenant than the Mosaic covenant.
    C. offered a better sacrifice than the sacrifices of Aaron.
    D. performed a better ministry than the Day of Atonement ritual of Leviticus 16.

2. **The author of Hebrews taught the following about the earthly tabernacle:**
    A. it was part of the Mosaic covenant.
    B. it was built according to instructions from God.
    C. it was a temporary and passing thing.
    D. All of the above.

3. **By placing the altar of incense in the Most Holy Place (9:4), the author has**
    A. connected it to the ritual of the Day of Atonement.
    B. made a mistake.
    C. made an important point about the need for incense in today's church meetings.
    D. indicated the importance of ritual for the Christian.

4. **According to the lesson, the first room of the tabernacle taught this important lesson:**
    A. the old religion offered a wonderful advance towards God's presence.
    B. The west wall of the Holy Place (the veil) was an obstacle to God's presence.
    C. the old religion satisfied man's every longing for access to God.
    D. the high priest was better off spiritually than the other priests.

5. **The title *Christ* means**
    A. High Priest.   C. Anointed One.
    B. Forerunner.   D. the Lord is salvation.

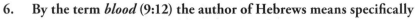

6. **By the term *blood* (9:12) the author of Hebrews means specifically**
   A. the release of spiritual life into believers.
   B. death.
   C. death by violence, by sacrifice.
   D. divine energy.

7. **Hebrews 9:12 teaches that**
   A. at the ascension Christ carried His blood to heaven.
   B. at the ascension Christ entered heaven by virtue of the blood He had shed upon the cross.
   C. Christ's death on the cross was in a spiritual sense connected with the Most Holy Place in heaven.
   D. None of the above.

8. **The term *redemption* means**
   A. deliverance from the punishment of sin.
   B. acquittal in God's courtroom.
   C. the satisfaction of divine wrath.
   D. deliverance by the payment of a ransom.

9. **The phrase "eternal Spirit" in 9:14 refers to**
   A. Christ's divine nature.
   B. Christ's human nature.
   C. the Holy Spirit.
   D. God the Father.

10. **God accepts us because Christ has entered the Most Holy Place in heaven as our**
    A. judge.   C. friend.
    B. lawyer.   D. representative.

What Do You Say?

Restate one difference between the ministry of the old covenant and the new.

Under the OC, the animal sacrifices were many and temporary. Under the NC, Christ's sacrifice is once-for-all and eternal.

Hebrews 10

In Hebrews 10:1-18 the author of the epistle gives his final verdict on the OT priesthood. He has already shown that Christ serves in a better sanctuary than the earthly tabernacle (8:1-6), that He instituted a better covenant than the one made with Israel at Sinai (8:7-13), and that He performed a better priestly ministry than the one performed annually by Aaron on the Day of Atonement (9:1-28). Now he will argue that the one sacrifice of Christ is superior to all the sacrifices offered on the Jewish altar.

The author's purpose is twofold: First, he has a practical purpose. A number of his readers are depressed by the thought that they can have nothing to do with the services of the Jewish sanctuary. The visible services in Jerusalem with their year-by-year ritual had great appeal. The author will seek to show that the very features that had such great appeal were in fact signs of its ineffectiveness and temporary nature (Westcott). Second, he has a theological or doctrinal purpose. In verses 1-18 the author will review the main thoughts of his argument:

The one sacrifice of Christ is superior to all the sacrifices offered on the Jewish altar.

1. Christ's one sacrifice is the complete fulfillment of God's will (10:1-10).
2. His one sacrifice perfectly accomplished all that the daily offerings of Judaism had failed to do (10:11-14).
3. His death has inaugurated a new and everlasting covenant (10:15-18).

HE OFFERED A BETTER SACRIFICE (10:1-18)

Because It Was the Accomplishment of God's Will Regarding Sacrifice (10:1-10)

The Inadequacies of the OT Sacrifices (10:1-4)

They were shadowy and unreal, 10:1. The word "for" in verse 1 serves to connect 10:1-18 with 9:23-28. The author will now further explain the finality of Christ's one sacrifice. Many of the original readers wanted to return to their old religion, Judaism. The author responds, "The law" was only a "shadow," but the work of Christ is the "true form," i.e., the essence or the reality. The work of Christ casts its shadow back over the rituals of the law. The law foreshadowed, typified, illustrated, or pointed to the reality of the work of Christ.

The phrase "good things to come" refers to all the good things Christ will bestow upon His people at His second coming (9:28).[1] Since the law only foreshadows these future realities, it did not have the kind of sacrifices that would prepare people to enter the coming kingdom.

The OT sacrifices did not make the OT believer "perfect," and by implication, they cannot make us "perfect" either. To perfect someone in Hebrews means to put them in a position in which they can come before God. The Law and its sacrifices were unable to do this. They were unable to remove the sinner's guilt and quiet their conscience.

> **The law and its sacrifices were unable to remove the sinner's guilt.**

They were repetitive, 10:2. The author points to the ongoing sacrifices in Jerusalem (he wrote the epistle before the destruction of the temple in AD 70). If animal sacrifices had provided true once-for-all cleansing of guilt ("once cleansed") and relief for the conscience ("consciousness of sins"), they would have ceased. By implication, of course, our author is saying that the sacrifice of Christ does remove our guilt and quiets our conscience.

They were burdensome, 10:3. Every year on the Day of Atonement the question of sin was raised again ("a reminder of sins every year"). The OT sacrifices were, in effect, a pardon bestowed for a year. They could never grant the same peace as a pardon bestowed once for all (F. F. Bruce). The

Lord's Supper suggests a wonderful contrast between the new covenant and the old. Under the old covenant there is a yearly reminder of sins. Under the new covenant there is a regular reminder of Christ, but our sins are remembered no more (1 Cor. 11:24; Heb. 10:17).

They were ineffective, 10:4. Our problem is the human problem of sin. The shedding of animal blood can have no effect upon the defilement of people. What was needed was the sacrifice of the God-man. As man, He died for mankind. As God, His sacrifice affects the spiritual realm and has infinite value.

The Superiority of the Sacrifice of Jesus Christ (10:5-10)

The author's quotation of Psalm 40:6-8, 10:5-7. How can the author prove to his Jewish-Christian reader that the OT animal sacrifices are ineffective and abolished from God's program? He does so by quoting from the OT.

He quotes a psalm written by David, probably at the time of his flight from his rebellious son Absalom (2 Sam. 15). God delivered him, and David asked if he should express his gratitude by offering animal sacrifices. No, he realized, it is not offerings that God wants, but obedience. So, David from then on sought to do God's will.

Yet David could only do God's will in a faltering way. In the ideal sense there is only One who can do God's will perfectly. That is David's greater Son, Jesus Christ (P. E. Hughes).

The author understands David's experience in Psalm 40 to be typical or prophetic of the experience of Christ. It is clear from verse 5 ("when Christ came into the world") that the author applies the psalm to Christ. He understands the words of verses 5-7 to have been spoken by the Son of God just as He was about to be born into the world. In the virgin's womb the Father prepared a body for Christ to do His will.

The author's exposition of Psalm 40:6-8; Heb 10:8-9. God neither desired nor took pleasure in the OT animal sacrifices.[2] The author does not say that God rejected sacrifice. Rather, He rejected *animal* sacrifice. He rejected the sacrifices of dumb, amoral, and unwilling creatures. What He accepted was a rational, human, spiritual sacrifice who performed the will of God. Christ has taken away the "first" order (the Mosaic law with its animal sacrifices) and has replaced it by a new ("second") order (the new covenant based on the sacrifice of Christ).

The author's application of Psalm 40:6-8, 10:10. When the author speaks of Jesus doing God's "will" in verses 7-10, he is not speaking of the *general* will of God, i.e., His will that Jesus keep the commandments. Rather he is speaking of the *gracious* will of God. God's gracious will was that

We have been set apart to worship and serve God.

Jesus Christ should obey the Father by offering Himself as a sacrifice that our sins might truly be forgiven. God did not prepare a body for Christ just so that He would be a good man. No, He came to earth to be a great High Priest. The Father prepared a body for Him that He might offer it and place sinful men and women in a cleansed spiritual relationship before God (J. Denney).

Christ's death was effective. He offered Himself "once" and that was enough. He does not need ever to offer Himself again. The result is that "we have been sanctified." By "sanctified" the author of Hebrews means that we have been set apart to worship and serve God. We are now free to approach Him, conscious that our sins are truly forgiven. This is positional sanctification.[3]

Because Christ Is Now a Seated Priest (10:11-14)

An Unrepeatable Sacrifice (10:11-13)

In verses 11-14 the author of Hebrews supplies further evidence that Christ's offering is the true and final offering for sin. Having made His offering, Christ "sat down at the right hand of God" (A. B. Davidson).

In verse 11 the author intensifies his argument. In verses 1-4 he has spoken of the inferior nature of the annual Day of Atonement sacrifices. Now he adds that the high priest's assistants ("every priest") offered an endless number of sacrifices on a daily basis. There are three points to be observed in verse 11:

1. The priests offered sacrifices "daily."
2. They stood as they did their work. There were no chairs in the tabernacle, for their work was never done.
3. The daily sacrifices "can never take away sins."

The verb *take away* literally means "to take off something that is wrapped around." Sin is like a robe we have made for ourselves. The plural "sins" speaks of all our individual acts of rebellion, hatred, deceit, disloyalty, immorality, and dishonesty. Our sins envelop us and need to be stripped away.

Verse 12 provides a sharp contrast with the OT priests. Christ offered one sacrifice in contrast to the thousands offered by the Jewish priests. Then He "sat down." Unlike the earthly tabernacle, the true tabernacle in heaven does have a chair, and Christ sat in it. "He sat down at the right hand of God." His work of sacrifice was completed and cannot be repeated.

Christ does not continue His work of sacrifice in heaven. Rather, He waits for the time when He will return to earth and all His enemies will be subjected to Him (10:13).

An Effective Sacrifice (10:14)

The word "for" in verse 14 introduces the reason Jesus Christ has taken His seat in heaven. His "single offering" perfects sinners. The verb *to perfect* does not mean to make sinlessly perfect. It literally means "to bring to an end or goal." The goal under discussion in Hebrews is freedom of access into God's presence. The barrier to that access is our sin. By bearing my punishment on the cross, Jesus has removed this barrier. In short, the verb *to perfect* in verse 14 simply means the forgiveness of sins.

As we learned in verse 10, the verb *to sanctify* means "to consecrate" or "to set apart."[4] It speaks of our new relationship to God. When a person receives Christ as Savior, they are consecrated to God, i.e., set apart to worship and serve Him.

Because the Inauguration of a New Covenant Proves That Sin Has Been Put Away (10:15-18)

The Testimony of the Holy Spirit (10:15)

Having stated that forgiveness is "for all time" (10:14), the author now offers proof from Scripture (Jer. 31:33-34). He says that it is the "Holy Spirit" who guarantees the correctness of his argument in verses 1-14.

Clearly the author believes three things about the Holy Spirit:

1. He believes in the deity of the Holy Spirit, i.e., he believes that He is God. In Jeremiah 31:33 the prophet Jeremiah explains that it is the LORD (Jehovah or Yahweh) who spoke these words. The author of Hebrews says that it was the Holy Spirit who spoke these words. Therefore, the Holy Spirit is the LORD or God.

2. He believes in the inspiration or divine authorship of the Scriptures. He quotes from Jeremiah, yet he says that the words in Jeremiah originated with the Holy Spirit.

3. He believes in the doctrine of the present witness of the Spirit. He believes that as we read or hear the Scriptures, the Holy Spirit will produce conviction in our hearts that these things are true (see John 16:8-11).

The original sense of the verb *to witness* (10:15) is "to bear witness to facts in legal proceedings." A witness is a person who can speak from direct knowledge. In Scripture the Holy Spirit

> **Jesus Christ has paid the debt of sin, and those who receive Him as Savior are debt-free.**

bears witness: He says in effect, "I saw Christ offered in sacrifice. I bear witness to the covenant that God made. I bear witness to his promise that all who hear the gospel and believe it will be forgiven forever" (4:2; 10:14, 17).

The Substance of His Testimony (10:16-17)

The author again quotes from Jeremiah 31 as he did in chapter 8 (see my comments on Heb. 8:10-12 in lesson 7). The point that the Holy Spirit makes in Jeremiah 31:33-34 is that on the basis of the new covenant, inaugurated at the death of Christ, sins are truly forgiven.

The Implications of His Testimony (10:18)

With this quotation from Scripture, the author has clinched his argument. Since the one offering of Christ provides forgiveness of sins, "there is no longer any offering for sin." There is no need for the sacrifices of Judaism nor any other sacrifice. The word *forgiveness* means "to send off." It was used in biblical times of releasing someone from a debt. Jesus Christ has paid the debt of sin, and those who receive Him as Savior are debt free.

Verse 18 contains a word of encouragement and a word of warning. The encouraging word is that no more sacrifice is needed. Whatever our sins, Christ forgives them. The word of warning is directed to those who would substitute something for the sacrifice of Christ. Our author affirms that no human deed (no sacrifice, good work, religious feeling) can bring forgiveness. Only the once-for-all offering of Christ will do.

III. Christ as High Priest: Superior in His Resources

(10:19 - 13:25)

> # A CALL TO STEADFASTNESS:
> # BASED ON A NEW ACCESS (10:19-39)

The author of Hebrews was a good preacher, and he asked himself the question every good preacher must ask: "What impact should this truth have upon my listeners or readers?" The word "Therefore" in 10:19 brings him to the practical implications of the argument he has developed in 7:1–10:18.

The Privileges and Duties of Christians (10:19-25)

Two Great Privileges (10:19-21)

He begins with a summary of the great privileges that belong to every Christian. This is really a summary of all that has been accomplished for believers by Christ (Westcott). He introduces each of the privileges by the phrase "we have."

We have free access, 10:19-20. In OT times the average Israelite could come as far as the brazen altar in the outer courtyard of the tabernacle. If he was a priest, he could go into the first chamber, namely, the Holy Place. If he was the high priest, he could go into the Most Holy Place, but only once a year. In short, under the old covenant nobody except the high priest could enter the Most Holy Place.

> **Under the new covenant all believers have the right to enter the Most Holy Place.**

Under the new covenant all believers ("brothers," 10:19) have the right "to enter the holy places." The Greek phrase (*parresian*) is incorrectly translated "boldness" (NKJV) or "confidence" (NASB) in our English versions. The original readers lacked boldness and confidence in their new covenant privileges. Unfortunately, this is also true of many Christians today. The Greek word literally means "freedom of speech." A better translation is, "We have the right (freedom of access) to enter." Whatever our failures and sins, we can at any time come before God's throne and speak freely (4:16).

Our means of access is "by the blood of Jesus." In other words, we have access to God's presence on the grounds of Christ's sacrifice upon the cross. The author reinforces this thought in verse 20. Here he says that Jesus "opened" (NASB has "inaugurated") a new way to God. Just as Jesus' death marked the dedication of a new covenant (9:18), it also marks the dedication of a new tabernacle in heaven.

The verb "open" may also be translated to "make available for use." Jesus has made available to His people a way of access, and this way was consecrated at the cross. It is a "new" way, i.e., new in time and new in quality. It never grows old. And it is "living." In other words it is effective. This way *works*. It brings the believer into God's presence.

Borrowing a picture from the tabernacle, the author says that we enter the Most Holy Place in heaven "through the curtain, that is, his flesh." The veil in the tabernacle was both a door and a barrier. It allowed the high priest to enter God's presence once a year, yet it barred everyone else. It reminded the Israelites that they could come so far but no farther. This reminded men and women of the barrier between mankind and God caused by sin. What the author is saying is that Jesus' body was a veil in just that way. It was a provision of mercy. It allowed sinners to approach God and have their sins forgiven. Yet it was also a barrier. Jesus' human nature was an obstacle to God's presence. His sinless life emphasized the distance between sinners and God. The veil had to be torn, which happened when Jesus died on the cross (see Matt. 27:51). The lesson is that an uncrucified Savior is no Savior at all (K. S. Wuest).

> **As we approach God in prayer, Jesus brings us into His very presence.**

We have a Great Priest, 10:21. Not only do we have an open way, but we have a powerful friend (A. B. Bruce). Jesus is our "great priest." He is great due to His dignity as the Son of God (1:2-4), due to His present exalted position (4:14), due to His present intercessory work (7:24-25) and, in this passage, due to the unique worth of His sacrifice. As we approach God in prayer, Jesus brings us into His very presence.

CONTRASTS BETWEEN THE SACRIFICE OF CHRIST AND THE SACRIFICES OF THE OLD COVENANT

The Contrasts	Levitical Offerings	Christ's Offering
Tabernacle	An "earthly" sanctuary (9:1) erected by man, a "copy and shadow" of the true one (8:5).	The "greater and more perfect tent" (9:11), i.e., the "true tent" in heaven (8:2).
Kind of Offerings	Bulls and goats, etc. (9:13, 25; 10:4).	Himself (9:12, 25).
Frequency of Offerings	The high priest, annually on the Day of Atonement (9:7); the other priests, daily (10:11).	Once for all (9:12, 26, 28).
Character of Offerings	Physically without blemish (Lev. 4:3, 23).	Morally "without blemish," i.e., sinless (9:14).
Punishment of The Offerings	The animals died (9:13). "Blood" = violent death by sacrifice.	Christ died (9:14). "Blood" = violent death by sacrifice.
Effectiveness of The Offerings	Did not make the sinner "perfect" nor cleanse his conscience (10:1-2). Ultimately the OT believer was forgiven on the basis of the death of Christ (9:15).	Christ by His self-offering obtained "eternal redemption" (9:12), sanctified His people (2:11; 10:14), and cleansed their consciences (9:14).
Outcome of The Offerings	The high priest entered the Most Holy Place only once a year (9:7, 25).	Christ, our High Priest, entered the Most Holy Place in heaven once-for-all (9:12).
Covenant	The Levitical priesthood was the basis of the old covenant (7:11-12).	Christ's offering ratified the new covenant (9:15).
The Promises	Levitical system foreshadowed the promises (9:24; 10:1).	Christ's offering ensures the fulfillment of the promises (9:15; see 6:17; 8:6).

Three Solemn Duties (10:22-25)

1. Our Godward duty: genuine worship and communion, 10:22a. The above privileges are the basis of a threefold exhortation to "faith" (10:22), "hope" (10:23), and "love" (10:24). Each exhortation begins with the expression, "Let us." Our first duty is to "draw near with a true heart." The tense of the Greek verb suggests repeated occasions. The high priest could enter the Most Holy Place once a year. We can come as often as we want. The plural "us" suggests that the author has in mind the local church as it gathers to praise God and give Him thanks.

In the OT the "house" of God was the tabernacle. In the NT the house of God is the local assembly or church (see Heb. 3:6). The worship apparatus of the OT was the tabernacle, while the worship apparatus of the NT is the church.[5] When believers "draw near," they do not actually ascend physically or mystically into heaven. Rather, we who are on earth come before God who is in heaven through prayer and the mediation of Christ (see Heb. 13:15). Our Great Priest is the connecting link between God's tabernacle in heaven and God's house on earth.

> **Believers are to consider how they might stir one another up to love and good works.**

We should draw near "with a true ["sincere," NASB] heart." Our worship and communion with God should not be a mechanical thing. It should be hearty. We should put our hearts into it. We are to come into God's presence "in full assurance of faith," i.e., we are to come trusting in the finished work of Jesus Christ.

The author never lets his readers forget that it is through our Great Priest that we may come. We come "with our hearts sprinkled clean from an evil conscience and our bodies washed with pure water." The imagery here goes back to the OT where priests were sprinkled with blood and bathed with water when they were consecrated for service (Ex. 29:4, 19-20; Lev. 8:6, 23). The reference to hearts and bodies suggests that the work of Christ ultimately affects the person as a whole: body, soul, and spirit. The word "blood" suggests propitiation, i.e., God's wrath has been poured out upon Christ in our place. The word "water" suggests cleansing.

2. Our duty selfward: unwavering perseverance, 10:23. God promises in Scripture to keep His people secure (see Isa. 41:13; Rom. 8:28-30; John 10:27-30). That is His responsibility, and He "is faithful." Our responsibility is to "hold fast the confession of our hope." This is an exhortation to perseverance or endurance. We are to hold fast to the spiritual values and instruction we have received. The term *confession* does not refer here to the personal witness of Christians but to the body of truth they believe in. The term *hope* does not refer here to the attitude of hope but to the object of our hope, viz., the return of Christ and the establishment of His kingdom.

3. Our duty manward (or churchward): mutual encouragement, 10:24-25. Believers are to consider how they might stir up one another to "love and good works." We do this by gathering together with other Christians and encouraging one another in the meetings of the church. "Some" of the original readers were "neglecting" the meetings. The verb *to forsake* means "to abandon, to desert." It is a terrible thing to abandon fellow Christians. We are not to do to one another what God never does to us (J. Moffatt).

The Greek word used here for "to meet together" is an interesting one. It is used in only one other verse in the NT (2 Thess. 2:1) where it refers to our being gathered to Christ at His coming. Each time the early Christians assembled, they broke bread (Acts 2:46; 20:7), i.e., they celebrated the Lord's Supper. As the apostle Paul wrote, Christians will only celebrate the Lord's Supper "until He comes" (1 Cor. 11:26). Their incentive to assemble together was the imminent return of Christ ("all the more as you see the Day drawing near").

The Peril of Rejecting Christ (10:26-31)

The Danger of Forsaking the Son of God (10:26)

The word "for" at the beginning of verse 26 introduces an explanation of the significance of the approaching "Day" in verse 25. The author wants his readers to understand the problem of forsaking Christ in view of future judgment. They must see present sin in view of future consequences.

The author warns his readers of willful sin. By willful sin he does not mean the sin of true Christians. He recognizes that believers sin (12:1) and are chastened for it (12:6). He tells believers to go to their High Priest where they will find mercy (4:14-16). He knows there are things (including sins) in the lives of believers that make Christ's intercession necessary (7:25). He is confident that the once-for-all sacrifice of Christ is effective for believers, even if they repeatedly sin (10:17).

Willful sin is the same thing as falling away in 6:6 and "to fall away from the living God" in 3:12. The author is aware of some who have forsaken the meetings of the church. There are two possible explanations for this:

1. They may be genuine, albeit apathetic and backslidden believers. This is a possibility in a church where there is so much immaturity (5:11-14).
2. They may be apostates, i.e., threshold Christians. They are people who at one time came right to the threshold of believing in Christ. They may even have professed to believe in Christ, but now they are departing from the local assembly and that profession of faith. It is this second possibility that our author addresses in verses 26-31.

The author is writing of the person who is outwardly a professing Christian yet inwardly lost. Such persons have never trusted Christ to forgive their sins. He warns these professing Christians that if they turn their back on Christ, there is no other way of salvation. If we reject the one true sacrifice for sins, there is no other. "There no longer remains a sacrifice for sins."

The Nature of Forsaking the Son of God (10:28-29)

In verses 28-29 the author argues that the higher the privilege, the more severe should be the penalty. In OT times a person who turned from God and went after idols was stoned to death ("dies without mercy") if there were "two or three witnesses" (see Deut. 13:8; 17:2-7). All kinds of sin were forgiven in OT times, such as perjury (Lev. 5:1), sexual immorality (19:20-22), adultery, and murder (2 Sam. 11-12). The one sin that could not be forgiven was defiant, willful sin. If an Israelite demonstrated unbelief in God, rejected His law, and removed himself from the covenant, he could not be forgiven. If rejecting God's OT law brought physical death, then those who have had the higher privilege of hearing the message about Jesus Christ will face "worse punishment."

He presents God's triple indictment of the apostate (Westcott):

1. One who completely and finally rejects Christ tramples "underfoot the Son of God" and treats the God-man with flagrant contempt.
2. Not only does an apostate reject Christ's person but also His work. He or she weighs the facts and decides that the death of Christ was a "common thing" (the blood of the covenant). It has no more power to forgive sin than the blood of any other person. The phrase "by which he was sanctified" simply means that this person was at one time outwardly identified with the people of God but, unfortunately, not inwardly set apart.

3. The apostate is a person who has "outraged the Spirit of grace." He or she has seen the Spirit's work of grace in changing the lives of many in the assembly (see Heb. 4:16; 13:9). This person has heard the Spirit's testimony about Christ from the Scriptures (see Heb. 10:15) and has inwardly rejected that testimony.

The Punishment for Forsaking the Son of God (10:27, 29-31)

Judgment is certain for apostates and all who reject Christ. Our translation speaks of the "expectation of judgment." It is unlikely, however, that the apostate is expecting judgment. The thought is rather that the judgment is expecting or waiting for the sinner. The translation "fearful prospect of judgment" (RSV) is better. The author pictures God's judgment as a fire that consumes the enemies of God. He captures the awfulness of apostasy in the word "adversaries." To profess at one time to be a Christian and then to end up numbered with God's enemies ("adversaries") is a horrible tragedy.

God's enemies are punished; His people are delivered.

Verse 29 poses a solemn question ("How much worse punishment?"), and verses 30-31 supply the answer. The word "for" (10:30) introduces a reason. Judgment is certain because God says so. The author drives the awesome warning of future punishment home with two quotations from Deuteronomy 32:35-36. Hell is not a temporary place of reformation. It is a place where God takes revenge ("vengeance") upon those who deserve it.

Then he says, "The Lord will judge his people." In the OT context the word *judge* has the idea "to vindicate." The thought is that while God's enemies are punished, His people are delivered. When God judges, He will separate the true from the false. Our author's words are terrifying. The hands of God that today are extended in grace offering pardon to sinners will one day inflict punishment upon all who reject His Son and His sacrifice.

The Need for Endurance and the Promise of Reward (10:32-39)

The Evidence of Past Endurance (10:32-34)

Although the author worries that a number of his readers are potential apostates, he is convinced that the majority are possessors of genuine faith and life. The word "but" (10:32) contrasts the hopeful condition of the readers with the hopeless state of those in verses 26-31. In the past the readers gave evidence they were genuine believers. They had suffered, and the cause of that suffering was that they had been "enlightened," i.e., they had received the knowledge of the truth about Christ (see Heb. 10:26). They had suffered verbal abuse ("reproach," 10:33), physical abuse ("affliction") and the confiscation of their property ("the plundering of your property," 10:34). They had shown loving sympathy to fellow Christians who were thrown in prison because of their Christian beliefs. They no doubt visited them and fed them. Such suffering had sharpened their priorities by making them realize that their most important possession could not be stolen or destroyed.

The Need for Present Endurance (10:35-36)

The readers have given every evidence of true faith, so ("therefore") they should press on. He says, "Do not throw away your confidence." The Greek word translated "confidence" (*parrēsia*) means "freedom of access" (see 10:19). The author tells his readers (and us) that they are not to throw away their wonderful privilege of access to God's throne of grace. To press on will result in "great reward." The Lord Jesus Christ and His apostles taught that the reward of Christians will be authority and honor in the future kingdom upon the earth (Luke 19:11-27; James 1:12; Rev. 2:10; 1 Peter 5:4). The implication of various NT passages (Matt. 25:14-28; 1 Cor. 3:8, 14-15; 2 Cor. 5:10) is that there will be differences in reward depending on our faithfulness.

Why should the readers not cast away their access to God's throne? The author introduces his reason with the word "for" in verse 36. They (and we) need endurance, and the source of strength for such endurance is their High Priest who sits at God's right hand. The author links "endurance" and doing the "will of God." God's will for them (and us) is that they endure. The result of such endurance is that "you may receive what is promised." Only those who endure will receive "what is promised." Endurance is evidence of genuine faith. In Hebrews "what is promised" is the promised inheritance in the future rest (4:1), the heavenly country (11:16) of God's people.

The Incentives to Future Endurance (10:37-39)

In the concluding verses of the chapter, the author does three things:

1. He encourages his readers to endurance with the promise of Christ's imminent return.
2. He warns them of the necessity of endurance by reminding them of God's judgment upon apostates.
3. He assures them that he does not believe they are apostates.

First, he uses the positive incentive of our Lord's return, 10:37-38a. We should endure because in "a little while" Christ ("the coming one") will come to His people. The phrase "For, yet a little while" (10:37a) is taken from Isaiah 26:20, a passage that speaks of Israel's future deliverance at the second coming of Christ.

Those who live "by faith" will inherit the messianic kingdom in the life to come.

Verses 37b-38 are a quotation from Habakkuk 2:3-4, a passage that speaks of a threatened invasion of Judah by the Chaldeans. The prophet cries to God, and the Lord tells him that judgment will fall upon the enemy. The Hebrew Bible says that judgment is coming, but the Greek OT (LXX) says that a *person* is coming to deliver the people. The author of Hebrews is even more specific. He says that Christ ("the coming one") is coming to save His people.

How are God's people ("My righteous one") to live their daily lives in view of the Lord's imminent return? They are to live their lives "by faith," i.e., by believing God's promises. Those who do so will inherit the messianic kingdom in the life to come.

Second, he reminds them of God's judgment upon apostates, 10:38b. It is possible in any group of Christians that there may be those who only seem to be believers. An apostate is a person who believes "for a while" (Luke 8:13) but then "shrinks back" from Christ. Their faith was not genuine. Those who "shrink back" (10:39) prove they were not true believers to begin with, and their destiny is "[to be] destroyed," i.e., ruin. By "are destroyed" the author speaks of the eternal punishment of the wicked. God has "no pleasure" in the apostate, i.e., He does not approve of them.

Third, he assures them that he does not believe they are apostates, 10:39. In verse 39 the author makes it clear that he is sure that his readers are (for the most part, at least) true believers. Their destiny is in contrast to the destiny of the apostates. The apostates face judgment, but the readers are assured of preservation ("preserve their souls") through the future judgment of God. Unlike those who reject Christ, they will be kept safe.

SUMMARY

The Hebrew Christians were tempted to place saving value on the animal sacrifices of the OT. In chapter 10 the author argues that those sacrifices could not take away sin. The once-for-all sacrifice of Christ does provide complete forgiveness of sins. If Christ's offering of Himself does forgive my sins, I should not think that other sacrifices are necessary.

The Hebrew Christians did not appreciate fully their privileges as Christians. The author reminds them that they have free access into God's presence through their High Priest Jesus Christ. He exhorts them to worship, endurance, and mutual encouragement, and he warns them of the danger of apostasy. He is encouraged by evidence of endurance in the past, and he encourages more of the same as they anticipate the certain return of the Lord.

Endnotes

[1] The phrase *"good things to come"* has been understood in three ways: (1) It refers to the sacrifice of Christ and the true forgiveness it provides at the present time. (2) It refers to the two aspects of the new covenant, i.e., forgiveness and access to God at the present time, and to the complete fulfillment of the Abrahamic promises in the age to come. (3) It refers primarily to the future blessings to be bestowed at Christ's second coming. The immediate context (9:28) favors the third view.

[2] The author of Hebrews does not say that the OT sacrifices were evil or worthless. During OT times they had great value: (1) They taught the Israelites the seriousness of sin. (2) They taught the righteousness of God. God's holiness demanded payment for sin. (3) They taught the necessity of atonement. (4) They taught the Israelites in type of the Savior who would one day put away sin.

[3] Bible teachers often distinguish among three aspects of sanctification in the NT: (1) *Positional Sanctification.* This speaks of an event that takes place once-for-all at conversion. All believers are completely sanctified, or set apart to God, in this sense. With the exception of one verse, the author of Hebrews always speaks of sanctification in this sense. (2) *Progressive Sanctification.* This is a process of Christian growth that begins at conversion. Believers differ in their level of maturity

or sanctification. Hebrews 12:14 is the one example of progressive sanctification in the epistle. (3) *Prospective* or *Ultimate Sanctification.* This speaks of the future resurrection of believers when they will be completely conformed to Christ. See 1 Thessalonians 5:23-24.

[4] In view of the usage of the verb elsewhere in Hebrews, the participle translated "being sanctified" should probably be translated simply "sanctified" (NASB).

[5] The term *church* always refers to the people of God in the NT. It never refers to the building in which they meet.

LESSON 9 EXAM

Use the exam sheet at the back of the course to complete your exam.

1. **Under the Law, there was "a reminder of sins"**
   A. twice a day.
   B. once a day.
   C. every year.
   D. seven times a year.

2. **The words in Hebrews 10:5-7 were spoken by Christ**
   A. just before His birth.
   B. just after His birth.
   C. just before His second coming.
   D. just before His death.

3. **Hebrews 10:10 speaks of**
   A. positional sanctification.
   B. ultimate sanctification.
   C. progressive sanctification.
   D. prospective sanctification.

4. **The phrase "perfected for all time" in verse 14 means that**
   A. the believer has free access into God's presence.
   B. the believer has received the forgiveness of their sins.
   C. the cross of Christ has achieved its intended goal.
   D. All of the above.

5. **The author of Hebrews believed that the Holy Spirit**
   A. is God.
   B. is a person.
   C. inspired the Scriptures.
   D. All of the above.

6. **Hebrews 10:19 means that**
   A. the original readers had a bold faith.
   B. the original readers were characterized by confidence in Christ.
   C. the original readers had free access into God's presence.
   D. the original readers needed boldness in their hearts.

7. **The veil in Hebrews 10:20 speaks of**
   A. the crucified human body of Jesus Christ.
   B. the doorway of the Old Testament tabernacle.
   C. the barrier blocking the way into the Most Holy Place in the earthly tabernacle.
   D. the doorway into the Most Holy Place in the tabernacle.

8. **When the author speaks of our "confession" in 10:23, he means**
   A. our witness to unbelievers.
   B. the body of truth we believe in.
   C. our testimony at the time of baptism.
   D. the doctrinal statement of our local church or assembly.

9. **The greatest of all sins is**
   A. murder.
   B. perjury.
   C. sexual immorality.
   D. rejecting Christ.

10. **The imminent return of Christ should inspire believers to**
    A. faith and endurance.
    B. fear and self-condemnation.
    C. self-reliance.
    D. give away all earthly possessions.

What Do You Say?

According to verses 5-18 of chapter 10 how is Christ's sacrifice superior to all other sacrifices ever offered for sins?

A man + God, not an animal. He only did it once for all and sat down, not daily. By Him, there is truly no more remembrance of sins. The atonement once a year was a reminder of sin.

Hebrews 11

Chapter 11 does not introduce a new subject. Instead, the author goes on to develop what he has said in 10:35-39. In those verses the author sketches the life situation of his readers. They are Jewish Christians undergoing external and internal pressures to draw back from Christ and return to Judaism. The author has encouraged them not to turn back but to endure and press on in the Christian faith that they might inherit the promised kingdom of heaven. In 10:39 he assures his readers of his confidence in them. "We," he says in charitable fashion, shall not waver, for we have faith ("we … have faith," 10:39).

The author's exhortation to endurance (10:35-39) culminated in his statement (10:39) that it is faith that is the key to perseverance. In 10:38 he quoted Habakkuk 2:4, "my righteous one shall live by faith."[1] Faith is to be an ongoing principle of daily living. Believers are to live daily by faith. Faith will enable them to endure.

The word *faith* is a hook word that links chapters 10 and 11. In chapter 11 the author develops the thought that faith enables the believer to overcome every obstacle and triumph in the darkest of situations. This chapter makes two contributions to the original readers:

1. It gives several illustrations of what enduring faith is like. The lesson is that although God's promises are unseen, they are real, and the man and woman of faith must endure.
2. It reminds the Jewish readers that if they forsake Christ for Judaism, they will not be departing *to* the faithful but *from* the faithful (Lenski).

A CALL TO FAITH: BASED ON HISTORICAL ILLUSTRATIONS (11:1-40)

The Nature of Faith (11:1-3)

The Description of Faith (11:1)

Verse 1 is not a definition of faith.[2] Rather, it describes faith. It tells us what faith does, not what faith is (M. Dods).[3] "Faith," says the author, "is the assurance of things hoped for." This does not mean that faith makes something real that is not yet real. The author's point is this: faith's function is to make the promises of God about the future as real to the soul as material things are to the human eye. He adds that faith is "the conviction of things not seen." Just as physical eyesight provides evidence of the physical world, so faith enables people to see the invisible world (the actions, activities, inhabitants of the heavenly realm). In short, faith enables the believer to treat the future as present and the invisible as seen.

> **Faith enables the believer to treat the future as present and the invisible as seen.**

The Testimony of Faith (11:2)

The word "for" introduces the proof of the power of faith. It wins God's approval. The original readers of Hebrews had great regard for the OT and its heroes. Because of their faith these OT heroes ("the people of old") were approved by God ("received their commendation"). This commendation of God has been placed on permanent record in Scripture (F. F. Bruce).

The Perception of Faith (11:3)

In the remainder of the chapter, the author will give examples of those who exercised faith on the stage of history. Before he does, he pauses long enough to say something about how the stage itself came into existence (Davidson). Faith is required when we read the very first page of the Bible (Lenski). When we read it believingly, we understand that by a single utterance of the divine will ("the word of God"), the whole scheme of time and space ("universe," lit. "ages") came into being (J. B. Phillips). Matter is not eternal. The material world we see was created out of nothing ("not made out of things that are visible").

Faith in the Antediluvian (Pre-Flood) Era (11:4-7)

It will be helpful if we distinguish between two aspects of genuine faith (R. T. Kendall):

1. *Saving faith.* Saving faith has to do with initial cleansing and conversion. It is that faith which sinners exercise when they acknowledge that they are lost sinners and believe in God's promise of forgiveness through the shed blood of Jesus Christ. Saving faith is primary and fits us for the kingdom of heaven.

2. *Experimental, enduring or continuing faith.* Once sinners have been cleansed, they do not stop believing God. We are called upon to believe God daily. We do not do this in order to be cleansed but because we have been cleansed. This second aspect of faith may be called experimental faith because it is a faith that proves itself in the laboratory of life by good works. Hebrews 11 is concerned primarily with experimental, enduring, or continuing faith.

The Faith of Abel (11:4)

Although the main emphasis of Hebrews 11 is upon experimental or continuing faith, there is one example of initial, saving faith in the chapter, and that is Abel. The story of Abel is found in Genesis 4:2-8. Cain and Abel each brought an offering to the Lord. Abel's offering was accepted, and Cain's was rejected. The reason is that Abel "offered to God a more acceptable sacrifice."

Why was Abel's sacrifice "more acceptable?" Our author says it was "more acceptable" because it was offered "by faith." *Faith* throughout Hebrews 11 is believing what God says. Evidently Cain and Abel had been instructed about the importance of blood sacrifice. Abel believed God, and Cain did not. Abel's sacrifice was a confession of sin and a desire for forgiveness (Bengel).

God testified to Abel's sacrifice. Abel was made "righteous," i.e., he was made right before God. Abel's faith won him a place in Scripture, and from its pages, although he is dead, he "still speaks." He tells us that one must take God at His word about the importance and value of the blood sacrifice of Christ.

The Faith of Enoch (11:5-6)

Once a person has been cleansed like Abel it is God's desire that they walk with Him, i.e., have fellowship or communion with Him. The OT account of Enoch (Gen. 5:18-24) says that "Enoch walked with God ... 300 years." Such a walk would involve progress, growth in the knowledge of the Lord, and a surrendered will (see Amos 3:3). Unlike all those who lived before him, Enoch did not

> **Once a person has been cleansed it is God's desire that they walk with Him.**

die. God simply removed him from the earth. Evidently God promised Enoch that he would not die. Enoch believed God, and "by faith [he] was taken up so that he should not see death." He was nowhere to be found even though men looked for him.

The lesson is that God is pleased by faith (11:6). Faith, says the author, has two ingredients:

1. To come to God, either for the first time for cleansing or habitually thereafter, we must believe that He truly exists.
2. We must believe in the integrity of His promises. He will reward such faithfulness in the world to come.

There are various degrees of seeking God. There is initial conversion, illustrated in Abel. There is subsequent obedience and fellowship with God, illustrated by Enoch.

The Faith of Noah (11:7)

The story of Noah (see Gen. 5:28–6:22) illustrates the fact that the daily life of faith is unique for each believer. Each of us will face obstacles and trials that are distinctive to us and no one else. God warned Noah about something (a coming flood and the destruction of mankind) that had never taken place before ("events as yet unseen"), and Noah believed Him. "In reverent fear" he built an ark, and his family was delivered. By his simple faith "he condemned the world" of unbelievers around him. Such "righteousness," says the author, bestows an inheritance to all who practice it.

Faith in the Patriarchal Era (11:8-22)

The Faith of Abraham (11:8-19)

The OT does not explicitly speak of the faith of Abel, Enoch and Noah. The faith of Abraham, however, is clearly spelled out. Genesis 15:6 says, "And he believed the LORD, and he counted it to him as righteousness." The call of Abraham marks the beginning of the messianic nation. He was to become the father of the Jewish people, from whom Christ would come. The people of God are to be morally separate from the world. Thus, all his life Abraham is portrayed as a pilgrim on his way to the land of promise. This pilgrim character continues with Isaac and Jacob, who are characterized as "strangers and exiles on the earth" (11:13).

The obedience of faith, 11:8. Abraham's faith is first seen by his readiness to leave all at God's call. Abraham was not chosen ("called") by God because of his godliness. We learn in Joshua 24:2 that when he was called in Ur (S. Iraq), Abraham was in the dark hole of idolatry and unbelief. In grace (unmerited favor) God called Abraham and told him to leave Ur.[4] It is clear from Genesis 12:6-7 that Abraham did not know that Canaan was the land of promise until after he had left Ur ("not knowing where he was going"). The thing to notice in verse 8 is the close relationship between faith and obedience. Obedience is the outward evidence of inward faith.

The endurance of faith, 11:9-10. In verses 9-10 the author cites the second evidence of Abraham's faith, namely, his patient waiting in the land of promise. Even after arriving in Canaan, Abraham did not receive possession of it. Instead he ("with Isaac and Jacob") lived as an alien ("living in tents") never receiving the promises (see 11:13). The secret of Abraham's greatness is that he believed God ("by faith"). All his life he believed that he would one day dwell in the city of God. He will one day, when he is resurrected and enters the kingdom.

> **Obedience is the outward evidence of inward faith.**

The fulfillment of faith, 11:11-12. At this point the author brings Sarah into his discussion. Abraham and his wife had been promised a son (see Gen. 18:9-10). From the human perspective this was impossible in that they were well past their fertile years ("past the age" ... "as good as dead"). Sarah believed God ("she considered Him faithful") and was enabled to conceive and bear promised Isaac. She stands in Scripture as a picture of those who trust God to do what human reason says is impossible. Abraham did not live to see it, but his posterity is today innumerable ("as the stars ... as the grains of sand").

The pilgrim outlook of faith, 11:13-16. The patriarchs—Abraham, Isaac, and Jacob ("these all")—died "not having received the things promised." Yet they died "in faith," still believing those promises. Faith radically alters a person's attitude to death and to this present life. They openly proclaimed ("acknowledged") to their acquaintances and neighbors that they were "strangers and exiles on the earth" (a better translation is "in the land"). This present world was not their true home. They sought a "homeland" in Canaan (11:14). If the patriarchs had not believed God's promise of the land (see 11:9), they would have returned to the country they had come from (11:15). Of course, the patriarchs did not belong to Canaan *as it then was.* They looked forward to Canaan *as it was going to be* ("a better country") in the future kingdom of Christ. Because of their faith God honored the patriarchs by being called their God, "the God of Abraham, the God of Isaac, and the God of Jacob" (see Acts 3:13; 7:32).

The test of faith, 11:17-19. The third example of Abraham's faith is his offering of Isaac on Mt. Moriah (see Gen. 22:1-19). It is the greatest act of faith in the life of a great man of faith. The OT account says that "God tested Abraham." He told him to offer Isaac "as a burnt offering." There are two kinds of tests. The first is the temptation to do evil. In James 1:13-14 we learn that God does not tempt His creatures this way. The second kind is not a temptation to do evil. It is a proving. God tests believers to prove, or show off their faith. The testing of Abraham was of this second kind.

> **God tests believers to prove, or show off, their faith.**

In this account we learn that faith is not a mere passive acceptance of a creed, although many creeds are rich in doctrinal truth that must be believed. It is also something that calls for action. The great test for Abraham was that Isaac was the child of promise. It was through the line of Isaac that the promises were to be fulfilled (11:18).

Verse 17 says that Abraham "offered up Isaac." The author views the event ("offered up") as an accomplished fact. In his heart Abraham had decided to do it. How could he do it? He did it "by faith." He believed that God would raise Isaac from the dead and fulfill the promises. In a sense, God did just that. Abraham's faith rested on the doctrine of God's power or omnipotence (see 11:19, "God was able").

The Faith of Isaac (11:20)

The next three men of faith all illustrate the truth of verse 13, "These all died in faith, not having received the things promised." In the OT record (Gen. 26-27) Isaac appears to be a rather ordinary person who lived in the shadow of a strong father, a protective mother and a domineering wife. Of his two sons, Isaac preferred the elder, Esau, even though he knew that the Lord had promised the younger, Jacob, the inheritance of the blessing (see Gen. 25:21-26). "By faith" he yielded to the choice of God in blessing Jacob (see Gen. 27:33). Jacob became the heir in the line of promise. That promise[5] would be fulfilled in the work of Christ and the establishment of His kingdom (A. Saphir). The lesson is that faith gives priority to the will of God over personal preferences (Kendall).

The Faith of Jacob (11:21)

The author mentions two acts of Jacob's faith that took place "when dying." First, he "blessed each of the sons of Joseph." Joseph had brought his sons Manasseh and Ephraim to his father to be blessed (see Gen. 48:8-20). Over Joseph's protests, Jacob gave the chief blessing to the younger son (Ephraim), making him the primary heir. The lesson here is that faith submits to God's will even if the will of a man (Joseph) must be opposed. The story also tells us that spiritual blessing has nothing to do with nature (age, physical strength or appearance, intellect, etc.). It has everything to do with God's grace.

Jacob's second act of faith was in his worship (see Gen. 47:27-30). He bowed "in worship over the head of his staff." The staff, symbolizing his old age, draws attention to the endurance of Jacob. At the end of his life he still believed and "worship[ed]."

The Faith of Joseph (11:22)

As Joseph lay dying (see Gen. 50:22-26), he thought about the future exodus of the Israelites from Egypt to Canaan ("made mention of the exodus of the Israelites"). Appearances (good land, comfort, wealth) favored staying in Egypt. Joseph, however, remembered God's promise to the three patriarchs, Abraham, Isaac, and Jacob (see Gen. 50:24). The promise had come to Abraham 200 years earlier. The exodus was still 400 years in the future. Joseph believed ("by faith") God's promises about the land and knew they would be fulfilled. Furthermore, he asked that "his bones" be taken by the Israelites back to Canaan. Joseph believed that God's promises would be literally fulfilled. He knew that God would one day raise the patriarchs from the dead and would restore Israel to the land according to His promise (W. Kelly).

Faith in the Era of the Exodus (11:23-29)

The Faith of Amram and Jochebed (11:23)

The story of Moses begins with the faith of his parents (see Ex. 2:1-10). The Pharaoh of Egypt, viewing the Jewish people as a dangerous minority, ordered that all newborn male children be drowned in the Nile. Moses' parents would not obey the Pharaoh's command, "because they saw that the child was beautiful." In some way the Lord showed them that the child was "beautiful" to Him (see Acts 7:20). They perceived that this was no ordinary child but one chosen by God to accomplish great things for his people (F. F. Bruce). They "were not afraid of the king's edict" and entrusted their child to the safekeeping of God.

The Faith of Moses (11:24-28)

The renunciation of faith, 11:24-26. Moses grew up the privileged son of Pharaoh's daughter. When he was forty years old (see Acts 7:23), he made a decision not to capitalize on his royal position. He "refused to be called the son of Pharaoh's daughter." He made this choice "by faith." He responded to a word from God and identified himself with the suffering people of God. He renounced the wealth and satisfactions of power ("the fleeting pleasures of sin") rather than depart from known revealed truth from God. The lesson of the story of Moses is that the life of faith may involve the loss of wealth, influence, and prestige in this world.

> **The life of faith may involve the loss of wealth, influence, and prestige in this world.**

Moses was motivated by the future "reward." In Hebrews the reward involves the promised rest, the inheritance of the land of Canaan by the children of Abraham (Buchanan). For this he was willing to leave "the treasures of Egypt" and accept "the reproach of Christ."

In the ancient world it was a "reproach" (disgrace or insult) to a nation if it was captured and enslaved. Why does the author speak of "the reproach of Christ"? We must remember Moses' words to Pharaoh, "Israel is my firstborn son" (Ex. 4:22). Israel as a nation is God's son in that the history of the nation prefigures Jesus Christ, the Son of God. By aligning himself with the typical nation in its sufferings, Moses bears the reproach of Christ.

The courage of faith, 11:27. Moses stands out from other prophets of his era, for the Scriptures say that God spoke to him "mouth to mouth, clearly" (Num. 12:8). The author sees another illustration of Moses' faith in his flight to Midian after killing the Egyptian (see Ex. 2:11-15). Initially he was afraid because he had trusted his own thoughts and feelings. Later, however, he leaned on the Lord ("by faith … seeing him who is invisible"), and his fear gave way to courage ("not being afraid of the anger of the king").

> The Passover is a wonderful picture of the one offering of Christ that is effective forever.

The security of faith, 11:28. A long period of time (40 years, see Acts 7:30) takes place between verses 27 and 28. During that time a new pharaoh came to the throne. The Lord appeared to Moses in a burning bush and sent him back to Egypt. God used him to bring judgment upon the Egyptians by a series of plagues. In verse 28 the author of Hebrews alludes to the tenth plague, which caused the death of the firstborn male in every Egyptian family. God revealed to Moses that the firstborn children of Israel would be protected if their families applied the blood of the Passover lamb to the door posts of their homes (see Ex. 11–12).

Moses believed God and instituted the Passover, and the firstborn children were protected from the judgment of the angel of death ("the Destroyer of the firstborn"). We should note that the author mentions a single instance of being "sprinkled." Passover's most unique feature, the placing of the blood on the doorway, was never repeated. This is a wonderful picture of the one offering of Christ that is effective forever.[6]

The Faith of the People of Israel (11:29)

The Lord told the people of Israel to cross the Red Sea to escape the Egyptians (see Ex. 14:15-16). Although the parting of the sea was an act of God (14:14, 21), the author of Hebrews ascribes the safe passage of the Israelites to the fact that they believed God ("by faith"). There is a clear illustration here of the different consequences of belief and unbelief. Bengel wrote, "When two do the same thing, it is not the same thing." Both

Israelites and Egyptians crossed the Red Sea. Those with faith were saved, but those without faith perished.

Faith in the Era of the Conquest (11:30-31)

The Faith of the People of Israel (11:30)

The author moves ahead forty years to the time of Israel's entrance into Canaan. The hero of the conquest of Jericho was Joshua, for he believed God (see Josh. 5:14-15). The author of Hebrews includes the faith of the people for they followed the instructions (encircle the city "for seven days") which on the surface seemed foolish. The fall of Jericho suggests at least two lessons of faith:

1. The need of endurance. The people did not give up after any of the first six days.
2. The influence that one believer—in this case, Joshua—may have for good.

The Faith of Rahab (11:31)

The next example is startling in that Rahab was a prostitute and a Gentile. Two spies from the Israelites came to Jericho, and she hid them. Rahab believed ("by faith") that the Lord was the true God and had given the land to the Israelites (see Josh. 2:9-11). Her story suggests a number of lessons:

1. Belief in God's promise of deliverance brings salvation from judgment (she "did not perish").
2. Salvation is universal, i.e., it is for Gentiles as well as Jews.
3. Faith leads to works. She "had given a friendly welcome to [and had hidden] the spies."

Faith in the Era of the Judges, the Kings, and the Exile (11:32-35a)

In a sense, verses 8-31 form a complete cycle (Westcott). The history from the call of Abraham to the occupation of the Promised Land is a type or foreview of the spiritual history of man. That history begins with the call of God and is fulfilled in the inheritance of the kingdom. The author cannot continue to examine every example in detail. At this point his survey becomes more general. The phrase, "And what more shall I say?" is a transition to this more general section.

Representative Heroes (11:32)

The next six names are not listed in chronological or biblical order. Four are judges and two are from the period of the kingdom. The student is urged to take time to read of Gideon (Judg. 6–9), Barak (Judg. 4–5), Samson (Judg. 13–16), Jephthah (Judg. 11–12), David (1 Sam. 16–2 Sam. 24) and Samuel (1 Sam. 1–16).

Characteristic Achievements (11:33-35a)

Because of their faith the Israelites achieved military victory ("conquered kingdoms"), integrity in government ("enforced justice"), and spiritual reward ("obtained promises").[7] Daniel's faith "stopped the mouths of lions" (Dan. 6), and the faith of his friends "quenched the power of fire" (Dan. 3). Elijah and Elisha escaped execution ("the edge of the sword," 1 Kings 19; 2 Kings 6). Also mentioned are the resuscitations to life of children ("women received back their dead by resurrection," 1 Kings 17:17-24; 2 Kings 4:17-37).

Other Miscellaneous Illustrations (11:35b-38)

Verses 32-35a are a record of those who openly triumphed over trials and difficulties. In verses 35b-38, however, the author reminds his readers that there are those who seem to fail in this life and are outwardly unrewarded. Some were "tortured" to death. Others were "stoned" to death, "sawn in two," and "killed with the sword."

It is to be noted that some believers were "killed with the sword" (11:37) and others "escaped the edge of the sword" (11:34). Whether one lives or dies is not the issue. What is important in God's eyes is that both acted "by faith."

> **All believers will be raised to life in the age to come and will never die.**

Those who died by faith will "rise again to a better life" (11:35b). They will one day rise from the dead to inherit the Promised Land. What does the author mean by "a better life"? As we noted in verse 35a, he refers to women who received their dead raised to life again. The two boys to whom he refers (1 Kings 17; 2 Kings 4) were resuscitated to mortal life, only to die again. Someday, however, all believers will be raised to life in the age to come and will never die ("a better life").

Others endured great hardship and sufferings short of death (homelessness, poverty, mockery, whippings, and other discomforts). In a splendid phrase the author describes these faithful people of God, "of whom the world was not worthy." Many of God's people have been outlawed as people who were unfit for sophisticated and civilized society. The truth is that sophisticated and civilized society was unfit for them (F. F. Bruce).

The Culmination of Faith (11:39-40)

The author has now concluded his lengthy list of illustrations. He looks back at "all these" and says they are honored by God. They have been "commended," i.e., they have gained divine approval for their faith. He again observes that it was a faith that endured. This is seen in the fact that they all died without receiving "what was promised."

What was "promised" for which they waited? Some Bible teachers and scholars have argued that the promise has been fulfilled by the cross of Christ. The author says that the "last days" have come (1:2), and the benefits of the new covenant are ours. While these things are true, they are not the author's point here. In this passage he is encouraging endurance. He would hardly say that we need to endure if the fulfillment of the promise has already been granted.

Others have correctly concluded that by "what was promised" the author means the yet future benefits of the work of Christ. In 10:36 he has told his readers that a time of endurance is necessary for them before they receive "what was promised." The OT believer sought fulfillment of the promise made to Abraham, namely, permanent possession of the land, prosperity, and rest. In this present chapter "what was promised" includes a land (11:9), a city (11:10), and a homeland (11:14). The promise is not heaven. It is the establishment upon this earth of the kingdom of God.

> **Both OT believers and church age believers will be made perfect.**

In verse 40 the author says that God has provided "something better for us." The word "that" introduces what this "something better" is. God had something better than simply the perfection of the OT saints. His better plan involved "us," i.e., the millions who have been made a part of the church, the people of God, in the era since the cross. Both OT believers ("they") and church age believers ("us") will "be made perfect."

In one sense the perfection of which the author speaks is the present possession of the believer. Both OT and NT believers now enjoy the forgiveness of sins and unrestricted access to God. Yet in the fullest sense of the word, perfection will only be complete at the resurrection of the body when God's people enter the Promised Land and ultimately the Promised City. At that time the access that is theirs in a spiritual sense will become actual. "He [God] will dwell with them ... and God himself will be with them as their God" (Rev. 21:3; see Isa. 2:2-3).

SUMMARY

In chapter 11 the author illustrates the life of faith using believers from the time of Abel right through the OT era. What emerges from his exposition is a picture of God's people as pilgrims (see Heb. 11:9) wandering this world toward the promised inheritance or reward (11:7, 8, 26) in the future city of God (11:10, 16). Living in a time of promise, not fulfillment, their lives were marked by enduring faithfulness. The readers are reminded (11:39-40) that they, too, are part of the history of faith. The OT saints will be brought to perfection but not without them.

Endnotes

[1] Habakkuk 2:4 is quoted twice by the apostle Paul (Rom. 1:17; Gal. 3:11). The author of Hebrews uses the text a bit differently than does Paul. For Paul, faith is a backward look at the cross. He views faith as the moment when a sinner looks at the cross and trusts Christ to make them right with God. In Hebrews, however, faith is primarily a forward look. Faith looks to the future and the fulfillment of God's great promises to His people.

[2] The Greek word faith (*pistis*) is related to a verb (*pisteuō*) which means "to rely on," "to trust," "to believe." We may define faith as "believing God." It is "belief in," "trust of," "reliance upon" the God of the Bible and His declarations or promises.

3 To illustrate, the following statements are descriptions, not definitions: Knowledge is power. The sky is blue. Water is wet. Fire is hot.

4 When God called Abraham in Ur, he believed and was justified (made right with God). The author of Hebrews does not elaborate on this because Abel is his illustration of initial saving faith.

5 For further discussion of the promise, see Lesson 5.

6 Elsewhere in the NT the Passover is explained as a type of Christ (1 Cor. 5:7). The author of Hebrews does not mention this. He does not want to detract from the lesson he has already drawn about the Day of Atonement.

7 God promised many things (e.g., victories to Gideon, Barak, and David) that were fulfilled. All of these fulfilled promises pointed to the final fulfillment of the promise to Abraham in the age to come.

LESSON 10 EXAM

Use the exam sheet at the back of the course to complete your exam.

1. **The hook word that joins Hebrews chapters 10 and 11 is**
   A. hope.
   B. faith.
   C. love.
   D. endurance.

2. **According to verse 1,**
   A. faith may be defined as assurance.
   B. faith may be defined as conviction.
   C. faith may be defined as believing God.
   D. faith's function is to make God's promises about the future real and to enable the believer to see the invisible world.

3. **True faith is based on**
   A. God's Word, i.e., what God says.
   B. God's Word and church tradition.
   C. the believer's emotions.
   D. the believer's feelings.

4. **The stories of Scripture demonstrate that daily faith is**
   A. something that pleases God.
   B. unique for each believer.
   C. believing in God's existence and integrity.
   D. All of the above.

5. **The one illustration of initial, saving faith in Hebrews 11 is**
   A. Abel.
   B. Abraham.
   C. Enoch.
   D. Noah.

6. **In Hebrews 11 the promise of God involves**
   A. a land.
   B. a city.
   C. a country.
   D. All of the above.

7. **The Old Testament character whose faith was demonstrated by worship was**
   A. Jacob.
   B. Isaac.
   C. Joseph.
   D. Gideon.

8. **The reason Joseph asked that his bones be taken to Canaan (11:22) was so that**
    A. he might be buried among his people for sentimental reasons.
    B. he might inspire the Israelites to leave Egypt.
    C. he might prevent the Egyptians from making his tomb a place of idolatry.
    D. he might have a part in the restoration of the land of Israel to the Israelites at the time of the resurrection.

9. **Moses' first great test of faith was**
    A. pleasure.   C. fear.
    B. wealth.   D. affliction.

10. **Which of the following heroes of the faith was not an Israelite?**
    A. Abraham.   C. Barak.
    B. Rahab.   D. Samson.

What Do You Say?

Which person mentioned as an example of faith impresses you the most and why?

The faith of Rahab is a beautiful reminder that no past is to great for God to redeem. Also that He is the only way of salvation from judgment.

Hebrews 12

The author of Hebrews is writing to a group of Hebrew Christians to encourage them to endure in the Christian life (see 10:36). Because of the reproaches and hostilities they have faced as believers, they are in danger of becoming discouraged in their Christian walk. In chapter 12 the author seeks to inspire hope in their hearts by doing three things:

1. He points to Jesus as the great example for all Christians to follow.
2. He presents a brief doctrinal lesson to inform them of God's ways in disciplining or chastening His children.
3. He reminds them of their glorious destiny in the heavenly Jerusalem.

In addition to the words of encouragement and hope to his readers, the author also has words about the danger of refusing the message of forgiveness through the finished work of Christ. Believers in Christ have a secure future in the kingdom of God, but those who refuse Christ face the dreadful prospect of an angry God.

> ## A CALL TO HOPE: BASED ON CHRIST'S ENDURANCE (12:1-29)

Endurance in the Christian Life (12:1-2)

Verses 1 and 2 are transitional. They end the exposition of the life of faith, begun in chapter 11, with the example of Jesus ("the founder and perfecter of our faith"). They also announce the next section with a call to endurance based on Jesus' example.

Our Inspiration for the Race

In the opening verses of chapter 12, the author uses the dramatic picture of an amphitheater in which thousands of people have gathered to watch a race of long-distance runners. The readers of the epistle are the runners on the track, and the great heroes of the faith are the spectators ("so great a cloud of witnesses") in the stands.

The Greek word (*martus*) translated "witnesses" has been understood in two ways. Some scholars understand the word to mean spectators. The faithful believers of chapter 11

> **The Christian race is not optional for the believer.**

have finished the race and are now in heaven shouting, as it were, their encouragement as they watch us run the race. Other scholars argue that it is not what they see in us that is the point, but what we see in them. They shout their encouragement to us from the pages of Scripture. However we understand the word—and both ideas may be correct—the faithfulness of believing men and women of the past should be an encouragement to us today. Now we are on the track. It is our turn to be faithful.

Our Enrollment in the Race

The Christian race is not an optional thing for the believer. The race is "set before us." The day a person becomes a Christian they are not placed at the finish line, but on the starting blocks. God has appointed us to run. We must run. Growth in Christ will require effort on the part of the believer.

Our Instructions for the Race

The author is like a coach who gives instructions to a cross-country running team. He gives three guidelines for running:

1. *Keep your weight down.* He tells his readers to "lay aside every weight." A "weight" ("encumbrance," NASB) is anything that undermines your energy for God's things. It can be something (a habit, hobby, friendship, reading material, amusement, career) that is harmless to others, but wrong for you.
2. *Keep your limbs free.* The readers are also to lay aside "sin which clings so closely." Sin is pictured here as a piece of clothing that entangles and trips up the runner. The Christian race is difficult to run with known sin in one's life.

3. *Keep your eyes up.* The believer is to look to Jesus as the forerunner, the One who is our great example in the race.

Our Example for the Race

It is significant that our author speaks of "Jesus," not "Christ," "the Lord," or "the Lord Jesus Christ." He uses His human name, not a divine or messianic title. His focus is upon the true human nature of our Lord. The author speaks of "looking to Jesus." The NASB translates tris, "fixing our eyes on Jesus." The earthly life and human nature of Jesus are subjects for serious contemplative thought. We may do this (contemplate our Lord) by the regular reading and study of His life in the Gospels (W. Wiersbe).

The author here describes Jesus as "the founder and perfecter of our faith." The word translated "founder" should be translated "leader." The writer of Hebrews is not describing the divine work of awakening faith in the believer. Rather, he is describing Jesus as our great example in the race of faith. He is the pattern to be imitated. He is the "perfecter" of faith. He is the One who exercised complete faith. He is the man of faith *par excellence* (P. E. Hughes).

Just as in chapter 11, where the author focused on specific examples of faith in the lives of the OT heroes, so here he focuses on a specific illustration of faith in the life of Jesus. He focuses on the cross. How did Jesus endure the cross with the taunting, scourging, crucifying, and forsakenness? He did so by sheer faith in God (F. F. Bruce).

Discipline in the Christian Life (12:3-11)

In this section of the chapter, the author changes his picture a bit. We now see that the track is not clear. There are obstacles or hurdles on the track that the runners must conquer. The author refers to these hurdles as "discipline." This section is one of the most significant passages in the Bible on the subject of discipline (chastening) in the life of the believer.

It is written to a group of Christians who have reason, humanly speaking, to be discouraged. Because of their faith in Christ, their goods have been stolen, their homes seized, and their persons ridiculed and vilified (see Heb. 10:32-34). So the author writes these verses to teach them that God uses such disciplines to further the process of their spiritual growth.

The Example of Jesus (12:3a)

The author has some difficult teaching to give his readers, but he sweetens the lesson by turning their attention to Jesus ("consider him"). The verb *to consider* was used in NT times in a mathematical sense ("to reckon up, to total up, to calculate"). The readers are to total up or calculate Jesus' sufferings, going over them again and again, point by point (Westcott). They have not been doing this, yet understanding Jesus is the key to their problems, the cure for all their doubt and hesitation (A. T. Robertson). The author's implication is that the disciplines of the Lord have a pattern in the Son of God.

The Danger of Discouragement (12:3b-4)

The phrase "so that" introduces the purpose for considering the example of Jesus. The author is afraid that his readers are growing "weary" in the Christian race. They need their second wind, and a consideration of Jesus will give it to them.

Verse 4 indicates the cause of their weariness and discouragement. They have had a struggle against sin. The author does not mean their own sin. He means the sin of the enemies of Christ who by various kinds of violence and persuasion have been trying to turn them from Christianity. This is no time for the readers to lose heart. Others remained faithful amid sufferings much worse ("shedding your blood") than theirs (or ours).

The Appeal to Scripture (12:5a)

As a good preacher and Bible teacher, the author now turns his readers' attention to Scripture. He tells them that Proverbs 3:11-12 will help them put things in perspective. All the difficulties and trials of life are to be viewed in light of what the Bible teaches. The Scripture, he says, "addresses you." The verb here translated "to address" means "to discuss, conduct a conversation." As we intelligently read the Scriptures, they speak to us and reason with us.

The Nature of Discipline (12:5b-11)

Using verses from Proverbs, the author makes seven observations about discipline in the believer's life (E. Sauer):

  1. *Discipline is a process in the ways of God, 12:5-6.* The Greek word (*paideia*) has the idea of "upbringing, training and instruction."

Discipline is the holy training of a fatherly God. God seeks to educate us in divine things, and this involves discipline. In the case of the Hebrew Christians, discipline involved persecution, public ridicule, and suffering. Other Christians have found that the hurdles on the track are quite ordinary: financial losses, illness, job tensions, family crises, the treachery of a friend, etc. The author reminds us that God uses such disciplines to further the process of our Christian growth.

2. *Discipline is a proof of the Fatherhood of God, 12:7.* The readers may have felt that if God was fatherly they would be spared all hardship. Why would God allow His own children to suffer? The author's argument in verse 7 is this: "You readers have got it all wrong! It is not *in spite of* His Fatherhood, but *because of* His Fatherhood that discipline is necessary." He asks, "What son is there whom his father does not discipline?"

3. *Discipline is a proof of the love of God, 12:6.* "Why me?" the Christian may ask as they face the trials of life. "I thought God loved me." The author responds, "He does love you." The sufferings of life prove that God is interested in us. "The Lord disciplines the one he loves."

> **All the difficulties and trials of life are to be viewed in light of what the Bible teaches.**

4. *Discipline is a proof of the understanding of God, 12:10.* The average Christian can look back at their earthly home and see that their earthly father, no matter how wise, made mistakes. But our heavenly Father ("the Father of spirits," 12:9) never makes mistakes. He is infinitely wise and knows exactly what is best for us ("for our good").

5. *Discipline is a scourge from the hand of God, 12:5-6, 11.* Some discipline is for our moral and spiritual training. Some may be for correction or punishment. This is brought out by the word "chastises" in verse 6. This word is related to a word meaning "whip."

6. *Discipline has a purpose in the plan of God, 12:7, 11.* Endurance through discipline produces morally and spiritually trained believers ("those who have been trained by it"). The sufferings of God's redeemed children have a deeper meaning than their outward appearance. God's plan is being worked out in all the difficulties, injustices, and losses of the believer's life.

7. *Discipline has as its product the holiness of God, 12:10-11.* God is at work in the disciplines of life to show us the values that truly matter. He seeks to free us from the illusions of this life and give us a longing for the heavenly country (see 12:22-24). Discipline, the author truthfully admits, can be painful. Yet when the Christian race is over ("later")[1] and we arrive at the heavenly city, we shall discover that the disciplines of God have made us "share his holiness."

It is important that the believer learn to accept discipline as something designed by their heavenly Father for their good. Such a person will not be resentful and rebellious. Rather, their soul will be calmed ("peaceful") and will become fertile ground for the cultivation of a righteous life ("fruit of righteousness," F. F. Bruce).

Perseverance in the Christian Life (12:12-17)

In verses 12-17 there are two changes from the previous paragraph:

1. In verses 3-11 the author has stressed the believers' passive acceptance of fatherly correction. In verses 12-17 he stresses the Christian's active pursuit of spiritual priorities and ideals.
2. In verses 1-11 he presented the Christian life as a strenuous race. In verses 12-17 the picture of a race gives way to the metaphor of the Christian life as a journey or pilgrimage (R. Brown, W. L. Lane).

The Overcoming of Discouragement and Spiritual Depression (12:12-13)

The word "therefore" introduces the inference or conclusion the readers are to draw from the author's teaching on chastening (12:3-11). They are like athletes or pilgrims ready to collapse ("drooping hands and ... weak knees"). They are discouraged and depressed by the trials and disappointments of life. Now that they have been instructed that these things are really disciplines from the hand of a loving God, they should press on. They should brace themselves and again get involved in spiritual activity.

The author adds that they are to "make straight paths for your feet" (12:13). The picture is of runners on a track (or pilgrims on a journey) that has debris and potholes which will aggravate their lameness. They should clear away the clutter in their lives (religious ceremonies, sinful activities, worldly attitudes) that is tripping them up.

The Pursuit of Peace and Sanctification (12:14)

In verse 14 the author gives a twofold command regarding the believer's contact with the world.

1. The aim of their contact is to "strive for peace with everyone." The verb *pursue* suggests earnest pursuit, like a hunter after game or a runner in a race. In a world marked by warfare and greed the Christian must seek to cultivate a peaceful relationship with all people (W. Lane).

2. The limitation upon their contact with the world is found in the command to "strive for ... holiness." They are not to pursue peace with all people if it compromises their holiness. The author is here speaking ("holiness") of progressive sanctification, i.e., the process of moral renewal that begins at conversion and is completed at the resurrection. It is clear from the author's words that sanctification is not a passive thing but something to be actively pursued. His epistle makes clear that the author believes that all true Christians will pursue holiness. The unbeliever does not pursue holiness and will never see the Lord Jesus Christ in the sense of enjoying fellowship with Him.

The Need of Pastoral Vigilance (12:15-17)

The Greek expression translated "See to it" occurs only one other place in the NT (1 Peter 5:2), where it is translated "exercising oversight." The author is here clearly addressing those who occupy a position of responsibility and authority in the assembly, namely, the elders or overseers or pastors. He warns them of three tendencies in the congregation, each introduced by the words "that no," which will hinder progress.

1. *Failing to obtain the grace of God.* Grace is God's favor towards those who do not deserve His favor. The author warns the elders[2] of the church that there are those in the congregation who have never truly accepted God's gracious offer of cleansing. They are members of the assembly, but their claim to know Christ is a hollow one. They are in danger of missing out on the blessings of God in the future kingdom of heaven.

2. *Causing trouble as a root of bitterness.* The author here alludes to Deuteronomy 29:18, where the Israelites are warned of the sin of

idolatry. The bitterness the author speaks of is not the attitude of bitterness; Christians may occasionally be angry or bitter against one another. Rather, he is speaking of one of the evidences of apostasy. Apostasy may be the cause when a person becomes embittered and rebellious. Bitter against Christ, they embitter others against Christ (Lenski).

3. *Squandering blessings for immorality and worldliness.* In verses 16-17 the author refers to the story of Esau in Genesis 25. Unchecked apostasy will bear bad fruit. Although the passage in Genesis does not refer to it, our author says that Esau was guilty of sexual immorality. He was "sexually immoral." One sad lesson of church history is that departure from the truth is often accompanied by sexual sin. The author also says that Esau was "unholy." He "sold his birthright." All the privileges of the firstborn son of the family (head of family, double inheritance, blessings of the covenant) were his. He gave it all away for a single meal. He had a worldly-minded or secular attitude toward the things of God. Esau later had regrets about his hasty action (Gen. 27:34-40). The term translated "repent" (12:17) probably has the sense of "second thoughts." No doubt he wanted the material benefits of his inheritance. The author intends for Esau to be an illustration of the terrible danger of apostasy. Yes, an apostate may have occasional regrets about their rejection of Christianity, yet true repentance is impossible for such a person (see Heb. 6:4-6).

Departure from the Christian Life (12:18-29)

The Privileges Awaiting the Pilgrims (12:18-24)

Verse 18 begins with the word "for," which introduces a reason. It serves to connect verses 18-24 with verses 12-17. In verses 12-17 the author encouraged the readers to endurance and holiness. Now he gives a reason: our high privileges under the new covenant make a holy life imperative. He tells his readers of their position and prospects as new covenant pilgrims.

Their position stated negatively: You have not come to Mt. Sinai, 12:18-21. Believers under the new covenant are not like the Israelites of the days of the exodus. Their relationship to God is illustrated by the events that took place at Mt. Sinai at the time of the giving of the Law (see Ex. 19:16-19; 20:18-21; Deut. 4:11-12). The rugged heights of Sinai crackled with thunder and lightning. No one, not even an animal, was allowed to touch the mountain. The lesson that was taught at Sinai was the sheer majesty and absolute unapproachability of God. The way to Him was not open, and whoever tried to approach Him met death (W. Barclay).

Their position stated positively: You have come to Mt. Zion, 12:22a. The word "but" introduces a contrast between the old and the new covenants. Mt. Sinai symbolized the old covenant in its unapproachable, earthly, and temporal aspects. Mt. Zion symbolizes the new covenant in its approachable, heavenly and eternal aspects. The OT Israelites were forbidden to draw near. The NT pilgrims are invited to draw near.

> **Christians are given citizenship in the kingdom of heaven.**

The author writes, "You have come to Mount Zion" (12:22). The tense of the verb suggests that the author is looking at an actual fact. The readers came to Mt. Zion at the time of their conversion to faith in Jesus Christ. In physical reality, of course, they are still on earth, climbing, as it were, toward "the city of the living God." Yet when they became Christians, they were given citizenship in the kingdom of heaven (see Phil. 3:20). So, during the time of their earthly pilgrimage, they live in two worlds. They are pilgrims on earth and citizens of the heavenly city.

Their prospects, 12:22b-24. Verses 22-24 are actually prophetic; they not only describe our present position but also what awaits us in the future. The author gives a list of seven things that await the pilgrim in the life to come:

1. "The heavenly Jerusalem." The name "Zion" was virtually synonymous in the OT with Jerusalem (see Ps. 78:68-69). The OT city was a type of the city of God in heaven that will one day descend to this earth and be the dwelling place of God's people (Rev. 21:2).

2. "Innumerable angels." The phrase "to the assembly" literally means a gathering, especially at festive occasions. It should probably be attached to the phrase "innumerable angels." The pilgrims shall arrive in heaven to find an immortal fellowship of angels gathered in joyful praise and celebration.

3. "The assembly of the firstborn." All of God's people will eventually be reunited in the heavenly city. The expression "firstborn" was used of the son who received a double inheritance. It here speaks of the honors and privileges that await the church in heaven.

4. "God, the judge of all." This phrase may be rendered, "a judge,

who is God of all." This is a solemn reminder to all who claim to be pilgrims. They will all meet God, either as His children to be evaluated for reward (2 Cor. 5:10), or as His enemies to be condemned to the lake of fire (Rev. 20:11-15).

5. "The spirits of the righteous made perfect." This refers to those of OT times who were justified, i.e., acquitted of all guilt. In the future resurrection they will be "made perfect," i.e., glorified.

6. "Jesus, the mediator of a new covenant." The pilgrims will meet their Savior who offered a sacrifice that inaugurated a new covenant by which they have forgiveness.

7. "The sprinkled blood." Instead of comparing the death of Jesus with the OT sacrifices that inaugurated the old covenant, the author turns to Genesis 4 and speaks of the murder of Abel. The blood of Abel cried out for vengeance. The blood of Jesus "speaks a better word." It speaks of redemption (9:12), the putting away of sins (9:26), of cleansed consciences (9:14) and of free access into heaven (10:19).

The Peril Facing the Pilgrims (12:25-29)

In view of these marvelous contrasts with Mt. Sinai, the readers are warned of the dangers of rejecting the Gospel.

The danger of unbelief, 12:25. The author confronts his readers with the need to make a decision. They must not "refuse him who is speaking." To refuse the message is the same thing as rebelling against the living God (3:12), treating God's Word with contempt (6:5-6), and trampling underfoot the blood of the covenant (10:29).

In OT times the exodus generation was continually characterized by hardness of heart. They refused to give heed to God's Word as it was delivered by Moses. They did not escape God's judgment but died in the wilderness (Num. 14:22-24; Deut. 1:35-36). Today we have been offered a better covenant than the one given at Sinai, so we are in much greater danger. The OT Israelites heard God through Moses on a mountain. We have heard the Word of God from the Son in heaven. We shall not escape God's judgment if we reject the offer of forgiveness through the blood of Jesus.

The certainty of judgment, 12:26-27. God's voice "shook the earth" at Mt. Sinai (Ex. 19:18). Quoting Haggai 2:6, the author says that the world in which we live is heading for destruction. God is going to shake heaven and earth "yet once more." This shaking of the earth and the heavens ("things that have been made") involves their complete removal and destruction (see 2 Peter 3:10-12; Rev. 20:11; 21:1). Everything and everyone hostile to God will be purged from the universe. Only "the things that cannot be shaken," namely, the kingdom of God and its citizens, will remain.

The motives for endurance, 12:28-29. The chapter closes with a strong note of encouragement. The author is sure that most of his readers are true believers in spite of their weariness. He encourages them to press on in faithful service to God. He provides them with three powerful motives:

1. *The unshakeable kingdom of God.* Verse 28 begins with "Therefore." Because the readers will one day reign and rule with Christ in the millennial kingdom, they should press on in their pilgrimage. The verb "receiving" is a futuristic present. Our ownership of the kingdom is certain, even though the actual possession of it awaits the future. That kingdom "cannot be shaken." When the present creation passes away, the citizens of the kingdom will survive and enter a new heaven and a new earth (Rev. 21:1-3).

    > **We shall not escape God's judgment if we reject the offer of forgiveness through the blood of Jesus.**

2. *The available grace of God.* The author reminds his readers of the resource that will enable them to press on in reverent service to God. Earlier in the epistle he spoke of the throne of God where grace is dispensed (4:16). Now he again tells them to come to that throne for help ("let us be grateful").[3]

3. *The awesome holiness of God.* We are to serve God with "reverence and awe" for this reason: "Our God is a consuming fire." God is a holy God and all mankind will one day be evaluated by His searching judgments. Elsewhere in the NT (see 1 Cor. 3:10-15) the believer is warned that his service will be tested, and all that is worthless will be burned up. The false believer who falls away from the truth in apostasy will face the fire of everlasting punishment (Heb. 10:27, 29-31; Rev. 20:10, 15).

SUMMARY

In chapter 12 the author tells his readers not to become discouraged in the trials of the Christian life but to be encouraged by the great saints of the OT and by the example of Jesus who endured so much (12:1-3). Quoting Proverbs 3:11-12, he argues that these trials are evidence of the sonship of Christians and benefit the children of God by conforming them to God's holy character (12:7-13).

Even though they are being persecuted (12:3-4), the readers are commanded to pursue peace with all men but not if it compromises their pursuit of holiness. Only those who pursue holiness (namely, genuine believers) will see Christ at His coming. Using the example of Esau, the author again warns against the danger of faithlessness and apostasy (12:14-17).

The word "for" in 12:18 introduces the reason the circumstances in verses 15-16 cannot be allowed: the higher the privilege, the higher the responsibility. The position of Christians is not that of Jewish people under the law (12:18-21), but of blood-bought sons of God and citizens of the heavenly Jerusalem (12:22-24). If those under the law did not escape God's punishment for rejecting His Word, it is certain that those who have rejected the message of the Son from heaven (see Heb. 1:2) will not escape. In light of the fact ("Therefore," 12:28) that the readers belong to the new order, they should serve God, depending on His grace.

Endnotes

[1] The word "later" has been interpreted in three ways: (1) Afterward in this life, that is, whenever discipline is exercised by God and accepted by the believer, it yields fruit. (2) Afterward in the life to come, that is, after this life is over and the believer is in the kingdom of heaven, they will find that the disciplines of life have yielded their beneficial effects in ultimate sanctification or glorification. (3) Views 1 and 2 are both true.

[2] In Hebrews those who carry out the pastoral responsibilities of the church are called simply "leaders" (13:17) or "those who rule over you" (NKJV). In NT times such leaders were called "elders," or "overseers," and they were said "to shepherd" ("pastor") the flock. See Acts 20:17, 28; 1 Timothy 3:1-7; 1 Peter 5:1-5.

[3] Some commentators and translations (e.g., NASB) translate "let us show gratitude" instead of "let us have grace (12:28 NKJV)." If this translation is followed, then the author is saying that gratitude is the motivating force of Christian service and endurance.

LESSON 11 EXAM

Use the exam sheet at the back of the course to complete your exam.

1. **The "witnesses" of verse 1 are**
   A. the New Testament apostles.
   B. the Old Testament prophets.
   C. all the heroes of the faith mentioned in chapter 11.
   D. the Old Testament patriarchs.

2. **The name *Jesus* in verse 2 draws attention to**
   A. our Lord's human nature.
   B. our Lord's messianic office.
   C. our Lord's deity.
   D. our Lord's sinless nature.

3. **The phrase "struggle against sin" in verse 4 refers to**
   A. the sin of the readers.
   B. persecution by the enemies of Christ.
   C. attacks by Satan.
   D. the sin of the OT heroes of the faith.

4. **The term *discipline* (12:5-11) means**
   A. chastening.
   B. upbringing.
   C. training and instruction.
   D. All of the above.

5. **The term *holiness* in Hebrews 12:14 refers to**
   A. positional sanctification.   C. progressive sanctification.
   B. sinless perfection.   D. peace with all people.

6. **In verse 15 the author is addressing**
   A. the entire congregation.
   B. the women of the church.
   C. the leaders (elders or pastors) of the congregation.
   D. the diligent members of the congregation.

7. **An Old Testament illustration of a person who squandered future blessing for immorality and worldliness is**
   - A. Esau.
   - B. Jacob.
   - C. Joseph.
   - D. Moses.

8. **Mt. Sinai and Mt. Zion (12:18-22) are used by the author to contrast**
   - A. Moses and Jesus.
   - B. the Israelites under the Law and Christians under the new covenant.
   - C. Jacob and Esau.
   - D. Joseph and Pharaoh.

9. **The "spirits of the righteous made perfect" (12:23) are**
   - A. OT saints.
   - B. the NT saints.
   - C. the most holy of the OT saints.
   - D. the 12 apostles.

10. **Hebrews 12:26-28 teach that**
    - A. this present universe is eternal.
    - B. all that is hostile to God will one day be removed from this universe.
    - C. only the unsaved need to show reverence to God.
    - D. only the unsaved need to have "awe" concerning future judgment.

What Do You Say?

How do the values of God's discipline encourage you to respond positively to His discipline in your life?

Knowing that He sees and loves me as a daughter, I'm not left alone to figure out what to do. He uses trials to conform me to His holiness, which is for my good. He is good.

LESSON 12

Hebrews 13

The author of Hebrews sees the Christian life as a pilgrimage. The Christian is a person on a journey from the city of destruction (the present world that will one day be destroyed, 12:26-27) to the celestial city (Mt. Zion, the city of God in heaven, 12:22). In chapter 13 he tells his readers of the kind of behavior that should characterize the pilgrim on their journey. The chapter, with its ethical, practical, and personal comments, is similar to the conclusions of other NT epistles.

> ## A CALL TO LOVE:
> ## BASED ON GOD'S GRACE (13:1-25)

Ethical Imperatives for Christian Pilgrims (13:1-6)

The Imperative of Brotherly Love (13:1-3)

"Let brotherly love continue." The dominant theme of chapter 13 is love, just as the dominant theme of chapter 11 is faith, and the dominant theme of chapter 12 is hope. The term "brotherly love" (*philadelphia*) occurs a total of five times in the NT.[1] It reflects the teaching of the NT that all Christians are brothers and sisters. Earlier in Hebrews the author taught that Christ died to make us members of God's family ("sons," see 2:10). Just as our brotherhood derives from Christ, so also does our love as brothers. His infinite love for us is the source and motivation of our love for each other (P. E. Hughes). Jesus said, "A new commandment I give to you, that you love one another: just as I have loved you" (John 13:34).

Verse 1 is a command. This suggests that these pilgrims were not only weakening in their zeal for their journey (see Heb. 12:1, 12) but also in the fervor of their love for each other (Hughes). The author is concerned because a lack of love for fellow Christians is invariably a sign that we are growing cold in our love for Christ (see 1 John 4:8).

In verses 2 and 3 the author makes two specific applications of verse 1. In verse 2 he speaks of the imperative of brotherly love concerning hospitality. Hospitality ("to show hospitality to strangers") is considered very important by the writers of the NT, and there are repeated commands to engage in it (see Rom. 12:13; 1 Peter 4:9; Heb. 13:2). Christians are to open their homes to traveling servants of Christ (see Matt. 10:11-12; Acts 9:43; 16:15; 21:8; Phil. 22), to local Christians for meetings (Acts 2:46), and to needy brothers and sisters (Matt. 25:34-40). Such hospitality promotes brotherly love.

> **Our common human lot should make us sympathetic with believers who suffer.**

By being hospitable, says the author, some believers "have entertained angels unawares." He is probably referring to an incident in the life of Abraham when he entertained three strangers who turned out to be angels of God (Gen. 18:1-33). The Greek word for angel (*angelos*) means "messenger." Most Christians will never entertain an angel. Yet most of us—if we "show hospitality to strangers"—will play host to people who will prove to be messengers of God. We will profit spiritually from having them in our homes.

In verse 3 the author speaks of the imperative of brotherly love concerning compassion. The early Christians were marked by compassion for those who were ill treated. They went into action to visit fellow Christians who were imprisoned because of their faith in Christ. They ransomed others who were kidnapped by robbers and outlaws. The author reminds his readers, "You also are in the body." In other words, we all have bodies that expose us to physical suffering. Our common human lot should make us sympathetic with believers who suffer.

The Imperative of Sexual Purity (13:4)

The author's exposition of brotherly love leads naturally to an exposition of marital love. Some versions of the Bible (AV, NKJV) translate the verse as indicative ("Marriage is honorable among all"). The context, however, suggests that it be translated as an imperative ("Let marriage be held in honor among all"). We are to consider marriage an honorable thing and that it is dishonored by sexual impurity.

Sexual intercourse was created uniquely and solely for marriage to express the oneness of husband and wife (see Gen. 2:24-25). The marriage bed is defiled by adultery and fornication. Adultery is sexual unfaithfulness by a married person. The marriage bed has room for just two. It is defiled by the intrusion of a third person. The Greek word translated "sexually immoral" is related to a word (*porneia*) that broadly includes all forms of sexual intercourse outside of a heterosexual marital relationship. The author warns any "sexually immoral and adulterous" among his readers that "God will judge" them, for they are destroying an ordinance of God and ruining their marriages.

The Imperative of Financial Contentment (13:5-6)

The author now turns from unchastity to covetousness. He writes, "Keep your life free from love of money." The expression "free from love of money" literally means "not loving money, not greedy." The readers had faced financial losses because of their faith (see Heb. 10:32-34). This may have discouraged their liberality in giving and caused some of them to spend most of their time regaining their losses. In 1 Timothy 6:10 the apostle Paul says that the love of money is the root of all kinds of evil. The craving for money and things leads to anxiety and unhappiness.

The very opposite of this state of mind is contentment. The author admonishes his readers, "Be content with what you have." He reassures them of God's foreseeing care and protection by quoting Deuteronomy 31:6, "I will never leave you nor forsake you." In verse 6 he quotes Psalm 118:6, "The LORD is my helper; I will not fear; what can man do to me?" Believers are to trust God to provide them with what is best. We are to work hard, be generous with our possessions, and leave the rest to God (R. Brown).

Congregational Imperatives for Christian Pilgrims (13:7-17)

Remembering Our Godly Heritage (13:7)

A new paragraph begins with verse 7. This paragraph begins and ends with references to the leaders of the church (13:7, 17). This would suggest that everything enclosed between verses 7 and 17 is somehow related to that one idea. In this section the author is primarily concerned with the relationship of believers to the leaders of the congregation (G. H. Lang).

In verse 7 the author tells his readers to remember their leaders. He is speaking of the founders of the assembly, now dead and gone ("those who led you," NASB).[2] His reference to their leaders clearly indicates that the NT church is not an anarchy. There are recognized leaders who provide recognized functions. Nor is the assembly an absolute democracy with everyone going their own way. Rather, it is to be an orderly congregation governed by elders appointed by the Holy Spirit (Acts 20:28).

The founders of the church left a godly heritage, and they are to be esteemed ("remembered") for it. Their godly heritage includes two elements:

1. They spoke "the word of God" to the Hebrews. The phrase "spoke … the word of God" elsewhere means to preach the Gospel (see Acts 4:31; 8:25; 13:46). The phrase probably includes in this passage not only the work of evangelism but also the work of teaching new Christians "the basic principles of the oracles of God" (Heb. 5:12). The NT makes it clear that the central responsibility of the shepherds of God's people is to teach them God's Word (John 21:15-17; Acts 2:42; 6:2; 20:20-21, 27, 31-32).
2. They lived lives worth imitating. No doubt they lived out the virtues mentioned in verses 1-6: hospitality, compassion, sexual purity, and financial contentment. The unwritten lesson of our verse for leaders in the local church is that a leader is someone who should set an example. He should be a faithful role model whose faithful life others will imitate.

Considering Our Unchanging Lord (13:8-9)

The readers of Hebrews are immature, dull, and doctrinally unstable. Their first leaders have died and are no longer on the scene. After telling his readers to remember the teaching and lives of their faithful leaders, the author turns their attention to Christ (see Heb. 12:2-3).

The doctrinal standard, 13:8. They are to imitate the faith of their early leaders, for the object of their faith has not changed or passed away. "Jesus Christ" was the object of their dead leaders' faith, and He is the same Redeemer and Lord today. "Yesterday" He offered a fully effective sacrifice for the sins of the people when He offered up Himself (7:27; 9:12, 26; 10:10). "Today" He carries on a ministry of intercession for His people

(7:25). Whatever lies ahead in the future, His people may be sure that His help, grace, power, and guidance are "forever" at their disposal.

Leaders come and go. Every new generation needs to "lay hold" (1 Tim. 6:12) for themselves the doctrinal truths that were held fast by their spiritual fathers. "Jesus Christ" is the unchanging, living link that binds the succeeding generations of God's people together.

The doctrinal error, 13:9. There is always a tendency among immature believers to be susceptible to the idea that times have changed and the faith of Christians of previous generations is no longer relevant. Jesus Christ has not changed, argues the author, and consequently the truth about Him remains the same even today (H. Kent).

The author now warns his readers not to be swept off their feet by various false teachings. The reference to the "altar" in verse 10 and "the camp" in verse 11 clearly identifies the "strange teachings" of which the author is speaking. He is referring to the rituals of Judaism, specifically

> **Jesus Christ has not changed, and the truth about Him remains the same even today.**

to the arrangements of cleansing, i.e., the sacrifices, of the OT tabernacle. Although commanded in OT times, these sacrifices have now been canceled by the sacrifice of Christ. Some of the readers of the epistle were being carried away by the notion that those sacrificial rites were necessary for salvation. The author rejects this notion. His words condemn each and every way of salvation based on religious rituals and sacrificial rites (H. Koester).

By the term "foods" the author means sacrificial rites. The Jewish people believed that the use of certain "foods" ("meats," AV) had an influence upon our forgiveness and peace with God. All such distinctions of meats arose from the altar. Those animals that could be offered upon the altar were "clean," and it was those meats that could be eaten by Israelites (see Lev. 11). When our Lord did away with all Jewish distinctions about meats (see Mark 7:19), He in effect did away with the altar, which was the life and center of Judaism (J. Owen). Such meat distinctions did not spiritually profit the Jewish people. They did not bring them salvation and cleansing.

The author argues that "It is good for the heart to be strengthened by grace." The term *grace* speaks of God's favor upon those who do not deserve His favor. In this verse it speaks of the single deed of cleansing of sin that took place at the cross of Christ (see Heb. 1:3; 2:9). The Greek word (*bebaioō*) translated "strengthened" is a word that refers to legally guaranteed security. It stresses the security that is ours because of the effectiveness of the work of salvation performed by Christ at the cross. The lesson for today's reader is this: cleansing from sins is a free gift ("grace") of God. It is not ours through religious rites such as priestly garments, sacrifices, the use of incense, ceremonies, penances, fasting, or sacraments.

Responding to Correct Doctrine (13:10-16)

The correct doctrine: The only true sacrifice to God is that offered by Jesus Christ, 13:10-12. Some of the readers were troubled that Christianity had no visible priest, no tabernacle altar, and no sacrificial ritual. In this epistle the author has already shown his readers that Christ is our priest and our sacrifice. Now he assures them that Christians also "have an altar." The Christians' altar is the cross to which Christ was affixed at His death. It is upon Christ crucified that every believer is entitled "to eat."

To grasp the full force of the author's argument we must understand that he is here alluding to the annual ritual of the Day of Atonement (Lev. 16). On other days the priests were permitted portions

> **Cleansing from sins is a free gift of God.**

of meat from most sacrifices. But from daily sin offerings and from the annual Day of Atonement offering they were allowed nothing. The author's point is that the Christian altar is better than the Jewish one for two reasons:

1. The Day of Atonement was typical. It was only a foreshadowing of the true sacrifice, namely, Christ.
2. The sacrifices of the Day of Atonement could not be eaten. The sacrifice of Christ, however, is one upon which the sinner is commanded to feed.

The classic passage on eating from the Christian altar is John 6. In that passage Jesus invites people to come to Him and eat His flesh and drink His blood (John 6:48, 53-56). Jesus, of course, was speaking spiritually and not literally (6:35, 63). He explained that when He spoke of eating His flesh, He meant believing in Him. To believe in Christ is to eat His flesh; to eat is to believe and live (6:35-36).

The word "for" in verse 11 introduces a proof of the superior privilege of the Christian. We draw our spiritual sustenance from Christ, but the OT priests received no sustenance from the animals sacrifices because they were burned "outside the camp." The carcasses of the bullock and goat of the Day of Atonement were taken outside the encampment of Israel because they were "covered," as it were, with their sins.

The "so" at the beginning of verse 12 suggests that the events of the Day of Atonement had a typical-prophetic meaning.[3] The burning of the carcasses is typical of Jesus' death at Golgotha. The animals were "burned outside the camp" of Israel, and Jesus died "outside the gate" of Jerusalem (see Mark 15:20).

Three observations should be made about verse 12:

1. *The purpose.* Jesus suffered "in order to sanctify the people." Throughout the epistle the concept of sanctification means to make acceptable to God through the removal of defilement and guilt. Those who are sanctified are thereby set apart to worship and serve God.
2. *The price.* Jesus sanctified His people "through his own blood." The term *blood* suggests a death violently inflicted by sacrifice.
3. *The place.* Like the OT sacrifices Jesus was treated as a sin bearer. The nation classified Him with blasphemers (Lev. 24:14) and Sabbath breakers (Num. 15:35). He was an outcast and rejected by the people.

It is of great importance to the author of Hebrews that Jesus suffered "outside the gate." To be led outside the gate was to be put outside the holy city and outside the holy precincts of the temple. The author's point is that the death of Jesus marks a complete separation between Christianity and Judaism.

The proper response: The only true devotion to God is that offered to Jesus Christ, 13:13-14. The author now exhorts his readers to forsake Judaism with its altar, priesthood, and sacrifices. The true Christian can have no part in a system that had cast Jesus out. The lesson for today is that the Christian must forsake each and every religious system that rejects Jesus Christ. We are to "go to him outside the camp and bear the reproach he endured."

Like the OT pilgrims, Christians today are "strangers and exiles on the earth." We can see from Hebrews that a pilgrimage has four essential ingredients:

1. It entails a separation, a leaving home.
2. It involves a journey to a sacred place.
3. It is made for a definite purpose.
4. It involves hardship (W. G. Johnsson). Believers in Christ are pilgrims on their way to the heavenly Jerusalem. They "have no lasting city" on earth, but are seeking "the city that is to come."[4]

The appropriate worship: The only true worship of God is that offered through Jesus Christ, 13:15-16. Although the readers do not today offer animal sacrifices on an earthly altar in Jerusalem, they do have access to their High Priest in the heavenly tabernacle (see Heb. 8:1-2). "Through Him" they are to "offer up a sacrifice of praise to God." Jesus Christ is the mediator between God and His people, and it is through His priestly office that our prayers and praises reach God (see 1 Tim. 2:5-6).

God is not interested in calves slain before physical altars, but in the worship of thankful lips. We should give thanks for brotherly love and hospitality (13:1-2), for caring fellow Christians (13:3), for loyal spouses (13:4), for God's loving and protective care (13:5), and for teachers and leaders who have shared God's Word with us and given us a godly example (13:7, 17).

> **Jesus Christ is the mediator between God and His people.**

To the sacrifice of praise the author adds the sacrifice of kind and loving action in verse 16 (F. F. Bruce). Some of the readers may have been wondering how people who could no longer worship at the sanctuary in Jerusalem could possibly please God. The author of Hebrews would agree with James, who wrote, "Religion that is pure and undefiled before God the Father is this: to visit orphans and widows in their affliction, and to keep oneself unstained from the world" (James 1:27). The author of Hebrews tells his readers "to do good and to share." The term *to share* here refers to sacrificial financial giving. The early Christians took care of the needy in their midst. The author's lesson is clear. Pious participation in the outward forms of religious worship is no substitute for a compassionate concern for others.

Obeying Our Present Leaders (13:17)

It is evident from this paragraph (13:7-17) that there were recognized leaders in the church. No group, including the local assembly of Christians, can have order and peace without leadership. The responsibility of the congregation is to "obey [their] leaders and submit to them." Believers are to obey when they agree with what they are told to do and submit when they have a contrary opinion (Lenski).

The author tells his readers two things about the responsibility of the leaders:

1. They have a pastoral responsibility to the congregation. He says, "They are keeping watch over your souls." The verb *to watch*

literally means "to chase away sleep." Elders or pastors[5] lose sleep as they watch over and care for an assembly of Christians. The seriousness of their work is brought out by the word "souls" (see 4:12).[6] The leaders of the church are concerned that they bring their flock to salvation and not to judgment.

2. They are accountable to the Lord. Leadership is a responsibility for which a man must answer to God at the judgment seat of Christ (2 Cor. 5:10).

Cooperation on the part of the congregation makes the task of the elders easier. It allows them to discharge their task "with joy and not with groaning." Leaders face grief and discouragement when the flock is wayward. Disobedience hurts the Christian, and it hurts the assembly. It is "of no advantage," says the author. It brings defilement, trouble, and a bitter spirit to the church (see Heb. 12:15).

Closing Words for Christian Pilgrims (13:18-25)

A Request for Prayer (13:18-19)

The author's admonition regarding his readers' duty to their local leaders leads now to a consideration of their wider responsibility. There are probably problems in the group behind the request in verse 18, "Pray for us." The same willful attitude and dullness that is seen in their local church is seen in their attitude to outside Christian workers who seek to confront them about their dull condition (Westcott). So he seeks to get them involved in the Lord's work through the practical ministry of prayer. As is generally true, spiritual dullness had affected the regularity of their prayers. The present imperative form of the verb suggests that it is something at which they need to be constant: "Be praying, keep on praying."

We might expect the word "for" to introduce a list of the author's needs. Instead they are urged to pray on the basis of the author's "clear conscience."[7] The word "for" suggests that he is defending his conduct to them. It may be that the author is concerned that his severe statements earlier in the epistle will be misunderstood. He wants them to know that he has not spoken out of anger or other bad motives. Or perhaps his long absence (13:19) has led the readers to suspect him of lack of concern. He wants them to know this is not the case. Whatever his reason for writing like this, it is clear that the author agrees with other NT writers that a good conscience is necessary for Christian service (see Rom. 9:1; 2 Cor. 1:12; 1 Tim. 1:5, 19; 3:9; 2 Tim. 1:3). To be active in the Lord's work with a bad conscience about something can have a defiling and hardening effect upon a believer (W. Kelly).

The author asks that they would pray, "that I may be restored to you the sooner." The word "restored" implies that he had previously been associated with the readers, possibly in a leadership role. The word may also suggest that something—possibly his present ministry—was keeping him from returning.

A Prayer for Blessing (13:20-21)

God's work for us, 13:20. The author was a man who sought the prayers of others and who prayed for others. He now asks a blessing for his readers. He is confident that his prayer will be answered because of what God is like and what He has done. He calls upon God as "the God of peace," that is, He is the source of peace. This description of God suggests three things:

1. He is the God who establishes peace between rebellious sinners and Himself.
2. He is the God who can bring inner peace to Christians like the readers who faced a hostile and persecuting world (Heb. 10:32-33).
3. He is the God who can bring peace to a local church where Christians are at odds with one another (10:25) and rebellious toward their leaders (13:7, 17).

The author is also assured that his prayer will be answered because of the mighty acts that God has done. He mentions two of them:

1. He "brought again from the dead our Lord Jesus," and
2. He established "the eternal covenant" on the basis of "the blood" (sacrificial death) of Christ.

First, he mentions the resurrection. This is the first time in Hebrews that the author mentions the resurrection of Christ. He has saved it for his grand finale in his closing benediction or blessing. The resurrection assures us of Christ's victory over death and Satan (2:14-15) and of God's power to equip believers to do His will (13:21).

This is the only place in the epistle where the Lord Jesus is called "that great shepherd of the sheep." The readers would be aware that in Isaiah 63:11 Moses is described as the "shepherd" of Israel who "brought them up out of the [Red] sea." As elsewhere in the epistle, the events of the OT are a shadow of the new age (see Heb. 10:1). Moses was a shadow or type of Christ; the Red Sea was a shadow of the grave; the exodus was a shadow of the resurrection, and the old covenant was a shadow of the new covenant (Westcott).

God establishes peace between rebellious sinners and Himself.

The description of the Lord Jesus as the "great shepherd" comes from the Lord Himself (see John 10:11-28). The ideas underlying the title are of One who leads and rules His people in mercy and love, and who saves them at the cost of His life (V. Taylor). The title is especially appropriate in this passage. The very next phrase ("by the blood") suggests that Jesus died for His people, and such self-sacrifice is elsewhere explained by the figure of a shepherd (see John 10:15). Furthermore, the author refers three times in chapter 13 to the leaders of the church (Heb. 13:7, 17, 24). In such a context it is understandable that he would call the Lord Jesus a shepherd, for He is the prototype of all who shepherd local congregations.

The phrase "by the blood of the eternal covenant" introduces the second mighty act of God that serves to assure us that God can answer prayer. We may translate the word "by" as "because of." Jesus was raised "because of the blood,"—that is, He was raised because He had fulfilled God's will that He die. And because of His sacrifice the everlasting covenant[8] has been enacted. The new covenant is "eternal" for three reasons:

1. *Its basis*, namely the blood of the Lord Jesus. The one who died was the God-man. It was the sacrifice by One with an eternal Spirit in the eternal realm (9:14).
2. *Its effect*, namely, eternal life for His sheep. His sheep will never perish (John 10:11-28).
3. *Its duration*, that is, it will last forever. Unlike the covenant made through Moses, this one is completely effective and need never be replaced.

God's work in us, 13:21. This verse contains the substance of the author's prayer for his readers, namely, that God would enable them to live the Christian life. He describes the Christian life as doing "His will," i.e., as obedience. As he says elsewhere, the believer needs to be skillful "in the word of righteousness" (5:13). They need to know the Word of God and to obediently apply it to their life.

The author tells his readers that we are enabled to live the Christian life by the power of God working in us "through Jesus Christ." "We are to do, yet all the while God is doing" (Lenski). Jesus Christ is not only the High Priest whose sacrifice provides forgiveness of sins. He is also the agent by whom God's power is communicated to us for daily Christian living.

The Lord Jesus equips us "with everything good." The verb translated "equip" had a wide range of uses in the time Hebrews was written. It was used with these meanings: to adjust, to put in order, to restore, to mend, to set, to reconcile, to furnish, to equip, to prepare, to make ready. All these definitions suggest the multifaceted, enabling work of God in the life of the believer. The divine work in us involves restoring, repairing, equipping and enabling. The goal of the Christian life is to please the Lord.

The author concludes verse 21 by affirming that Jesus Christ is deserving of "glory forever and ever." The Greek word (*doxa*) translated "glory" is the one from which we get the word *doxology*. We praise our Lord Jesus because of His position of glory—that is, of power, splendor, dignity, majesty, and honor.

> **The believer needs to know the Word of God and to obediently apply it to life.**

Some Final Comments (13:22-25)

An appeal for receptivity, 13:22. The author urges his readers (both ancient and modern) to listen willingly to his letter as it is read to the congregation. It may appear to us to be a long letter, but it was probably, in its original form, a sermon (a "word of exhortation"). It can be read aloud in one hour, and that would not be a long sermon ("briefly") by first-century standards (see Acts 20:7-9). In any case, God's people are to be receptive to biblical teaching and preaching. One of the signs of the onset of revival in the life of an individual or a church is a hunger for and a renewal of powerful biblical preaching.

An announcement of Timothy's arrival, 13:23. The author joyfully informs his readers that Timothy, Paul's young companion, has just been released from prison. The author hopes to join him in a visit to this congregation of Jewish Christians.

A greeting to all the church, 13:24. Like many epistles in the NT, Hebrews concludes with a formal greeting by the author. He also sends greetings from Italian believers ("those who come from Italy") to his readers in Palestine. The elders and the congregation are to be greeted. The twofold use of the word "all" ("all your leaders … all the saints") may suggest that the author does not think the entire congregation would be there to hear his letter-sermon read. Because of their spiritual problems, some of the Hebrew Christians were not regularly attending the meetings of the church (10:25). The author wants even those who are absent to hear what he has to say.

A closing blessing, 13:25. The author closes with a prayer for God's grace upon his readers. Letters in his day often ended with a greeting such as "rejoice," "hail," or "farewell." The Christians substituted the

Grace is God's undeserved and free love toward people.

word "grace." Grace is God's undeserved and free love toward people. It is because of grace that Christ died as a substitute for sinners that they might be forgiven and live in the heavenly city of God (2:9-10). In Hebrews it is a term that describes God's loving concern for His people and His readiness to aid all who come to Him in time of need (4:16).

Some Bible translations include the word "Amen" at the end of this chapter. The expression "Amen" is a Hebrew word meaning "verily" or "truly." It was the common response of a congregation of believers when they approved a prayer or utterance of worship. In our passage (13:21, 25) we might translate it as "So let it be," "truly," "indeed," "May the Lord do so," "Right!" or "It is true." The author anticipates that his readers (both in his own day and ours) will be in agreement with his doxology and all that he has written.

SUMMARY

The dull faith of the readers has resulted in a weakening of their love for fellow believers. Their lives, our author says, should be marked by hospitality and compassion (13:1-3). Christian love, he warns, is opposed to marital infidelity and is stifled by the love of money (13:4-6). Love, he adds, should also be reflected in their relationship to their leaders (13:7-17).

The readers are to imitate the faith of their first leaders, for the object of their faith (Jesus Christ) has not changed or passed away (13:7-8). The author exhorts them to put a stop to their connection with the Levitical system with its impermanent city and sanctuary and fully identify themselves with Christ and the true and lasting city of God (13:9-14). He says their lives should be marked by thanksgiving, kind and loving activity, and obedience to their leaders (13:15-17). Along with personal matters, his closing remarks remind them that it is God's grace that is the source of their strength (13:18-25).

Endnotes

[1] In addition to Hebrews 13:1, see Romans 12:10; 1 Thessalonians 4:9; 1 Peter 1:22; 2 Peter 1:7.

[2] Some have argued that the leaders of verse 7 were still alive when the epistle was written. Most commentators, however, agree that the leaders of verse 7 were dead at the time of the epistle. This is suggested by the verb "remember" and by the tense of the verb "spoke," which suggests a work in the past, namely, the original proclamation of the Gospel to the group.

[3] For a review of the events of the Day of Atonement, see Lesson 8. Also read Leviticus 16.

[4] There is a solemn tone to Hebrews 13:14. The epistle was probably written around AD 68. The old order was about to crash. Within two years the words of verse 14 were confirmed, for in AD 70 the Romans destroyed the city of Jerusalem.

[5] It is clear from the NT that the ruling office in the local church is that of elder. It is also clear that the terms *elder, pastor* (or shepherd), and *overseer* all refer to the same office (see Acts 20:20, 28).

[6] The term *soul* refers to the immaterial nature of man and woman. It is their essential being, the seat of their personal identity. It is the whole inner life of a man or woman with their powers of will, reason and emotion (G. Harder and H. D. McDonald).

[7] The conscience may be defined as the faculty of man that gives the inner knowledge or awareness of, and sensitivity to, some moral standard, in this case the Word of God (R. B. Zuck). The author's conscience was good in that it was causing him no pain. He had a sense of duty done, of responsibility well discharged (F. F. Bruce).

[8] A covenant was a treaty, compact, bond, or agreement between two parties. Such covenants were sealed in blood to indicate they were irrevocable.

LESSON 12 EXAM

Use the exam sheet at the back of the course to complete your exam.

1. **The dominant theme of chapter 13 is**
   A. compassion.
   B. faith.
   C. hope.
   D. love.

2. ***Covetousness* refers to**
   A. contentment.
   B. anxiety.
   C. trust in God.
   D. greed and jealousy.

3. **Verses 7-17 are primarily concerned with**
   A. the eternality of Christ.
   B. the altar of the temple in Jerusalem.
   C. false doctrine.
   D. the relationship of the people of the congregation to their leaders.

4. **The "diverse and strange teachings" of verse 9 refer to**
   A. the doctrines of the Gnostics.
   B. the doctrines of the Essenes.
   C. the rituals of Emperor worship.
   D. the rituals of Judaism.

5. **In verses 10-11, the author is alluding to the sacrifices of**
   A. Passover.
   B. the Feast of Pentecost.
   C. the Feast of Trumpets.
   D. the Day of Atonement.

6. **The "altar" of the Christian (13:10) is the**
   A. Garden of Gethsemane.
   B. Person of Christ.
   C. communion table.
   D. cross of Christ.

7. **That Jesus "suffered outside the gate" means**
   A. He was rejected by the Jewish people.
   B. He was a sin bearer.
   C. there is now a complete break between Judaism and Christianity.
   D. All of the above.

8. **The sacrifices of the Christian are**
   A. praise.
   B. doing good.
   C. sharing.
   D. All of the above.

215

9. **That God is "the God of peace" suggests that**
   A. He establishes peace between sinners and Himself.
   B. He can bring inner peace to believers in a hostile world.
   C. He can bring peace to a local assembly torn by strife.
   D. All of the above.

10. **The "eternal covenant" is**
   A. the new covenant.
   B. the covenant made through Moses.
   C. the covenant made with Noah.
   D. the covenant made with David.

What Do You Say?

Which one of the commands given in chapter 13 challenges you the most, and why?

The command to be content with what I have. Love of money does indeed make giving difficult. And it isn't loving, but selfish to do this. I must be content in His Promise to always be there for me.

Since then we have a great High Priest who has passed through the heavens, Jesus, the Son of God, let us hold fast our confession. For we do not have a High Priest who is unable to sympathize with our weaknesses, but one who in every respect has been tempted as we are, yet without sin. Let us then with confidence draw near to the throne of grace, that we may receive mercy and find grace to help in time of need.

—Hebrews 4:14-16

EXAM SHEET
The Letter to the Hebrews

DIRECTIONS: 1) Use a pen or pencil. 2) Completely fill in the circle.
3) Erase or X any answer you wish to change. 4) Try not to make stray marks.

INCORRECT: ⊠ ⊘ ⊙ ⊝
CORRECT: Ⓐ ● Ⓒ Ⓓ

1-1. Ⓐ Ⓑ Ⓒ Ⓓ	4-1. Ⓐ Ⓑ Ⓒ Ⓓ	7-1. Ⓐ Ⓑ Ⓒ Ⓓ	10-1. Ⓐ Ⓑ Ⓒ Ⓓ
2. Ⓐ Ⓑ Ⓒ Ⓓ	2. Ⓐ Ⓑ Ⓒ Ⓓ	2. Ⓐ Ⓑ Ⓒ Ⓓ	2. Ⓐ Ⓑ Ⓒ Ⓓ
3. Ⓐ Ⓑ Ⓒ Ⓓ	3. Ⓐ Ⓑ Ⓒ Ⓓ	3. Ⓐ Ⓑ Ⓒ Ⓓ	3. Ⓐ Ⓑ Ⓒ Ⓓ
4. Ⓐ Ⓑ Ⓒ Ⓓ	4. Ⓐ Ⓑ Ⓒ Ⓓ	4. Ⓐ Ⓑ Ⓒ Ⓓ	4. Ⓐ Ⓑ Ⓒ Ⓓ
5. Ⓐ Ⓑ Ⓒ Ⓓ	5. Ⓐ Ⓑ Ⓒ Ⓓ	5. Ⓐ Ⓑ Ⓒ Ⓓ	5. Ⓐ Ⓑ Ⓒ Ⓓ
6. Ⓐ Ⓑ Ⓒ Ⓓ	6. Ⓐ Ⓑ Ⓒ Ⓓ	6. Ⓐ Ⓑ Ⓒ Ⓓ	6. Ⓐ Ⓑ Ⓒ Ⓓ
7. Ⓐ Ⓑ Ⓒ Ⓓ	7. Ⓐ Ⓑ Ⓒ Ⓓ	7. Ⓐ Ⓑ Ⓒ Ⓓ	7. Ⓐ Ⓑ Ⓒ Ⓓ
8. Ⓐ Ⓑ Ⓒ Ⓓ	8. Ⓐ Ⓑ Ⓒ Ⓓ	8. Ⓐ Ⓑ Ⓒ Ⓓ	8. Ⓐ Ⓑ Ⓒ Ⓓ
9. Ⓐ Ⓑ Ⓒ Ⓓ	9. Ⓐ Ⓑ Ⓒ Ⓓ	9. Ⓐ Ⓑ Ⓒ Ⓓ	9. Ⓐ Ⓑ Ⓒ Ⓓ
10. Ⓐ Ⓑ Ⓒ Ⓓ	10. Ⓐ Ⓑ Ⓒ Ⓓ	10. Ⓐ Ⓑ Ⓒ Ⓓ	10. Ⓐ Ⓑ Ⓒ Ⓓ
2-1. Ⓐ Ⓑ Ⓒ Ⓓ	5-1. Ⓐ Ⓑ Ⓒ Ⓓ	8-1. Ⓐ Ⓑ Ⓒ Ⓓ	11-1. Ⓐ Ⓑ Ⓒ Ⓓ
2. Ⓐ Ⓑ Ⓒ Ⓓ	2. Ⓐ Ⓑ Ⓒ Ⓓ	2. Ⓐ Ⓑ Ⓒ Ⓓ	2. Ⓐ Ⓑ Ⓒ Ⓓ
3. Ⓐ Ⓑ Ⓒ Ⓓ	3. Ⓐ Ⓑ Ⓒ Ⓓ	3. Ⓐ Ⓑ Ⓒ Ⓓ	3. Ⓐ Ⓑ Ⓒ Ⓓ
4. Ⓐ Ⓑ Ⓒ Ⓓ	4. Ⓐ Ⓑ Ⓒ Ⓓ	4. Ⓐ Ⓑ Ⓒ Ⓓ	4. Ⓐ Ⓑ Ⓒ Ⓓ
5. Ⓐ Ⓑ Ⓒ Ⓓ	5. Ⓐ Ⓑ Ⓒ Ⓓ	5. Ⓐ Ⓑ Ⓒ Ⓓ	5. Ⓐ Ⓑ Ⓒ Ⓓ
6. Ⓐ Ⓑ Ⓒ Ⓓ	6. Ⓐ Ⓑ Ⓒ Ⓓ	6. Ⓐ Ⓑ Ⓒ Ⓓ	6. Ⓐ Ⓑ Ⓒ Ⓓ
7. Ⓐ Ⓑ Ⓒ Ⓓ	7. Ⓐ Ⓑ Ⓒ Ⓓ	7. Ⓐ Ⓑ Ⓒ Ⓓ	7. Ⓐ Ⓑ Ⓒ Ⓓ
8. Ⓐ Ⓑ Ⓒ Ⓓ	8. Ⓐ Ⓑ Ⓒ Ⓓ	8. Ⓐ Ⓑ Ⓒ Ⓓ	8. Ⓐ Ⓑ Ⓒ Ⓓ
9. Ⓐ Ⓑ Ⓒ Ⓓ	9. Ⓐ Ⓑ Ⓒ Ⓓ	9. Ⓐ Ⓑ Ⓒ Ⓓ	9. Ⓐ Ⓑ Ⓒ Ⓓ
10. Ⓐ Ⓑ Ⓒ Ⓓ	10. Ⓐ Ⓑ Ⓒ Ⓓ	10. Ⓐ Ⓑ Ⓒ Ⓓ	10. Ⓐ Ⓑ Ⓒ Ⓓ
3-1. Ⓐ Ⓑ Ⓒ Ⓓ	6-1. Ⓐ Ⓑ Ⓒ Ⓓ	9-1. Ⓐ Ⓑ Ⓒ Ⓓ	12-1. Ⓐ Ⓑ Ⓒ Ⓓ
2. Ⓐ Ⓑ Ⓒ Ⓓ	2. Ⓐ Ⓑ Ⓒ Ⓓ	2. Ⓐ Ⓑ Ⓒ Ⓓ	2. Ⓐ Ⓑ Ⓒ Ⓓ
3. Ⓐ Ⓑ Ⓒ Ⓓ	3. Ⓐ Ⓑ Ⓒ Ⓓ	3. Ⓐ Ⓑ Ⓒ Ⓓ	3. Ⓐ Ⓑ Ⓒ Ⓓ
4. Ⓐ Ⓑ Ⓒ Ⓓ	4. Ⓐ Ⓑ Ⓒ Ⓓ	4. Ⓐ Ⓑ Ⓒ Ⓓ	4. Ⓐ Ⓑ Ⓒ Ⓓ
5. Ⓐ Ⓑ Ⓒ Ⓓ	5. Ⓐ Ⓑ Ⓒ Ⓓ	5. Ⓐ Ⓑ Ⓒ Ⓓ	5. Ⓐ Ⓑ Ⓒ Ⓓ
6. Ⓐ Ⓑ Ⓒ Ⓓ	6. Ⓐ Ⓑ Ⓒ Ⓓ	6. Ⓐ Ⓑ Ⓒ Ⓓ	6. Ⓐ Ⓑ Ⓒ Ⓓ
7. Ⓐ Ⓑ Ⓒ Ⓓ	7. Ⓐ Ⓑ Ⓒ Ⓓ	7. Ⓐ Ⓑ Ⓒ Ⓓ	7. Ⓐ Ⓑ Ⓒ Ⓓ
8. Ⓐ Ⓑ Ⓒ Ⓓ	8. Ⓐ Ⓑ Ⓒ Ⓓ	8. Ⓐ Ⓑ Ⓒ Ⓓ	8. Ⓐ Ⓑ Ⓒ Ⓓ
9. Ⓐ Ⓑ Ⓒ Ⓓ	9. Ⓐ Ⓑ Ⓒ Ⓓ	9. Ⓐ Ⓑ Ⓒ Ⓓ	9. Ⓐ Ⓑ Ⓒ Ⓓ
10. Ⓐ Ⓑ Ⓒ Ⓓ	10. Ⓐ Ⓑ Ⓒ Ⓓ	10. Ⓐ Ⓑ Ⓒ Ⓓ	10. Ⓐ Ⓑ Ⓒ Ⓓ

Form Identifier — DO NOT MARK

Write It Out!
The Letter to the Hebrews

These questions will be reviewed and responded to by your group leader or instructor.

1. HEAD: Explain what role(s) Jesus Christ is shown to fulfill throughout the book of Hebrews.

2. HEART: How does this course affect your perspective of or feelings towards God, yourself, or others?

3. HANDS: How does this course affect your actions today?

PRAYER REQUESTS OR QUESTIONS?

Your Information

First Name: Rachel   Last Name: Taylor

Address: 1541 FM 1831 B

City: Ralls   State: TX   ZIP: 79357

Email Address: racheltirzah@gmail.com

Group leader or Instructor: (If known)

Institution: (If applicable)

Cell Location: (If applicable) _____ ID # (If applicable)